P9-DUV-110

VOICES OF ISLAM

Volume 4

VOICES OF ART, BEAUTY, AND SCIENCE

Vincent J. Cornell, General Editor and
Volume Editor

PRAEGER PERSPECTIVES

Westport, Connecticut
London

Library of Congress Cataloging-in-Publication Data

Voices of Islam / Vincent J. Cornell, general editor.
  p. cm.
  Includes bibliographical references and index.
  ISBN 0–275–98732–9 (set : alk. paper)—ISBN 0–275–98733–7 (vol 1 : alk. paper)—ISBN
0–275–98734–5 (vol 2 : alk. paper)—ISBN 0–275–98735–3 (vol 3 : alk. paper)—ISBN 0–
275–98736–1 (vol 4 : alk. paper)—ISBN 0–275–98737–X (vol 5 : alk. paper) 1. Islam—
Appreciation. 2. Islam—Essence, genius, nature. I. Cornell, Vincent J.
  BP163.V65 2007
  297—dc22   2006031060

British Library Cataloguing in Publication Data is available.

Library of Congress Catalog Card Number: 2006031060
ISBN: 0–275–98732–9 (set)
        0–275–98733–7 (vol. 1)
        0–275–98734–5 (vol. 2)
        0–275–98735–3 (vol. 3)
        0–275–98736–1 (vol. 4)
        0–275–98737–X (vol. 5)

First published in 2007

Praeger Publishers, 88 Post Road West, Westport, CT 06881
An imprint of Greenwood Publishing Group, Inc.
www.praeger.com

Printed in the United States of America

The paper used in this book complies with the
Permanent Paper Standard issued by the National
Information Standards Organization (Z39.48–1984).

10 9 8 7 6 5 4 3 2 1

CONTENTS

——————————————— • ———————————————

VOICES OF ISLAM

———————————— • ————————————

Vincent J. Cornell

It has long been a truism to say that Islam is the most misunderstood religion in the world. However, the situation expressed by this statement is more than a little ironic because Islam is also one of the most studied religions in the world, after Christianity and Judaism. In the quarter of a century since the 1978–1979 Islamic revolution in Iran, hundreds of books on Islam and the Islamic world have appeared in print, including more than a score of introductions to Islam in various European languages. How is one to understand this paradox? Why is it that most Americans and Europeans are still largely uninformed about Islam after so many books about Islam have been published? Even more, how can people still claim to know so little about Islam when Muslims now live in virtually every medium-sized and major community in America and Europe? A visit to a local library or to a national bookstore chain in any American city will reveal numerous titles on Islam and the Muslim world, ranging from journalistic potboilers to academic studies, translations of the Qur'an, and works advocating a variety of points of view from apologetics to predictions of the apocalypse.

The answer to this question is complex, and it would take a book itself to discuss it adequately. More than 28 years have passed since Edward Said wrote his classic study *Orientalism,* and it has been nearly as long since Said critiqued journalistic depictions of Islam in *Covering Islam: How the Media and the Experts Determine How We See the Rest of the World.* When these books first appeared in print, many thought that the ignorance about the Middle East and the Muslim world in the West would finally be dispelled. However, there is little evidence that the public consciousness of Islam and Muslims has been raised to a significant degree in Western countries. Scholars of Islam in American universities still feel the need to humanize Muslims in the eyes of their students. A basic objective of many introductory courses on Islam is to demonstrate that Muslims are rational human beings and that their beliefs are worthy of respect. As Carl W. Ernst observes in the preface to his recent work, *Following Muhammad: Rethinking Islam in the*

Contemporary World, "It still amazes me that intelligent people can believe that all Muslims are violent or that all Muslim women are oppressed, when they would never dream of uttering slurs stereotyping much smaller groups such as Jews or blacks. The strength of these negative images of Muslims is remarkable, even though they are not based on personal experience or actual study, but they receive daily reinforcement from the news media and popular culture."[1]

Such prejudices and misconceptions have only become worse since the terrorist attacks of September 11, 2001, and the war in Iraq. There still remains a need to portray Muslims in all of their human diversity, whether this diversity is based on culture, historical circumstances, economic class, gender, or religious doctrine. Today, Muslims represent nearly one-fourth of the world's population. Although many Americans are aware that Indonesia is the world's largest Muslim country, most are surprised to learn that half of the Muslims in the world live east of Lahore, Pakistan. In this sense, Islam is as much an "Asian" religion as is Hinduism or Buddhism. The new reality of global Islam strongly contradicts the "Middle Eastern" view of Islam held by most Americans. Politically, the United States has been preoccupied with the Middle East for more than half a century. Religiously, however, American Protestantism has been involved in the Middle East for more than 150 years. Thus, it comes as a shock for Americans to learn that only one-fourth of the world's Muslims live in the Middle East and North Africa and that only one-fifth of Muslims are Arabs. Islam is now as much a worldwide religion as Christianity, with somewhere between 4 and 6 million believers in the United States and approximately 10 million believers in Western Europe. Almost 20 million Muslims live within the borders of the Russian Federation, and nearly a million people of Muslim descent live in the Russian city of St. Petersburg, on the Gulf of Finland.

To think of Islam as monolithic under these circumstances is both wrong and dangerous. The idea that all Muslims are fundamentalists or antidemocratic religious zealots can lead to the fear that dangerous aliens are hiding within Western countries, a fifth column of a civilization that is antithetical to freedom and the liberal way of life. This attitude is often expressed in popular opinion in both the United States and Europe. For example, it can be seen in the "Letters" section of the June 7, 2004, edition of *Time* magazine, where a reader writes: "Now it is time for Muslim clerics to denounce the terrorists or admit that Islam is fighting a war with us—a religious war."[2] For the author of this letter, Muslim "clerics" are not to be trusted, not because they find it hard to believe that pious Muslims would commit outrageous acts of terrorism, but because they secretly hate the West and its values. Clearly, for this reader of *Time,* Islam and the West are at war; however the "West" may be defined and wherever "Islam" or Muslims are to be found.

Prejudice against Muslim minorities still exists in many countries. In Russia, Muslim restaurateurs from the Caucasus Mountains must call themselves "Georgian" to stay in business. In China, being Muslim by ethnicity is acceptable, but being a Muslim by conviction might get one convicted for antistate activities. In the Balkans, Muslims in Serbia, Bulgaria, and Macedonia are called "Turks" and right-wing nationalist parties deny them full ethnic legitimacy as citizens of their countries. In India, over a thousand Muslims were killed in communal riots in Gujarat as recently as 2002. As I write these words, Israel and Hizbollah, the Lebanese Shiite political movement and militia, are engaged in a bloody conflict that has left hundreds of dead and injured on both sides. Although the number of people who have been killed in Lebanon, most of whom are Shiite civilians, is far greater than the number of those killed in Israel, television news reports in the United States do not treat Lebanese and Israeli casualties the same way. While the casualties that are caused by Hizbollah rockets in Israel are depicted as personal tragedies, Lebanese casualties are seldom personalized in this way. The truth is, of course, that all casualties of war are personal tragedies, whether the victims are Lebanese civilians, Israeli civilians, or American soldiers killed or maimed by improvised explosive devices in Iraq. In addition, all civilian deaths in war pose a moral problem, whether they are caused as a consequence of aggression or of retaliation. In many ways, depersonalization can have worse effects than actual hatred. An enemy that is hated must at least be confronted; when innocent victims are reduced to pictures without stories, they are all too easily ignored.

The problem of depersonalization has deeper roots than just individual prejudice. Ironically, the global village created by international news organizations such as CNN, BBC, and Fox News may unintentionally contribute to the problem of devaluing Muslim lives. Depictions of victimhood are often studies in incomprehension: victims speak a language the viewer cannot understand, their shock or rage strips them of their rationality, and their standard of living and mode of dress may appear medieval or even primitive when compared with the dominant cultural forms of modernity. In her classic study, *The Origins of Totalitarianism,* Hannah Arendt pointed out that the ideology of human equality, which is fostered with all good intentions by the international news media, paradoxically contributes to the visibility of difference by confusing equality with sameness. In 99 out of 100 cases, says Arendt, equality "will be mistaken for an innate quality of every individual, who is 'normal' if he is like everybody else and 'abnormal' if he happens to be different. This perversion of equality from a political into a social concept is all the more dangerous when a society leaves but little space for special groups and individuals, for then their differences become all the more conspicuous."[3] According to Arendt, the widespread acceptance of the ideal of social equality after the French Revolution was a major reason why genocide, whether of Jews in Europe, Tutsis in Rwanda, or Muslims in the former Yugoslavia, has become a characteristically modern phenomenon.

The idea of equality as sameness was not as firmly established in the United States, claimed Arendt, because the "equal opportunity" ideology of American liberalism values difference—in the form of imagination, entrepreneurship, and personal initiative—as a token of success.[4] This ideology enabled Jews in America to assert their distinctiveness and eventually to prosper in the twentieth century, and it provides an opportunity for Muslim Americans to assert their distinctiveness and to prosper today. So far, the United States has not engaged in systematic persecution of Muslims and has been relatively free of anti-Muslim prejudice. However, fear and distrust of Muslims among the general public is fostered by images of insurgent attacks and suicide bombings in Iraq, of Al Qaeda atrocities around the globe, and of increasing expressions of anti-Americanism in the Arabic and Islamic media. In addition, some pundits on talk radio, certain fundamentalist religious leaders, and some members of the conservative press and academia fan the flames of prejudice by portraying Islam as inherently intolerant and by portraying Muslims as slaves to tradition and authoritarianism rather than as advocates of reason and freedom of expression. Clearly, there is still a need to demonstrate to the American public that Muslims are rational human beings and that Islam is a religion that is worthy of respect.

Changing public opinion about Islam and Muslims in the United States and Europe will not be easy. The culture critic Guillermo Gomez-Peña has written that as a result of the opening of American borders to non-Europeans in the 1960s, the American myth of the cultural melting pot "has been replaced by a model that is more germane to the times, that of the *menudo chowder*. According to this model, most of the ingredients do melt, but some stubborn chunks are condemned merely to float."[5] At the present time, Muslims constitute the most visible "stubborn chunks" in the *menudo chowder* of American and European pluralism. Muslims are often seen as the chunks of the *menudo chowder* that most stubbornly refuse to "melt in." To the non-Muslim majoritarian citizen of Western countries, Muslims seem to be the most "uncivil" members of civil society. They do not dress like the majority, they do not eat like the majority, they do not drink like the majority, they do not let their women work, they reject the music and cultural values of the majority, and sometimes they even try to opt out of majoritarian legal and economic systems. In Europe, Islam has replaced Catholicism as the religion that left-wing pundits most love to hate. Americans, however, have been more ambivalent about Islam and Muslims. On the one hand, there have been sincere attempts to include Muslims as full partners in civil society. On the other hand, the apparent resistance of some Muslims to "fit in" creates a widespread distrust that has had legal ramifications in several notable cases.

A useful way to conceive of the problem that Muslims face as members of civil society—both within Western countries and in the global civil society that is dominated by the West—is to recognize, following Homi K. Bhabha, the social fact of Muslim *unhomeliness.* To be "unhomed," says Bhabha, is not to be homeless, but rather to escape easy assimilation or accommodation.[6] The problem is not that the "unhomed" possesses no physical home but that there is no "place" to locate the unhomed in the majoritarian consciousness. Simply put, one does not know what to make of the unhomed. Bhabha derives this term from Sigmund Freud's concept of *unheimlich,* "the name for everything that ought to have remained secret and hidden but has come to light."[7] Unhomeliness is a way of expressing social discomfort. When one encounters the unhomed, one feels awkward and uncomfortable because the unhomed person appears truly alien. Indeed, if there is any single experience that virtually all Muslims in Western countries share, it is that Islam makes non-Muslims uncomfortable. In the global civil society dominated by the West, Muslims are unhomed wherever they may live, even in their own countries.

This reality of Muslim experience highlights how contemporary advocates of Muslim identity politics have often made matters worse by accentuating symbolic tokens of difference between so-called Islamic and Western norms. The problem for Islam in today's global civil society is not that it is not seen. On the contrary, Islam and Muslims are arguably all too visible because they are seen as fundamentally different from the accepted norm. Like the black man in the colonial West Indies or in Jim Crow America, the Muslim is, to borrow a phrase from Frantz Fanon, "overdetermined from without."[8] Muslims have been overdetermined by the press, overdetermined by Hollywood, overdetermined by politicians, and overdetermined by culture critics. From the president of the United States to the prime minister of the United Kingdom, and in countless editorials in print and television media, leaders of public opinion ask, "What do Muslims want?" Such a question forces the Muslim into a corner in which the only answer is apologetics or defiance. To again paraphrase Fanon, the overdetermined Muslim is constantly made aware of himself or herself not just in the third person but in *triple person.* As a symbol of the unhomely, the Muslim is made to feel personally responsible for a contradictory variety of "Islamic" moral values, "Islamic" cultural expressions, and "Islamic" religious and political doctrines.[9]

In the face of such outside pressures, what the overdetermined Muslim needs most is not to be seen, but to be heard. There is a critical need for Islam to be expressed to the world not as an image, but as a narrative, and for Muslims to bear their own witness to their own experiences. The vast majority of books on Islam written in European languages, even the best ones, have been written by non-Muslims. This is not necessarily a problem, because an objective and open-minded non-Muslim can often describe Islam for a non-

Muslim audience better than a Muslim apologist. The scholars Said and Ernst, mentioned above, are both from Christian backgrounds. The discipline of Religious Studies from which Ernst writes has been careful to maintain a nonjudgmental attitude toward non-Christian religions. As heirs to the political and philosophical values of European liberalism, scholars of Religious Studies are typically dogmatic about only one thing: they must practice *epoché* (a Greek word meaning "holding back" or restraining one's beliefs) when approaching the worldview of another religion. In the words of the late Canadian scholar of religion Wilfred Cantwell Smith, it is not enough to act like "a fly crawling on the outside of a goldfish bowl," magisterially observing another's religious practices while remaining distant from the subject. Instead, one must be more engaged in her inquiry and, through imagination and the use of *epoché*, try to find out what it feels like to be a goldfish.[10]

Through the practice of *epoché*, the field of Religious Studies has by now produced two generations of accomplished scholars of Islam in the United States and Canada. Smith himself was a fair and sympathetic Christian scholar of Islam, and his field has been more influential than any other in promoting the study of Islam in the West. However, even Smith was aware that only a goldfish truly knows what it means to be a goldfish. The most that a sympathetic non-Muslim specialist in Islamic studies can do is *describe* Islam from the perspective of a sensitive outsider. Because non-Muslims do not share a personal commitment to the Islamic faith, they are not in the best position to convey a sense of what it means to *be* a Muslim on the inside—to live a Muslim life, to share Muslim values and concerns, and to experience Islam spiritually. In the final analysis, only Muslims can fully bear witness to their own traditions from within.

The five-volume set of *Voices of Islam* is an attempt to meet this need. By bringing together the voices of nearly 50 prominent Muslims from around the world, it aims to present an accurate, comprehensive, and accessible account of Islamic doctrines, practices, and worldviews for a general reader at the senior high school and university undergraduate level. The subjects of the volumes—*Voices of Tradition; Voices of the Spirit; Voices of Life: Family, Home, and Society; Voices of Art, Beauty, and Science;* and *Voices of Change*—were selected to provide as wide a depiction as possible of Muslim experiences and ways of knowledge. Taken collectively, the chapters in these volumes provide bridges between formal religion and culture, the present and the past, tradition and change, and spiritual and outward action that can be crossed by readers, whether they are Muslims or non-Muslims, many times and in a variety of ways. What this set does *not* do is present a magisterial, authoritative vision of an "objectively real" Islam that is juxtaposed against a supposedly inauthentic diversity of individual voices. As the Egyptian-American legal scholar and culture critic Khaled Abou El Fadl has pointed out, whenever Islam is the subject of discourse, the authoritative quickly elides into the authoritarian, irrespective of whether the voice of authority is

Muslim or non-Muslim.[11] The editors of *Voices of Islam* seek to avoid the authoritarian by allowing every voice expressed in the five-volume set to be authoritative, both in terms of individual experience and in terms of the commonalities that Muslims share among themselves.

THE EDITORS

The general editor for *Voices of Islam* is Vincent J. Cornell, Asa Griggs Candler Professor of Middle East and Islamic Studies at Emory University in Atlanta, Georgia. When he was solicited by Praeger, an imprint of Greenwood Publishing, to formulate this project, he was director of the King Fahd Center for Middle East and Islamic Studies at the University of Arkansas. Dr. Cornell has been a Sunni Muslim for more than 30 years and is a noted scholar of Islamic thought and history. His most important book, *Realm of the Saint: Power and Authority in Moroccan Sufism* (1998), was described by a prepublication reviewer as "the most significant study of the Sufi tradition in Islam to have appeared in the last two decades." Besides publishing works on Sufism, Dr. Cornell has also written articles on Islamic law, Islamic theology, and moral and political philosophy. For the past five years, he has been a participant in the Archbishop of Canterbury's "Building Bridges" dialogue of Christian and Muslim theologians. In cooperation with the Jerusalem-based Elijah Interfaith Institute, he is presently co-convener of a group of Muslim scholars, of whom some are contributors to *Voices of Islam,* which is working toward a new theology of the religious other in Islam. Besides serving as general editor for *Voices of Islam,* Dr. Cornell is also the volume editor for Volume 1, *Voices of Tradition;* Volume 2, *Voices of the Spirit;* and Volume 4, *Voices of Art, Beauty, and Science.*

The associate editors for *Voices of Islam* are Omid Safi and Virginia Gray Henry-Blakemore. Omid Safi is Associate Professor of Religion at the University of North Carolina at Chapel Hill. Dr. Safi, the grandson of a noted Iranian Ayatollah, was born in the United States but raised in Iran and has been recognized as an important Muslim voice for moderation and diversity. He gained widespread praise for his edited first book, *Progressive Muslims: On Justice, Gender, and Pluralism* (2003), and was interviewed on CNN, National Public Radio, and other major media outlets. He recently published an important study of Sufi-state relations in premodern Iran, *The Politics of Knowledge in Premodern Islam* (2006). Dr. Safi is the volume editor for Volume 5, *Voices of Change,* which contains chapters by many of the authors represented in his earlier work, *Progressive Muslims.*

Virginia Gray Henry-Blakemore has been a practicing Sunni Muslim for almost 40 years. She is director of the interfaith publishing houses Fons Vitae and Quinta Essentia and cofounder and trustee of the Islamic Texts Society of Cambridge, England. Some of the most influential families in Saudi

Arabia, Egypt, and Jordan have supported her publishing projects. She is an accomplished lecturer in art history, world religions, and filmmaking and is a founding member of the Thomas Merton Center Foundation. Henry-Blakemore received her BA at Sarah Lawrence College, studied at the American University in Cairo and Al-Azhar University, earned her MA in Education at the University of Michigan, and served as a research fellow at Cambridge University from 1983 to 1990. She is the volume editor for Volume 3, *Voices of Life: Family, Home, and Society.*

THE AUTHORS

As stated earlier, *Voices of Islam* seeks to meet the need for Muslims to bear witness to their own traditions by bringing together a diverse collection of Muslim voices from different regions and from different scholarly and professional backgrounds. The voices that speak to the readers about Islam in this set come from Asia, Africa, Europe, and North America, and include men and women, academics, community and religious leaders, teachers, activists, and business leaders. Some authors were born Muslims and others embraced Islam at various points in their lives. A variety of doctrinal, legal, and cultural positions are also represented, including modernists, traditionalists, legalists, Sunnis, Shiites, Sufis, and "progressive Muslims." The editors of the set took care to represent as many Muslim points of view as possible, including those that they may disagree with. Although each chapter in the set was designed to provide basic information for the general reader on a particular topic, the authors were encouraged to express their individual voices of opinion and experience whenever possible.

In theoretical terms, *Voices of Islam* treads a fine line between what Paul Veyne has called "specificity" and "singularity." As both an introduction to Islam and as an expression of Islamic diversity, this set combines historical and commentarial approaches, as well as poetic and narrative accounts of individual experiences. Because of the wide range of subjects that are covered, individualized accounts (the "singular") make up much of the narrative of *Voices of Islam,* but the intent of the work is not to express individuality per se. Rather, the goal is to help the reader understand the varieties of Islamic experience (the "specific") more deeply by finding within their specificity a certain kind of generality.[12]

For Veyne, "specificity" is another way of expressing typicality or the ideal type, a sociological concept that has been a useful tool for investigating complex systems of social organization, thought, or belief. However, the problem with typification is that it may lead to oversimplification, and oversimplification is the handmaiden of the stereotype. Typification can lead to oversimplification because the concept of typicality belongs to a structure of general knowledge that obscures the view of the singular and the different. Thus, presenting the voices of only preselected "typical Muslims" or "representative Muslims" in a work such as *Voices of Islam* would only aggravate the tendency of many Muslims and non-Muslims to define Islam in a single, essentialized way. When done from without, this can lead to a form of stereotyping that may exacerbate, rather than alleviate, the tendency to see Muslims in ways that they do not see themselves. When done from within, it can lead to a dogmatic fundamentalism (whether liberal or conservative does not matter) that excludes the voices of difference from "real" Islam and fosters a totalitarian approach to religion. Such an emphasis on the legitimacy of representation by Muslims themselves would merely reinforce the ideal of sameness that Arendt decried and enable the overdetermination of the "typical" Muslim from without. For this reason, *Voices of Islam* seeks to strike a balance between specificity and singularity. Not only the chapters in these volumes but also the backgrounds and personal orientations of their authors express Islam as a lived diversity and as a source of multiple wellsprings of knowledge. Through the use of individual voices, this work seeks to save the "singular" from the "typical" by employing the "specific."

Dipesh Chakrabarty, a major figure in the field of Subaltern Studies, notes: "Singularity is a matter of viewing. It comes into being as that which resists our attempt to see something as a particular instance of a general idea or category."[13] For Chakrabarty, the singular is a necessary antidote to the typical because it "defies the generalizing impulse of the sociological imagination."[14] Because the tendency to overdetermine and objectify Islam is central to the continued lack of understanding of Islam by non-Muslims, it is necessary to defy the generalizing impulse by demonstrating that the unity of Islam is not a unity of sameness, but of diversity. Highlighting the singularity of individual Islamic practices and doctrines becomes a means of liberating Islam from the totalizing vision of both religious fundamentalism (Muslim and non-Muslim alike) and secular essentialism. While Islam in theory may be a unity, in both thought and practice this "unity" is in reality a galaxy whose millions of singular stars exist within a universe of multiple perspectives. This is not just a sociological fact, but a theological point as well. For centuries, Muslim theologians have asserted that the Transcendent Unity of God is a mystery that defies the normal rules of logic. To human beings, unity usually implies either singularity or sameness, but with respect to God, Unity is beyond number or comparison.

In historiographical terms, a work that seeks to describe Islam through the voices of individual Muslims is an example of "minority history." However, by allowing the voices of specificity and singularity to enter into a trialogue that includes each other as well as the reader, *Voices of Islam* is also an example of "subaltern history." For Chakrabarty, subaltern narratives "are marginalized not because of any conscious intentions but because they represent moments or points at which the archive that the historian mines develops a degree of intractability with respect to the aims of professional history."[15] Subaltern narratives do not only belong to socially subordinate or minority groups, but they also belong to underrepresented groups in Western scholarship, even if these groups comprise a billion people as Muslims do. Subaltern narratives resist typification because the realities that they represent do not correspond to the stereotypical. As such, they need to be studied on their own terms. The history of Islam in thought and practice is the product of constant dialogues between the present and the past, internal and external discourses, culture and ideology, and tradition and change. To describe Islam as anything less would be to reduce it to a limited set of descriptive and conceptual categories that can only rob Islam of its diversity and its historical and intellectual depth. The best way to retain a sense of this diversity and depth is to allow Muslim voices to relate their own narratives of Islam's past and present.

NOTES

1. Carl W. Ernst, *Following Muhammad: Rethinking Islam in the Contemporary World* (Chapel Hill and London: University of North Carolina Press, 2003), xvii.

2. *Time,* June 7, 2004, 10.

3. Hannah Arendt, *The Origins of Totalitarianism,* rev. ed. (San Diego, New York, and London: Harvest Harcourt, 1976), 54.

4. Ibid., 55.

5. Guillermo Gomez-Peña, "The New World (B)order," *Third Text* 21 (Winter 1992–1993): 74, quoted in Homi K. Bhabha, *The Location of Culture* (London and New York: Routledge Classics, 2004), 313.

6. Bhabha, *The Location of Culture,* 13.

7. Ibid., 14–15.

8. Frantz Fanon, *Black Skin, White Masks* (London, U.K.: Pluto, 1986), 116. The original French term for this condition is *surdéterminé.* See idem, *Peau noire masques blancs* (Paris: Éditions du Seuil, 1952), 128.

9. Ibid., 112.

10. Wilfred Cantwell Smith, *The Meaning and End of Religion* (Minneapolis, Minnesota: The University of Minnesota Press, 1991), 7.

11. Khaled Abou El Fadl, *Speaking in God's Name: Islamic Law, Authority, and Women* (Oxford, U.K.: Oneworld Publications, 2001), 9–85.

12. Paul Veyne, *Writing History: Essay on Epistemology,* trans. Mina Moore-Rinvolucri (Middletown, Connecticut: Wesleyan University Press, 1984), 56.

13. Dipesh Chakrabarty, *Provincializing Europe: Postcolonial Thought and Historical Difference* (Princeton and Oxford: Princeton University Press, 2000), 82.

14. Ibid., 83.

15. Ibid., 101.

INTRODUCTION: BEAUTY, CULTURE, AND CREATIVITY IN ISLAM

————————————•————————————

Vincent J. Cornell

In "Diary of a Careless Woman" (*Yawmiyat Mar'a la Mubaliya*), the Syrian poet Nizar Qabbani, bemoaning the state of contemporary Arab culture, wrote: "Our culture! Nothing but bubbles in washtubs and chamber pots!"[1] Qabbani's complaint, which shocked readers at the time it was written, reflected what the French Arabist and culture critic Jacques Berque called the "ravaged subjectivity" of the Arab intellectual. "In aesthetic matters as in everything else," wrote Berque, "the Arabs suffer both from the valuation they place upon their classicism, and from their training on foreign models. They attach value to this training itself, since in most cases they take it as an index of modernity and a criterion of survival. Arabic expression is thus caught between two millstones, one coming from the depths of the ages, the other from the outside."[2]

Berque's analysis of the dilemma of Arab cultural expression can be applied to Islamic cultural expression as well. The two millstones of which he speaks —a formalistic classicism that leads to the idealized construction of a mythical past and a shallow and materialistic modernism, imported from the outside, which offers the allure of progress without the antidote of self-criticality— imprison the contemporary Muslim artist and intellectual between two dogmatisms that offer few avenues of escape. In response to this dilemma, the Muslim artist or intellectual often retreats into an antimodern or anti-Western stance in order to preserve the integrity of a classical ideal that is more metaphorical than real. However, what such artists and intellectuals fail to realize is that Muslims and Westerners are both caught in a similar dilemma. Both are born into the "original sin" of modernity, whether they live in Cairo or Cleveland, Tehran or Topeka, Lahore or Los Angeles. Because of this, any attempt to escape from modernity can only be made through modernity itself, by using modern concepts, strategies, and methodologies. Muslim artists and intellectuals make frequent and regular use of modern concepts and strategies whether they intend to do so or not. This is why the attempt to undo the loss of tradition often becomes a false front, the fetishization of an ideal, and an artificial invention of a pseudo-tradition.

This problem is not unique to the Muslim world. The invention of pseudo-tradition is as much a problem for Western conservatives as it is for Muslim revivalists. For example, speaking empirically, what makes the "Greatest Generation" of Americans who fought in World War II necessarily better than the present generation of Americans? How can one be sure that the present generation of Americans would not respond with the same courage and resolve if faced with the same challenges? Eric Hobsbawm has observed that the nostalgic reinvention of tradition is not a creative revitalization of the past but is instead a sterile process of "formalization and ritualization, characterized by reference to the past, if only by imposing repetition."[3] The Moroccan feminist writer Fatima Mernissi refers to the fetishization of tradition in the contemporary Muslim world as a *mal du présent,* a "sickness of the present," which leads Muslims to experience "a desire for death, a desire to be elsewhere, to be absent, to flee to the past as a way of being absent. A suicidal absence."[4]

Characteristic of the nostalgia for the past as described by Hobsbawm and Mernissi is the rejection of values labeled as "modern" by Muslim ideological conservatives. In the context of postcolonial Islam, this means a rejection of virtually everything that bespeaks Western liberalism. The Iranian essayist Abdolkarim Soroush, despite being highly critical of the Islamic Republic of Iran, supports the antiliberal stance of the Iranian Revolution when he writes, "The modern world is the ethical inverse of the old world. The ancient apocalyptic prophecies came true: Reason is enslaved to desire, the external governs the internal, and vices have supplanted the virtues."[5] In his famous manifesto *Ma'alim fi al-Tariq* (Signs along the Road), the Egyptian Muslim Brotherhood ideologue Sayyid Qutb (d. 1966) warns Muslim youth to avoid Western views of "the interpretation of human endeavor...the explanation of the origin of the universe, [and] the origin of the life of man.... It is... not permissible for a Muslim to learn them from anyone other than a God-fearing and pious Muslim, who knows that guidance in these matters comes from God."[6] The reason why Muslims must reject the products of Western culture, says Qutb, is that "these 'civilizations' that have dazzled many Muslims and have defeated their spirits, are nothing but an ignorant and godless system at heart, and this system is erroneous, hollow, and worthless in comparison with Islam.... We ought not to be defeated to such an extent that we start looking for similarities with Islam in current systems and in some current religions, or in some current ideas; we reject these systems in the East as well as in the West. We reject them all, as indeed they are retrogressive and in opposition to the direction in which Islam intends to take humankind."[7]

Such strikingly similar points of view from a conservative Muslim Brotherhood activist and an ostensibly progressive Iranian thinker remind us that the current confrontation between postcolonial Islam and the West is not only political but also cultural. As we have learned from recent debates in the United States over funding for the Public Broadcasting System and the National Endowment for the Humanities, culture wars are just as often fought over art and philosophy as over political ideologies. Certainly, there is much in Western secular culture that is profane and antireligious, and draws one's attention away from the spiritual and toward the material. But have the jeremiads of modern Muslim revivalists led to anything more culturally significant than a resurgent Islamic political activism? Have new schools of literature, music, or design developed, for example, among the different branches of the Muslim Brotherhood? Has there been a renaissance of Islamic arts, letters, or architecture to counteract the allegedly decadent cultural expressions of the West? In Iran, the Islamic Revolution created new markets for edited works of classical Islamic scholarship and produced a vivid poster art based largely on political themes. In addition, the works of Iranian filmmakers have appeared at Cannes and even in Hollywood. But has the official cultural environment of the Islamic Republic been conducive to an artistic and intellectual renaissance in general? The jury is still out on these questions, but most observers would probably respond in the negative. Creativity in today's Islam is more a product of the margins than of the center.

The Egyptian-American legal scholar and culture critic Khaled M. Abou El Fadl has noted that all too often, the image of Islamic culture among non-Muslims is associated not with beauty, but with everything ugly, unpleasant, and inhumane. "In these popular perceptions, Islam is a legalistic religion whose numerous laws vitiate the need for morality or ethics or for a sense of beauty. The encounter is rendered frustrating when a Muslim jumps up in the midst of a discussion and declares, 'Beauty is a corruption, and that is why there is no law in Shari'a which commands that we should care for beauty'."[8] If the image of contemporary Islam that Abou El Fadl describes is accurate, then the attempt by conservative Islamic ideologues to separate Islam retroactively from the spiritually corrosive effects of globalization and Westernization seems analogous to a doctor's attempt to amputate a gangrenous limb after the gangrene has already entered the bloodstream.

Virtually every Muslim in the world knows the saying of the Prophet Muhammad, "God is beautiful and He loves beauty" (*Allahu jamil wa yuhibbu al-jamal*). If this is the case, then where is the sense of beauty in contemporary Islam? Where is the sense of the spiritual aesthetics of form, substance, and expression that used to be characteristic of the arts of the Muslim world? While examples of beauty can still be found in modern Islam, it often appears, as Abou El Fadl suggests, that ugliness is taking over. First-time visitors to the Middle East often remark on the stark contrast between the elegance and majesty of premodern Islamic mosques and their ungainly modern counterparts, which are often lit garishly at night by green neon lights. Traditionally, mosques on the island of Java in Indonesia were built without minarets, following South Indian architectural models. In the twentieth century, Indonesian Muslim reformers, returning from the Middle East, sought to correct this "problem" by attaching new minarets to preexisting structures. In the Javanese city of Demak, there is a mosque dating to the fifteenth century CE, which the locals believe was constructed by the *Wali Songo*, the nine saints who first brought Islam to Java. This old mosque, which is topped by a low-slung tiled roof that shades the prayer hall and outer portico, is a place of peace and contemplation that evokes an immediate sense of spirituality. However, due to the zeal of modern reformers, a steel minaret that looks like an oil derrick now stands next to the mosque and utterly ruins the visual effect of the original building. In 2005 I visited Bosnia-Herzegovina as a member of an interreligious delegation headed by the Archbishop of Canterbury. Outside the city of Mostar, we saw a mosque under construction, endowed by donors from abroad, whose squat onion dome and arched portico made it look more like a crouching spider than a place of spiritual retreat and contemplation. A British Muslim scholar in the delegation wryly observed that it must have been a present to Bosnia-Herzegovina from the Klingon Empire of the *Star Trek* television series.

In an ironic correspondence that deserves its own separate analysis, the word that best describes the attitude of modern ideological Islam toward beauty and art is "Philistine." The dictionary definition of a Philistine is a materialistic person who is indifferent to or disapproving of artistic and intellectual achievements and values. In the city of Cairo, Egypt, there is a museum of Islamic art that contains some of the finest examples of Islamic artisanship to be found anywhere in the world. In this museum one can see beautifully illuminated Qur'an manuscripts from the Mamluk period (thirteenth to sixteenth centuries CE), embroidered textiles, carved woods, and pottery from the Fatimid period (tenth to twelfth centuries CE), and works of brass, mosaic, and calligraphy from different periods of Egypt's Islamic history. What surprised me as I visited this museum on several occasions was that it was almost always empty, save for the occasional Western tourist or researcher such as myself. Once when I visited Cairo, I hired an Islamist cab driver to take me to the places in the city where I was conducting research. He was an intelligent man and I enjoyed our discussions and debates about Islam and Egypt as we made our way through the heavy Cairo traffic. One day, I needed to visit the Islamic art museum, so I bought my driver a ticket, thinking that he might enjoy the chance to learn something about Egypt's Islamic artistic heritage. After passing through the first exhibit hall, I discovered that he had disappeared. Two hours later, as I exited the building, I found him sitting at the entrance of the museum, chatting with the ticket-taker. When I asked him where he had gone, he replied in an offhand way that he found the entire museum uninteresting.

This is what it means to be a Philistine. What makes the Islamist cab driver's behavior culturally significant is the contrast that one observes in Cairo between the Museum of Islamic Art, which is virtually empty, and the Egyptian Museum, which contains pre-Islamic art and is always crowded. Even more significant is the fact that the Egyptian Museum is filled not only with foreign tourists but also with large numbers of Egyptian visitors, including Islamist families with men wearing neatly trimmed beards and women veiled in *hijab*. Clearly, Pharaonic art is considered part of Egypt's cultural heritage in a way that Islamic art is not. One of the conclusions that I drew from this paradox was that the Philistinism of Egyptian Islamists is due, at least in part, to the ideological influence of religious fundamentalism. When one visits the artistic remains of the Pharaohs, one is led to recall the stories of the Prophets Joseph and Moses in the Qur'an. Although the Pharaohs were pagans, the cultural artifacts of their past can be legitimized on both nationalistic grounds (as the original Egyptian civilization) and on religious grounds, because the Pharaohs are protagonists in the stories of the Prophets that have been told to popular audiences throughout Islamic history. However, when a Sunni Muslim fundamentalist looks at the cultural artifacts of the Fatimid or Mamluk periods of Egyptian Islamic history, he or she merely observes the artifacts of Shiite "heretics" (the Fatimids) or cruel Turkish despots who oppressed the Egyptian people (the Mamluks). Typically, the fundamentalist observer overlooks the fact that the artistic themes in the Museum of Islamic Art are more Qur'anic in spirit than the artistic themes in the Egyptian Museum. Because the scriptural literalism and constricted historical vision of fundamentalism make little or no room for artistic imagination, the modern Islamist perspective can be nothing but Philistine in its approach to art and culture. This attitude is not unique to Islam, or even to Islamic fundamentalism. Fundamentalism is just as Philistine when it is found in Christianity or Judaism as well.

In an essay entitled, "Pearls of Beauty (on Re-Finding Our Lost Civilization)," Khaled M. Abou El Fadl discusses from the inside of Muslim experience the same dilemma that Jacques Berque noted nearly 30 years earlier as a sympathetic outsider. In the following passage from this essay, Abou El Fadl suggests that both the nostalgic classicism and the Philistinism of modern Islamic culture are consequences of a postcolonial sense of cultural deprivation and inferiority:

> The nomads of the Lost Civilization live frozen in fear—the fear of gazing at the corpse, confronting their loss, and relinquishing their grip over the fossils of antiquity. The chains of their once-glorious memories have condemned them to the mortification of an unrelenting redundancy. Old words and thoughts are uttered like chants in a sanctuary of hallowed memories. They supplicate in the name of a bygone oasis and every mirage becomes their prophecy. Finally, the nomads either settle in their makeshift shelters of ignorance or, if they search the oceans, they dare not open a single shell lest the pearls of perception reveal to them the full extent of their ignoble destitution and agonizing reality.

Yes, we are the displaced children of the Civilization of the Word, pariahs in the world of thought and literacy. We are the outcasts of the unthinkables and unmentionables, subsisting on the scraps of hardened ideas. We've forgone the pearls of knowledge in fear of being distracted from our sanctimonious memories. Even the word of God is preserved as a memory and not as a thought to be engaged, in search of the pearls it conceals and then reveals. But the life of a word is measured by the pearls that mark its development, not by the shrines that honor its memory.[9]

The chapters that were chosen for the present volume of *Voices of Islam* are all premised on the idea that Islamic civilization has been, and remains, the quintessential Civilization of the Word. In the divine discourse of Islam, as it is expressed in the Qur'an, the concepts of being, reality, and existence are conjoined in the terms, *al-Haqq*—the Truth—and *al-Haqiqa*—Reality, the Real, the "I am what I am" (to paraphrase the Bible), which connote God in the act of self-revelation. In *Surat Yasin* (Qur'an 36), a chapter of the Holy Qur'an that is believed to have an especially powerful surplus of meaning, God says of Himself: "We bring dead things to life and We determine their pasts and their futures; and We have contained all things in a self-revealing paradigm" (Qur'an 36:12). The translation of the Arabic phrase *imam mubin* in this verse as "a self-revealing paradigm" is derived from the French Islamic scholar and Qur'an translator René Blachère, who saw in the concept of *imam mubin* a justification for the popular belief in Islam that the paradigm for all knowledge is contained in the Qur'an.[10] The value of this concept for the present discussion lies in the fact that although the Qur'an comments on moral beauty more often than on aesthetic beauty, aesthetic beauty is still highly valued in the Qur'anic paradigm because God is the self-revealing Creator (*al-Khaliq*), Originator (*al-Bari'*), and Fashioner of Forms (*al-Musawwir*). "To Him belong the Most Beautiful Names" (Qur'an 59:24). Despite the famous hadith that proclaims, "God is beautiful and He loves beauty," *al-Jamil,* the Arabic term for "the Beautiful," is not one of the Divine Names in the Qur'an. However, as the Fashioner of Forms and Possessor of the Beautiful Names, beauty continually flows from God through His act of self-revelation.

Put another way, one can say that in the perspective of the Qur'an, God is the Supreme Artist. As Seyyed Hossein Nasr, the noted Islamic scholar and commentator on Islamic art, has observed: "God is not only the Grand Architect or Geometer; He is also the Poet, the Painter, the Musician... Being 'created in the image of God' and therefore a supreme work of art, man is also an artist who, in imitating the creative powers of his Maker, realizes his own theomorphic nature. The spiritual man, aware of his vocation, is not only the musician who plucks the lyre to create music. He is himself the lyre upon which the Divine Artist plays, creating the music which reverberates throughout the cosmos, for as Mevlana Jalaluddin Rumi says, 'We are like the lyre which Thou pluckest.'"[11] The lesson to be learned from Nasr's statement is this: When the reader of the present volume approaches chapters on the arts of calligraphy, music, garden design, poetry, literature, and medicine, he or she should always remember that ultimately, in the perspective of Qur'anic Islam, it is God who is the Writer, Designer, Musician, Poet, and Healer. As vicegerents of God, human beings exercise creativity in imitation of the Divine Creativity that brought them and the world into being.

This is an important point to remember because much of the ugliness that has been perpetrated in the name of modern Islam is the unintentional result of a superficial and literalistic understanding of the Word of God. This is not to say, however, that one should not be careful in interpreting the divine discourse. Pious caution has always been a legitimate and important part of tradition in world religions. Although the human being has been given the license to produce works of beauty after the fashion of the Maker, one must be careful not to assume that, like God, one can originate something out of nothing or create something completely without precedent. As Confucius said, "I do not create. I only tell of the past."[12] The challenge for the Muslim artist is how to create beauty out of words, sounds, colors, and materials without arrogating to oneself the role of ultimate Creator. Again, this problem is not confined to Islam alone. In fact, it is as old as the Greek myth of Pygmalion and Galatea and as universal as Mary Shelley's *Frankenstein*.

The question of creativity and its limits has a long history in Islam. In the medieval Islamic world, creativity was seen as related to inspiration and was discussed with reference to the Arabic term, *khatir* (pl. *khawatir*). In his influential *Treatise on Sufism*, the famous Sufi and scholar Abu al-Qasim al-Qushayri of Nishapur (d. 1074 CE) defines *khawatir* as "addresses that arise in the conscious mind" (*khitabat taridu 'ala al-dama'ir*). In other words, for Qushayri, inspirations are like voices inside the head, which may come from self-subsisting knowledge (*min ilqa' malakin*), from Satan (*al-Shaytan*), from the mind or ego-self (*al-nafs*), or from an encounter with God as the Truth (*al-Haqq*).[13] If inspirations come from self-subsisting knowledge, they are "ideas" (*ilham*); if they come from the mind or ego-self, they are "notions" (*hawajis*); if they come from Satan, they are "suggestions" (*wasawis*); if they come from God, they are "true intimations" or "true inspirations" (*khatir haqqin*). The truth of a new idea is proved or disproved by its correspondence to something already known or by testing it in the outer world. By contrast, notions of the ego-self are characterized by their drive to gratify the senses or enhance pride in the self. Satanic suggestions can be recognized because they lead to disobedience of God. However, a true inspiration from God is known because it always leads to success and has no harmful effects on the soul. The problem with creativity is that when it is associated with the mental processes that produce ideas and notions, it can be affected by outside factors, such as the appetites. In such a case, it might be that one cannot distinguish an inspired idea from a Satanic suggestion. Furthermore, says Qushayri, all of the Sufi masters agree that "the ego-self never tells the truth, but the heart never lies."[14] Thus, from the point of view of Sufi psychology, the modern concept of creativity, which stresses the originality of the individual, self-governed imagination, must always be suspected because the ego-self never tells the truth.

Today, when modern Arabic speakers talk about creativity, they use the term *ibda'*. This term is not used by Qushayri in his discussion of creativity, which suggests that the current use of the term *ibda'* for "creativity" may be a modern innovation. Etymologically, *ibda'* is related to *al-Badi'*, "the Originator," which is one of the Names of God in the Qur'an. It is also related to the word *bid'a*, "innovation," which has often been understood negatively in Islam. The medieval Arabic dictionary *Lisan al-'Arab* (The Language of the Arabs) by Abu al-Fadl Jamal al-Din ibn Manzur (d. 1321 CE) mentions the term *ibda'* twice. However, neither mention of the term corresponds to the modern understanding of creativity.[15] For Ibn Manzur, the signification of *ibda'* revolves around the idea of fashioning something: In the first example, it means the fashioning of an object, and in the second example, it refers to God's "fashioning" creation. The modern concept of creativity, in the sense of the creative artist fashioning something completely new, does not seem to have occurred to Ibn Manzur any more than it occurred to Qushayri. The closest approximation to the modern concept of creativity is conveyed in *Lisan al-'Arab* not by *ibda'*, but by the verbs *ibtada'a* and *abda'a*. These verbs, which are related in meaning to the disapproved religious concept of *bid'a*, signify the creation of an unwarranted innovation; in other words, the refashioning of tradition in illegitimate ways. This is expressed in the Qur'an, for example, by the use of the verb *ibtada'a* to characterize the Christian "innovation" of monasticism (Qur'an 57:27). Apparently, Ibn Manzur and Qushayri both agreed with the Qur'an and with Confucius that as far as creativity is concerned, one does not create but one only tells of the past.

The Islamic concept of *bid'a* is discussed at length in Volume 5 of *Voices of Islam* in the chapter "Creativity, Innovation, and Heresy in Islam" by Umar F. Abd-Allah. Thus, it does not need to be discussed any further here. However, it should be noted that the concepts of development (*tatawwur*), progress (*taqaddum*), renaissance (*nahda*), and renewal (*tajdid*), which have been associated with the notion of creativity in modern times, have histories in nineteenth and twentieth-century Islamic thought that make them problematical because they involve changing tradition in the sense expressed by the Qur'anic verb *ibtada'a*. Each of these terms has appeared historically in the context of either Arab secularism or Islamic modernism or both, and it has been suggested in certain quarters that the positivistic and progressivistic worldview they imply has contributed to the moral and aesthetic ugliness that pervades much of today's Islamic discourse. As the English Muslim scholar Martin Lings (under his Muslim name of Abu Bakr Siraj ad-Din) pointed out in a lecture at Al-Azhar University in 1964, from the perspective of the Qur'an, "progress" (*taqaddum*) is best defined in a religious sense not as the replacement of traditional beliefs with new and improved versions but as a series of steps (from the Arabic word *qadam*) toward spiritual and moral development. "Every individual should hope to progress, and that is the meaning of our prayer, 'Lead us along the Straight Path'" (Qur'an 1:6).[16]

The fact that an English convert to Islam made this observation, and not a Muslim from the Arab world, Iran, or South Asia, illustrates another aspect of creativity in Islamic civilization that is often overlooked by both nationalist and fundamentalist purists: its *hybridity*. The term, "hybridity," is associated with the writings of Homi K. Bhabha, a postcolonial theorist from Mumbai who grew up as a Zoroastrian Parsi in a city that was primarily Hindu and secondarily Muslim. As a culture critic, Bhabha purposefully locates his work on the margins of the dominant forms of cultural and intellectual discourse. For Bhabha, hybridity is the "location" of creativity in a globalized world.[17] It is a concept of displacement and dislocation, and was characteristic in colonial times both of the metropolitan colonialist who created a parody of European culture in a faraway land and of the colonial subject that mimicked metropolitan values in a morality play of contradictions. Today, hybridity is a major result of the global movement of populations from the former colonies of the Third World to European political and cultural centers, such as the United Kingdom, France, Germany, and now Italy and Spain. It also characterizes the emerging intellectual culture of the United States as the imagined center of a globalized world, a place where the "imaginary" of globalization has been recreated in microcosm, especially since the opening of U.S. borders to a greater mix of peoples from Latin America, Asia, and Africa following the reform of immigration laws in 1965. Hybridity thus expresses a place of unresolved tensions, recognitions, and mis-recognitions—a culture of borders and thresholds, of strikingly different references and frames of mind—a place where authoritarian attempts to "speak with one voice," whether it be in the realm of culture, religion, or even language are subverted.

"It is a mistake," says Benedict Anderson, "to treat languages in the way that certain nationalist ideologues treat them—as *emblems* of nation-ness, like flags, costumes, folk-dances, and the rest. Much the most important thing about language is its capacity for generating imagined communities, building in effect *particular solidarities*."[18] The same can be said about religion. The mimicry of classical styles in the creation of pseudo-tradition, the fetishization of scripture, and the ideological reformulation of the Islamic *Umma* into an "Islamic nation" are all recent examples of the attempt to treat the concept of the "Islamic" as an emblem, in the way that languages are used as emblems in nationalistic discourses. The emblematic approach to Islam stifles creativity because it turns selected aspects of Islamic civilization (such as Islamic Law, the Islamic State, Islamic dress, the community of the Prophet Muhammad and his Companions) into exhibits in what French critical theorists call the "museum of the imaginary" (*musée imaginaire*). More importantly, however, it also stifles creativity because it takes the point of "religion"—the bond between the individual human being and God—out of the religion of Islam. The Qur'an reminds Muslims: "Whoever submits himself fully to God and acts with goodness, has indeed grasped the most trustworthy hand-hold. And with God is the resolution of all affairs" (Qur'an 31:22).

The notion of hybridity subverts and undermines fundamentalist and other totalitarian models of religion and culture. Political Islamists resist the study of the full range of Islamic history because knowledge of Islamic history makes it impossible to turn the Arabic language, the Islamic state, or Islamic culture into emblems, and thus to ignore the importance of vernacular expressions of culture, such as Islamic art. The world of Islam has always been full of hybrid communities where many "vernacular languages" of art, politics, and even science have been expressed and many "imagined communities" have arisen within larger communities of discourse. The artistic and creative traditions of Islam have always exhibited what Bhabha calls "vernacular cosmopolitanism," unique local expressions of art and culture that claim the right to "difference in equality" while maintaining "symbolic citizenship" in the Islamic Umma.[19] Vernacular cosmopolitanism can be seen in the traditional Javanese mosque without a minaret, where the muezzin's call to prayer is assisted by the beating of a large drum. It can be seen in Islamic calligraphy from Borneo that merges elements of native Iban decorative motifs with classical Islamic calligraphic styles. It can be seen in the walk-in *mihrab* of the North African and Andalusian mosque, which not only designates the direction of prayer but also recalls the Virgin Mary's use of the *mihrab* as a refuge in the Qur'an (Qur'an 3:37; 19:11). It can even be seen, despite the ideological tendency toward uniform Islamist dress, in the fashion shows of *hijab* styles for women that take place every year in Lebanon, Egypt, and the Gulf. The existence of the vernacular and its stubborn insistence on "difference in equality" is why there has always been a debate about an idealized "Tradition of Islam" versus the historical reality of *traditions* of Islam. Traditionalism is not vernacular. As an idealized construct and an ideology, it speaks with a single, authoritatively imposed voice. This is why traditionalism is oppressive whereas actual traditions allow some degree of creativity. "Oh humankind! We created you from male and female and made you into cultures (*shu'ub*) and tribes so that you may know each other," says the Qur'an (Qur'an 49:13). For contemporary Muslims, this verse should be taken as a reminder that where creativity is concerned, "Globalization must always begin at home."[20]

A common characteristic of the authors in this volume is that they are all products of hybridity and express the tradition of vernacular cosmopolitanism in a modern Islamic context. Martin Lings, as noted above, was an English convert to Islam who lived in Egypt for many years. In this, he is similar to Emma C. Clark, who spent time in Iran and now teaches at the Prince of Wales' School of Traditional Arts. Frithjof Schuon was an Alsatian, from the border between France and Germany, who lived in Switzerland and the United States and embraced Islam in colonial Algeria. Titus Burckhardt, his longtime friend and collaborator, was German-Swiss and was related to the famous Swiss explorer Jean-Louis Burckhardt. Jean-Louis Michon is French-Swiss and lived for many years in Morocco. Shawkat M. Toorawa's family is from the island of Mauritius in the Indian Ocean; he was born in England, grew up in France and Singapore, and teaches at Cornell University in upstate New York. Virginia Gray Henry-Blakemore has homes in Louisville, Kentucky and Cairo, Egypt. Laleh Bakhtiar, who is of Iranian descent, is a licensed psychologist and psychotherapist who, despite her nontraditional training, writes about traditional Islamic medicine and healing.

In addition, some of the best-known authors in this volume, such as Schuon, Burckhardt, and Lings, are representatives of the so-called Traditionalist school. Writers of the Traditionalist school have been criticized by some modernist and historicist scholars of Islam for maintaining an idealized notion of tradition, for supporting conservative and antimodernist political and cultural positions, and for adhering to a perennial philosophy that is based largely on Neo-Platonism. Certainly, when Schuon writes, in the lead chapter of this volume, "Islamic art is contemplative, whereas Gothic art is volitional," and that Renaissance art is "worldly, hypocritical, sensual, and ostentatious," he is expressing an opinion formed from a particular view of religious expression. However, it is also an opinion derived from a deep comparative knowledge of religious art and from a spiritually profound understanding of *tawhid*, the Islamic theological concept of divine unity. For Schuon, Islamic art is the crystalline unfolding of *tawhid* in countless facets of expression, each reflecting a different perspective of the same divine light. It is crucial to remember that Schuon and his collaborators do not read Islam through Europe; rather, they read Europe through Islam. In doing so, they are not less Islamically authentic than the philosopher Ibn Sina (Avicenna, d. 1037 CE), whose perennial philosophy interpreted Plato and Aristotle (the "cutting-edge" theorists of his day) through the lens of *tawhid*.

The hybridity that is represented in this volume of *Voices of Islam* should remind the reader that the community of Muslims—the *Umma Muslima*— is today as it always has been: a "community envisaged as a project—at once a vision and a construction."[21] At one point in its history, the construction project of Islamic culture was centered on the Arab world. At another point, it was centered on Iran and Central Asia. In another period, it drew inspiration from Turkey and South Asia. Today Islamic culture is fully global and has as much to do with Europe, America, and Southeast Asia as it does with its former cultural centers. The perspective that one obtains from each of these centers of Islamic culture is as valid as another is.

This being the case, the task of the creative interpreter of Islamic culture is not to erase the past or to impose an artificial homogeneity of cultural expression. Rather, it is to engage, within one's own intellectual or artistic medium, in the time-honored and fully legitimate process of Islamic interpretation as *ta'wil*—to "go back to the beginning" (*ta'awwala*) in order to take Islamic cultural expression beyond where it is at present. Particularly important is to open new horizons of art and creativity by reconnecting Muslims to the transcendent consciousness that created the miracle of Islam in the first place. In the words of Bhabha, a perspective on art and culture that is born of hybridity "does not merely recall the past as social cause or aesthetic precedent; it renews the past, refiguring it as a contingent, 'in-between' space that innovates and interrupts the performance of the present. The 'past-present' becomes part of the necessity, not the nostalgia, of living."[22] Such a perspective is indeed "otherwise than modern," but it should not be misconstrued as antimodern. Rather, it is what Bhabha terms *contra-modern*. It is born of modernity and contingent to modernity, but it is resistant to the oppressive homogenization of modernity and its tendency toward totalitarianism.

NOTES

1. Jacques Berque, *Cultural Expression in Arab Society Today* (Langages arabes du présent), trans. Robert W. Stookey (Austin and London: University of Texas Press, 1978), 197. This poem originally appeared in Nizar Qabbani's 1968 *Diwan* (Collection).

2. Ibid., 198.

3. Eric Hobsbawm, "Introduction: Inventing Traditions," in *The Invention of Tradition,* ed. Eric Hobsbawm and Terence Ranger (Cambridge, U.K.: Cambridge University Press, 1984), 4.

4. Fatima Mernissi, *Women and Islam: An Historical and Theological Enquiry,* trans. Mary Jo Lakeland (reprint of Basil Blackwell original, New Delhi: Kali for Women, 1991), 15. This work was published in the United States as *The Veil and the Male Elite: A Feminist Interpretation of Women's Rights in Islam* (Reading, Massachusetts: Addison Wesley Publishing, 1991).

5. Abdolkarim Soroush, "Life and Virtue: The Relationship Between Socioeconomic Development and Ethics," in *Reason, Freedom, and Democracy in Islam: Essential Writings of Abdolkarim Soroush,* ed. Mahmoud Sadri and Ahmad Sadri (New York and Oxford: Oxford University Press, 2000), 43.

6. Seyyid Qutb, *Milestones* (Damascus: Dar al-'Ilm), 109–110. See also, the Arabic edition of this work, Sayyid Qutb, *Ma'alim fi al-Tariq* (Beirut: Dar al-Shuruq, 2000), 139.

7. Ibid., 136–137.

8. Khaled M. Abou El Fadl, *Conference of the Books: The Search for Beauty in Islam* (New York and Oxford: University Press of America Inc., 2001), 114.

9. Ibid., 266–267.

10.   Berque, *Cultural Expression,* 171.

11.   Seyyed Hossein Nasr, "Traditional Art as Fountain of Knowledge and Grace," in Nasr, *Knowledge and the Sacred* (Albany, New York: State University of New York Press, 1989), 257.

12.   Nasr, "What Is Tradition?" in Nasr, *Knowledge and the Sacred,* 65.

13.   For the full text on inspiration and creativity as *khawatir,* see Abu al-Qasim 'Abd al-Karim al-Qushayri, *al-Risala al-Qushayriyya fi 'ilm al-tasawwuf,* ed. Ma'ruf Zurayq and 'Ali 'Abd al-Hamid Beltarji (Beirut: Dar al-Jil, 1990), 83–85.

14.   Ibid., 84.

15.   See Abu al-Fadl Jamal al-Din ibn Manzur, *Lisan al-'Arab,* vol. 8 (1883; repr., Beirut: Dar al-Sadir, n.d.), 6–8.

16.   Abu Bakr Siraj ad-Din, "The Spiritual Function of Civilization," in *The Sword of Gnosis: Metaphysics, Cosmology, Tradition, Symbolism,* ed. Jacob Needleman (London, Boston, and Henley: Arkana Publications, 1984), 104.

17.   See Homi K. Bhabha, *The Location of Culture* (London and New York: Routledge, 1994).

18.   Benedict Anderson, *Imagined Communities: Reflections on the Origin and Spread of Nationalism* (London and New York: Verso, 1991), 133.

19.   Bhabha, "Preface to the Routledge Classics Edition," *The Location of Culture,* xvi–xvii.

20.   Ibid., xv.

21.   Ibid., 4.

22.   Ibid., 10.

1

ISLAMIC ART

·

Frithjof Schuon

The nonfigurative or abstract arts of Judaism and Islam must not be overlooked. The former art was revealed in the Torah and is exclusively sacerdotal. Islamic art is akin to Judaic art by its exclusion of human and animal representations. As to its origin, Islamic art issued from the sensory form of the revealed Book; that is, from the interlaced letters of the verses of the Qur'an, and also, paradoxical though this may seem, from the forbidding of images. This restriction in Islamic art, by eliminating certain creative possibilities, intensified others, the more so since it was accompanied by the express permission to represent plants; hence, the capital importance of arabesques, and of geometrical and botanical decorative motifs. Islamic architecture, the themes of which were inherited from neighboring civilizations, was transmuted by its own particular genius, which tended at the same time both to simplification and to ornamentation. The purest expression of this genius is perhaps the art of the Maghrib (the Islamic West), in which no preexisting formalism invited concessions. In Islam, the love of beauty compensates for the tendency to austere simplicity. It lends elegant form to simplicity and partially clothes it in a profusion of precious and abstract lacework. "God is Beautiful," said the Prophet, "and He loves beauty."

Islamic art allies the joyous profusion of vegetation with the pure and abstract severity of crystals. A prayer niche adorned with arabesques owes something to a garden and to snowflakes. This mixture of qualities is already to be met with in the Qur'an, where the geometry of the ideas is as it were hidden under the flamboyance of forms. Islam, being possessed by the idea of Unity (*tawhid*), if one may so put it, also has an aspect of the simplicity of the desert, of whiteness and of austerity, which, in its art, alternates with the crystalline joy of ornamentation. The cradle of the Arabs is a landscape of deserts and oases. Let us also mention the verbal theophany, which is the psalmodized recitation of the revealed texts,[1] calligraphy being its visual mode,[2] or again, in Islam, the canonical prayer, the majestic movement of which expresses the sacred in a manner that from the point of view in question is not without relation to the *mudras* of India.

Christianity corresponds to a volitional decision between the here below and the hereafter. Islam, on the other hand, is a sapiential choice of the Truth, and in the light of this Truth, all must be known and evaluated. In metaphysical truth, there is neither here below nor hereafter. Everything is contained in it, and this can be seen in Islamic art. Everything natural to the human being finds its place in this truth. The world is seen in God and thus is given its meaning and spiritual efficacy.

It is understandable that the smiling grace of Islamic architecture should have appeared to many Christians as something worldly and "pagan"; the volitional perspective envisages the "here below" and the "beyond" only as levels of existence that mark separation and opposition, and not as universal essences that unite and make things identical. In Renaissance art, virtue becomes crushing, lugubrious, and tiresome; beside the Alhambra, the palace of Charles V in Granada seeks to be grave and austere, but only achieves a heaviness and an opacity, which banish all higher intelligence, contemplation, and serenity.

After looking at the Alhambra for hours, it became clearer than ever to me that Islamic art is contemplative, whereas Gothic art is volitional, not to speak of the Renaissance, in which the volitional becomes worldly, hypocritical, sensual, and ostentatious. For Charles V the Alhambra was worldly because it is beautiful and joyful, and to this apparent worldliness, he opposed the dull, oppressive, and completely unspiritual ostentatiousness of his palace. Here, ugliness and stupidity wish to pass themselves off as virtues: namely, seriousness, strength, and otherworldliness. The otherworldly is seen purely in "volitional" fashion, as something negative and not as something spiritual that reveals itself in creation.

After the Alhambra and the Alcázar of Seville, I have never seen anything that appeased my spirit more than the Mosque at Córdoba, and I have seldom seen anything that so aroused my indignation as the Christian addition to this mosque. The Catholicism of the Renaissance shows itself here in its most horrible form, a proof that exotericism is aware of only a fraction of the devil's power, and indeed beyond certain limits allows it free play: to be precise, in those realms which concern the Intellect. There is only one ancient and beautiful Madonna there, and one other good old picture. But enough of this.

Islamic art shows in a very transparent way how art should repeat nature—understood in the widest possible sense—in its creative modes without copying it in its results. It is abstract, but also poetical and gracious. It is woven out of sobriety and splendor. The style of the Maghrib (Islamic Spain and North Africa) is perhaps more virile than are the Turkish and Persian styles; but these—and especially the latter—are by way of compensation more varied.[3]

The spiritual intention of Islam is brought clearly to view in its art. Just as its art captures the all-pervading and the all-inclusive, and avoids narrowness of every kind, so does Islam itself seek to avoid whatever is ugly and to keep in sight that which is "everywhere Center." For this reason, it replaces, so to speak, the "cross" by the "weave." A center is a center only at a definite point, it rejects the cross as "association" (*shirk*). It wishes to dissolve a priori every individualistic entanglement. It knows only one Center: God. Every other "center," such as the Prophet Muhammad, or Islam itself, is loosened as in a rhythm or in a "weaving." The Ka'ba too is in its center a world-containing web.

NOTES

This chapter will also appear in the forthcoming volume, *Frithjof Schuon on Universal Art: Principles and Criteria,* edited by Catherine Schuon (Bloomington, Indiana: World Wisdom, 2007). Slight editorial changes have been made to the original for consistency of style and for purposes of clarification. The general editor of this set thanks the editors of World Wisdom Books for permission to reproduce this work.

1.   For instance, the chanting of the Qur'an, which can be in various styles, is an art. A choice can be made between one style and another, but nothing can be added to them. One can chant the Qur'an in certain ways, but not in others. The modes of chanting express different rhythms of the spirit.

2.   Outside of the Far East, there are scarcely any but the Muslim people who possess calligraphies equivalent to the Chinese ideograms, thanks not only to the richness and plasticity of the Arabic characters but also to the concentration—due to religious reasons—of the pictorial instinct on writing alone.

3.   Persian miniatures integrate things in a surface without perspective, and thus in a sense without limits, like a piece of weaving; it is this which makes them compatible—at any rate as "worldly" objects—with the Islamic perspective. In a general way, Muslims distrust any "materialization" of religious subjects, as if in fear that spiritual realities might become exhausted through an excess of sensory crystallization. The sculptured and dramatic imagery of the Roman Church has indeed proven to be a two-edged sword; instead of making it "sensitive" and popular, the Church ought to have maintained in it the hieratic abstraction of Romanesque statuary. It is not the sole obligation of art to come down toward the common people; it should also remain faithful to its intrinsic truth in order to allow men to rise toward that truth.

2

The Foundations of Islamic Art

•

Titus Burckhardt

"God is beautiful and He loves beauty."

—The Prophet

Unity, in itself eminently "concrete," nevertheless presents itself to the human mind as an abstract idea. This fact, together with certain considerations, connected with the Semitic mentality, explains the abstract character of Islamic art. Islam is centered on Unity, and Unity is not expressible in terms of any image.

The prohibition of images in Islam is not, however, absolute. A plane image is tolerated as an element in profane art, on condition that it represents neither God nor the face of the Prophet;[1] on the other hand, an image "that casts a shadow" is only tolerated exceptionally, when it represents a stylized animal, as may happen in the architecture of palaces or in jewelry.[2] In a general way, the representation of plants and fantastic animals is expressly allowed, but in sacred art stylized plant forms alone are admitted.

The absence of images in mosques has two purposes. One is negative, namely, that of eliminating a "presence" which might set itself up against the Presence—albeit invisible—of God, and which might in addition become a source of error because of the imperfection of all symbols; the other and positive purpose is that of affirming the transcendence of God, since the Divine Essence cannot be compared with anything whatsoever.

Unity, it is true, has a participative aspect, insofar as it is the synthesis of the multiple and the principle of analogy; it is in that aspect that a sacred image presupposes Unity and expresses it in its own way; but Unity is also the principle of distinction, for it is by its intrinsic unity that every being is essentially distinguished from all others, in such a way that it is unique and can neither be confused nor be replaced. This last aspect of Unity reflects most directly the transcendence of the Supreme Unity, its "Non-Alterity" and its absolute Solitude. According to the fundamental formula of Islam: "There is no

divinity other than God" (*la ilaha illalah*), it is through the distinction of the
different planes of reality that everything is gathered together beneath
the infinite vault of the Supreme Unity: once one has recognized the finite
for what it is one can no longer consider it "alongside of" the Infinite, and
for that very reason the finite reintegrates itself with the Infinite.

From this point of view the fundamental error is that of projecting the
nature of the absolute into the relative, by attributing to the relative an
autonomy that does not belong to it: the primary source of this error is
imagination, or more precisely illusion (*al-wahm*). Therefore, a Muslim sees
in figurative art a flagrant and contagious manifestation of the said error;
in his view the image projects one order of reality into another. Against this
the only effective safeguard is wisdom (*hikma*), which puts everything in its
proper place. As applied to art this means that every artistic creation must
be treated according to the laws of its domain of existence and must
make those laws intelligible; architecture, for example, must manifest the
static equilibrium and state of perfection of motionless bodies, typified in
the regular shape of a crystal.

This last statement about architecture needs amplification. Some people
reproach Islamic architecture with failing to accentuate the functional aspect
of the elements of a building, as does the architecture of the Renaissance,
which reinforces heavily loaded elements and lines of tension, thus conferring
on constructional elements a sort of organic consciousness. But according to
the perspective of Islam, to do so implies nothing less than a confusion
between two orders of reality and a lack of intellectual sincerity: if slender
columns can in fact carry the load of a vault, what is the good of artificially
attributing to them a state of tension, which anyhow is not in the nature of
a mineral? In another aspect, Islamic architecture does not seek to do away
with the heaviness of stone by giving it an ascending movement, as does
Gothic art; static equilibrium demands immobility, but the crude material is
as it were, lightened and rendered diaphanous by the chiseling of the arabesques and by carving in the form of stalactites and hollows, which present
thousands of facets to the light and confer on stone and stucco the quality
of precious jewels. The arcades of a court of the Alhambra, for example, or
of certain Northwest African mosques, repose in perfect calm; at the same
time they seem to be woven of luminous vibrations. They are like light made
crystalline; their innermost substance, one might say, is not stone but the
Divine Light, the creative Intelligence that resides mysteriously in all things.

This makes it clear that the "objectivity" of Islamic art—the absence of a
subjective urge, or one that could be called "mystical"—has nothing to do
with rationalism, and anyhow, what is rationalism but the limitation of
intelligence to the measure of man alone? Nevertheless that is exactly what
the art of the Renaissance does through its "organic" and subjectively
anthropomorphic interpretation of architecture. There is but one step
between rationalism and individualistic passion, and from these to a

mechanistic conception of the world. There is nothing of that sort in Islamic art; its logical essence remains always impersonal and qualitative; indeed, according to the Islamic perspective, reason (*al-ʿaql*) is above all the channel of man's acceptance of revealed truths, and these truths are neither irrational nor solely rational. In this resides the nobility of reason, and consequently that of art: therefore to say that art is a product of reason or of science, as do the masters of Islamic art, does not in any sense signify that art is rationalistic and must be kept clear of spiritual intuition, quite the contrary; for in this case reason does not paralyze inspiration, it paves the way toward a non-individual beauty.

The difference that divides the abstract art of Islam from modern "abstract art" may be mentioned here. The moderns find in their "abstractions" a response that is ever more immediate, more fluid, and more individual to the irrational impulses that come from the subconscious; to a Muslim artist, on the other hand, abstract art is the expression of a law, it manifests as directly as possible Unity in multiplicity. The writer of these lines, strong in his experience of European sculpture, once sought to be taken on as a hand by a Northwest African master decorator. "What would you do," said the master "if you had to decorate a plain wall like this one?" "I would make a design of vines, and fill up their sinuosities with drawings of gazelles and hares." "Gazelles and hares and other animals exist everywhere in nature," replied the Arab, "Why reproduce them? But to draw three geometrical rose patterns, one with eleven segments and two with eight, and to link them up in such a way that they fill this space perfectly, that is art."

It could also be said—and this is confirmed by Muslim masters—that art consists in fashioning objects in a manner conformable to their nature, for that nature has a virtual content of beauty, since it comes from God; all one has to do is to release that beauty in order to make it apparent. According to the most general Islamic conception, art is no more than a method of ennobling matter.

The principle which demands that art should conform to the laws inherent in the objects it deals with is no less respected in the minor arts, for example, that of rug making, so characteristic to the world of Islam. The restriction to geometrical forms alone, which are faithful to the flat surface of the composition, and the absence of so-called proper images, have proved to be no obstacle to artistic fertility, on the contrary, for each piece—apart from those mass produced for the European market—expresses a creative joy.

The technique of the knotted rug is probably of nomadic origin. The rug is the real furniture of the nomad, and it is in rugs of nomadic origin that one finds the most perfect and the most original work. Rugs of urban origin often show a certain artificial refinement, which deprives the shapes and colors of their immediate vigor and rhythm. The art of the nomadic rug-maker favors the repetition of strongly marked geometrical forms, as well as abrupt alternations of contrast and a diagonal symmetry. Similar preferences are

apparent throughout almost the whole of Islamic art, and this is very significant with respect to the spirit which those preferences manifest; the Islamic
mentality shows a relationship of the spiritual plane to what the nomadic
mentality is on the psychological plane: an acute sense of the fragility of the
world. A conciseness of thought and action and a genius for rhythm are
nomadic qualities.

When one of the first Muslim armies conquered Persia, they found in the
great royal hall of Ctesiphon an immense "carpet of spring" with decorations
of gold and silver. It was taken with other booty to Medina where it was
simply cut into as many pieces as there were ancient companions of
the Prophet. This apparent act of vandalism was, however, not only in
conformity with the rules of war as laid down by the Qur'an, but it also
gave expression to the profound suspicion felt by Muslims for every work of
man that seeks to be absolutely perfect or eternal—the carpet of Ctesiphon
incidentally portrayed the earthly Paradise, and its division among the
companions of the Prophet is not without spiritual significance.

This too must be said: although the world of Islam, which is more or less
coextensive with the ancient empire of Alexander,[3] includes many peoples
with a long sedentary history, yet the ethnic waves, which have periodically
renewed the life of these people, and imposed on them their domination
and their preferences, have always been of nomadic origin: Arabs, Seljuks,
Turks, Berbers, and Mongols. In a general way, Islam combines badly with
an urban and bourgeois "solidification."[4]

Traces of the nomadic mentality can be found even in Islamic architecture,
although architecture belongs primarily to sedentary culture. Thus, constructional elements such as columns, arches, and portals have a certain autonomy,
despite the unity of the whole; there is no organic continuity between the
various elements of a building; when it is a case of avoiding monotony—
and monotony is not always considered an evil—it is achieved less by the
gradual differentiation of a series of analogous elements than by incisive
changes. The "stalactites" in stucco hung from the inner surfaces of the
arches and the patterns of the arabesques "carpeting" the walls certainly keep
alive some reminiscences of nomadic "furnishings," consisting as they do of
rugs and tents.

The primitive mosque, in a form of a vast hall of prayer with its roof
stretched horizontally and supported by a palm-grove of pillars, comes near
to the nomadic environment; even an architecture as refined as that of
the mosque at Cordova, with its superposed arcades, is reminiscent of a
palm-grove.

The mausoleum with a cupola and a square base accords with the nomadic
spirit in the conciseness of its form.

The Islamic hall of prayer, unlike a church or a temple, has no center
toward which worship is directed. The grouping of the faithful round a
center, so characteristic of Christian communities, can only be witnessed in

Islam at the time of the pilgrimage to Mecca, in the collective prayer round the Ka'ba. In every other place, believers turn in their prayers toward that distant center, external to the walls of the mosque. But the Ka'ba itself does not represent a sacramental center comparable to the Christian altar, nor does it contain any symbol which could be an immediate support to worship,[5] for it is empty. Its emptiness reveals an essential feature of the spiritual attitude of Islam: whereas Christian piety is eager to concentrate on a concrete center—since the "Incarnate Word" is a center, both in space and in time, and since the Eucharistic sacrament is no less a center—a Muslim's awareness of the Divine Presence is based on a feeling of limitlessness; he rejects all objectivation of the Divine, except that which presents itself to him in the form of limitless space.

Nonetheless, a concentric plan is not alien to Islamic architecture, for such is the plan of a mausoleum roofed with a cupola. The prototype of this plan is found in Byzantine as well as in Asiatic art, where it symbolizes the union of Heaven and Earth, the rectangular body of the building corresponding to the Earth and the spherical cupola to Heaven. Islamic art has assimilated this type while reducing it to its purest and clearest formulation: between the cubical body and the more or less ogival cupola, an octagonal "drum" is usually inserted. The eminently perfect and intelligible form of such a building can dominate the indeterminate spaciousness of an entire desert landscape. As the mausoleum of a saint it is effectively a spiritual center of the world.

The geometrical genius, which asserts itself so strongly in Islamic art, flows directly from the kind of speculation favored by Islam, which is "abstract" and not "mythological." There is moreover no better symbol in the visual order of the internal complexity of Unity—of the passage from the Indivisible Unity to "Unity in multiplicity" or "multiplicity in Unity"—than the series of the regular geometrical figures contained within a circle, or that of the regular polyhedra contained within a sphere.

The architectural theme of a cupola with ribs resting on a rectangular body, to which it is connected in many different ways, has been abundantly developed in the Islamic countries of Asia Minor. This style is found on the art of building in brick, and from it Gothic architecture, with all its speculative spirit, probably received its first impulses.

The sense of rhythm, innate in nomadic people, and the genius for geometry: these are the two poles which, transposed into the spiritual order, determine all Islamic arts. Nomadic rhythmicality found its most direct expression in Arab prosody, which extended its influence as far as the Christian troubadours, while speculative geometry belongs to the Pythagorean inheritance very directly taken over by the Muslim world.

Art to the Muslim is a "proof of the divine existence" only to the extent that it is beautiful without showing the marks of a subjective individualistic inspiration; its beauty must be impersonal, like that of the starry sky. Islamic art does indeed attain to a kind of perfection that seems to be independent of its author; his triumphs and his failures disappear before the universal character of the forms.

Whenever Islam has assimilated a preexisting type of architecture, in Byzantine countries as well as in Persia and in India, subsequent development has been in the direction of a geometrical precision having a qualitative character—neither quantitative nor mechanical—which is attested by the elegance of its solutions of architectural problems. It is in India that the contrast between the indigenous architecture and the artistic ideals of the Muslim conquerors is without doubt most marked. Hindu architecture is at once lapidary and complex, elementary and rich, like a sacred mountain with mysterious caverns; Islamic architecture leans toward clarity and sobriety.

Wherever Islamic art appropriates incidental elements from Hindu architecture, it subordinates their native power to the unity and the lightness of the whole.[6] There are some Islamic buildings in India that are numbered among the most perfect in existence; no architecture has ever surpassed them.

But Islamic architecture is most faithful to its peculiar genius in the *Maghrib,* the West of the Muslim world. Here, in Algeria, in Morocco and in Andalusia it realizes the state of crystalline perfection that turns the interior of a mosque—or of a palace—into an oasis of freshness, a world filled with a limpid and almost unworldly beatitude.[7]

The assimilation of Byzatine models by Islamic art is exemplified with special clarity in the Turkish variations on the theme of the Hagia Sophia. As is well known, the Hagia Sophia consists of an immense central dome flanked by two half-cupolas, which in their turn are amplified by several vaulted apses. The whole covers a space more extensive in the direction of one axis than of the other; the proportions of the resulting environment are highly elusive and seem to be indefinite owing to the absence of conspicuous articulations. Muslim architects like Sinan, who took up the theme of a central cupola amplified by adjacent cupolas, found new solutions more strictly geometrical in conception. The Selimiye mosque at Edima is a notably characteristic example; its huge dome rests on an octagon with walls alternately flat and curved into apses, resulting in a system of plane and curved facets with clearly defined angles between them. This transformation of the plan of the Hagia Sophia is comparable to the cutting of a precious stone, made more regular and more brilliant by polishing.

Seen from inside, the cupola of a mosque of this type does not hover in indefinity, nor does it weigh upon its pillars. Nothing expresses effort in Islamic architecture; there is no tension, nor any antithesis between Heaven and Earth. "There is none of that sensation of a heaven descending from above, as in the Hagia Sophia, nor the ascending tendency of a Gothic cathedral. The culminating point in the Islamic prayer is the moment when the forehead of the believer prostrated on the rug touches the floor, that mirror-like surface which abolishes the contrast of height and depth and makes space a homogeneous unity with no particular tendency. It is by its immobility that the atmosphere of a mosque is distinguished from all things ephemeral. Here infinity is not attained by a transformation from one side of a dialectical antithesis to the other; in this architecture the beyond is not merely a goal, it is lived here and now, in a freedom exempt from all tendencies; there is a repose free from all aspiration; its omnipresence is incorporated in the edifice so like a diamond" (after Ulya Vogt-Goknil).[8]

The exterior of Turkish mosques is characterized by the contrast between the hemisphere of the dome, more in evidence than in the Hagia Sophia, and the needles of the minarets: a synthesis of repose and vigilance, and of submission and active witness.

In the arabesque, the typical creation of Islam, the geometrical genius meets the nomadic genius. The arabesque is a sort of dialectic of ornament, in which logic is allied to a living continuity of rhythm. It has two basic elements, the interlacement and the plant motif. The former is essentially a derivative of geometrical speculation, while the latter represents a sort of graphic formulation of rhythm, expressed in spiraloid designs, which may possibly be derived not so much from plant forms as from a purely linear symbolism. Ornaments with spiraloid designs—heraldic animals and vines—are also found in the art of Asiatic nomads, the art of the Scythians is a striking example.

The elements of Islamic decorative art are drawn from the rich archaic heritage that was common to all the peoples of Asia as well as to those of the Near East and of northern Europe. It came to the surface again as soon as Hellenism, with its essentially anthropomorphic art, had gone into retreat. Christian medieval art picked up this same heritage, brought to it by the folk-lore of immigrant peoples from Asia, and by insular art, both Celtic and Saxon, itself one of the most astonishing syntheses of prehistoric motifs. But this heritage was soon obscured and diluted in the Christian world by the influence of Graeco-Roman models, assimilated by Christianity. The Islamic spirit has a much more direct affinity with this vast current of archaic forms for they are in implicit correspondence with its conscious return toward a primordial order, toward the "primordial religion" (*din al-fitra*). Islam assimilates these archaic elements and reduces them to their most abstract and most generalized formulations; it levels them out in a certain sense, and thereby eliminates any magical qualities they may have possessed; in return, it endows them with a fresh intellectual lucidity, one might almost say—with a spiritual elegance.

The arabesque, which is the outcome of this synthesis, has also analogies in Arab rhetoric and poetry; a rhythmical outpouring of thought is given precision by parallels and inversions strictly interlinked. The Qur'an itself uses the same means of expression; in its periods they become elements in a spiritual algebra and rhythms of incantation. Thus, the Divine witness of the Burning Bush, which the Hebrew Bible conveys in the words "I am that I am" is rendered in the Qur'an by the paraphrase: "I am God, beside whom there is no divinity but I."

At the risk of pressing the point too hard, let it be said that for a Muslim the arabesque is not merely a possibility of producing art without making images; it is a direct means for dissolving images or what corresponds to them in the mental order, in the same way as the rhythmical repetition of certain Qur'anic formulae dissolves the fixation of the mind on an object of desire. In the arabesque, all suggestions of an individual form are eliminated by the indefinity of a continuous weave. The repetition of identical motifs, the flamboyant movement of lines and the decorative equivalence of forms in relief or incised, and so inversely analogous, all contribute to this effect. Thus, at the sight of glittering waves or of leafage trembling in the breeze, the soul detaches itself from its internal objects, from the "idols" of passion, and plunges, vibrant within itself, into a pure state of being.

The walls of certain mosques, covered with glazed earthenware mosaic or a tissue of delicate arabesques in stucco, recall the symbolism of the curtain (*hijab*). According to a saying of the Prophet, God hides Himself behind 70,000 curtains of light and the darkness; "if they were taken away, all that His sight reaches would be consumed by the lightnings of His Countenance." The curtains are made of light in that they hide the Divine "obscurity," and of darkness in that they veil the Divine Light.

Islam regards itself as the renewal of the primordial religion of humanity. The Divine Faith has been revealed through the mediation of the prophets or the "messengers," at very different times to the most diverse people. The Qur'an is but the final confirmation, the "seal," of all these numerous revelations, the sequence of which goes back to Adam; Judaism and Christianity have the same title to inclusion in the sequence as the revelations that preceded them.

This is the point of view that predisposes Islamic civilization to take to itself the heritage of more ancient traditions, at the same time stripping the legacy of its mythological clothing, and reclothing it with more "abstract" expressions, more nearly in conformity with its pure doctrine of Unity. Thus it is that the craft traditions, such as persisted in Islamic countries to the very threshold of our times, are generally said to have come down from certain pre-Islamic prophets, particularly from Seth, the third son of Adam, who reestablished the cosmic equilibrium after the murder of Abel by Cain. Abel represents nomadism, the rearing of animals, and Cain sedentarism, the cultivation of the earth; Seth is therefore synonymous with the synthesis of the two currents.[9]

Pre-Islamic prototypes preserved in the craft tradition also came to be connected with certain parables in the Qur'an and with certain sayings of the Prophet, in the same way as pre-Christian traditions assimilated by Christianity were connected with Gospel parables analogous to them.

In speaking of his ascent to Heaven (*mi'raj*) the Prophet describes an immense dome made of white mother-of-pearl and resting on four corner pillars, on which are written the four parts of the Qur'anic formula: "in the name—of God—the Compassionate—the Merciful," and from which flow four rivers of beatitude, one of water, one of milk, one of honey and one of wine. This parable represents the spiritual model of every building with a dome. Mother-of-pearl or white pearl is the symbol of the Spirit (*al-ruh*), the "dome" of which encloses the whole creation. The universal Sprit, which was created before all other creatures, is also the Divine Throne which comprehends all things (*al-'arsh al-muhit*).

The symbol of this Throne is invisible space extending beyond the starry sky; from the terrestrial point of view, which is natural to man and affords the most direct symbolism, the stars move in concentric spheres more or less remote from the earth as center, and surrounded by limitless space which in its turn is "enclosed" by the universal Spirit considered as the metaphysical "situation" of all perception or knowledge.

While the dome of a sacred building represents the universal Spirit, the octagonal "drum" that supports it symbolizes the eight angels, "bearers of the Throne," who in their turn correspond to the eight directions of the "rose of the winds." The cubical part of the building then represents the cosmos, with the four corner pillars (*arkan*) as its elements, conceived as principles both subtle and corporeal.

The building as a whole expresses equilibrium, the reflection of the Divine Unity in the cosmic order. Nevertheless since Unity is always Itself, whatever the degree at which It is envisaged, the regular shape of the building can also be transposed *in divinis;* the polygonal part of the building will then correspond to the "facets" of the Divine Qualities (*al-sifat*) while the dome recalls undifferentiated Unity.[10]

A mosque generally comprises a court with a fountain, where the faithful can make their ablutions before accomplishing their prayers. The fountain is often protected by a small cupola shaped like a baldaquin. The court with a fountain in the middle, as well as the enclosed garden watered by four runnels rising in its center, are made in the likeness of Paradise, for the Qur'an speaks of the gardens of Beatitude, where springs of water flow, one or two in each garden, and where celestial virgins dwell. It is in the nature of Paradise (*janna*) to be hidden and secret; it corresponds to the interior world, the innermost soul. This is the world which the Islamic house must imitate, with its inner court surrounded with walls on all four sides or with an enclosed garden furnished with a well or fountain. The house is the *sacratum* (*haram*) of the family, where woman reigns and man is but a guest. Its square shape is in conformity with the Islamic law of marriage, which allows a man to marry up to four wives, on condition that he offers the same advantages to each. The Islamic house is completely closed toward the outer world—family life is withdrawn from the general social life—it is only open above, to the sky, which is reflected beneath in the fountain court.

The spiritual style of Islam is also exemplified in the art of clothing, and particularly in the masculine costume of purely Islamic countries. The part played by costume has a special importance, because no artistic ideal established in painting or sculpture can replace or relativize the living presence of man in his primordial dignity. In one sense, the art of clothing is effective and even popular; it is nevertheless indirectly a sacred art, for the masculine costume of Islam is as it were a priestly costume generalized, just as Islam "generalized" the priesthood by abolishing the hierarchy and making every believer a priest. Every Muslim can perform the essential rites of his tradition by himself; anyone, provided that his mental faculties are intact and his life conforms to his religion, may in principle preside as *Imam* over any gathering great or small.

The example of the Mosaic law makes it clear that priestly costume as such is a branch of sacred art in the strictest sense of the word. Its formal language is determined by the dual nature of the human form, which is the most immediate symbol of God and at the same time, because of its egocentricity and subjectivity, the thickest of the veils that hide the Divine Presence. The hieratic garments of Semitic peoples hide the individual and subjectively "passionate" aspect of the human body, and emphasize on the contrary its "god-like" qualities. These qualities are brought out by combining their microcosmic evidences, more or less veiled by the polyvalence of the human form, with their macrocosmic evidences; thus, in the symbolism of the clothing, the "personal" manifestation of God is united with His "impersonal" manifestation, and through the complex and corruptible form of man, the simple and incorruptible beauty of the stars is projected. The golden disk which the High Priest in the Old Testament wore on his breast corresponds to the sun; the precious stones which adorn various parts of his body and are placed so as to correspond to the subtle centers of the *shekhina*, are like stars; his headdress is like the "horns" of the crescent moon: and the fringes of his vestments recall the dew or the rain of Grace.[11] Christian liturgical vestments perpetuate the same formal language, while relating it to the sacerdotal function of the Christ, who is both officiant and victim of the sacrifice.[12] Alongside the priestly vestment with its solar characteristics, there is the monastic garment, which serves only to efface the individual and sensual aspects of the body,[13] whereas the costume of the laity, with the exception of the insignia of consecrated kings and the heraldic emblems of nobles,[14] originates merely in plain necessity or in worldliness. In this way, Christianity make a distinction between the priest, who participates by virtue of his impersonal function in the glory of the Christ, and the profane person, whose whole attire can be but vanity, and who is integrated with the formal style of the tradition only when he assumes the garb of the penitent. It may be noted in this connection that modern masculine attire shows a curious

inversion of these qualities: its negation of the body, with its natural supple-
ness and beauty, becomes the expression of a new individualism, hostile to
nature and coupled with an instinctive hatred of all hierarchy.[15]

The masculine costume of Islam is a synthesis of the sacerdotal and
the monastic attire, and at the same time it affirms masculine dignity. It is
the turban which, according to the saying of the Prophet,[16] is the mark of
spiritual, and therefore sacerdotal dignity, together with the white color of
the clothing, the cloak with board folds and the *haik* enveloping the head
and shoulders. Certain articles of clothing appropriate to dwellers in the
desert have been generalized and "stylized" for a spiritual purpose. On the
other hand, the monastic character of the Islamic costume is affirmed by its
simplicity and by the more or less strict prohibition[17] of golden ornaments
and of silk. Women alone may wear gold and silk, and then it is not in public
but only in the interior of the house—which corresponds to the inner world
of the soul—that they may display such finery.

Wherever an Islamic civilization is beginning to decay, the turban is
the first thing that is banished, and next the wearing of loose and pliable
garments that facilitate the movements of the ritual prayer. As for the
campaign that is waged in certain Arab countries in favor of the hat, it is
aimed directly at the abolition of the rites. For the rim of a hat prevents the
forehead from touching the ground in the prostration; the cap with the peak,
so peculiarly suggestive of the profane, is no less inimical to the tradition.
If the use of machines necessitates the wearing of such clothes, it simply
proves that, from the point of view of Islam, reliance on machines draws
man away from his existential center, where he "stands upright before God."

This description of Islamic costume would not be complete without some
mention of the "sacred vestment" (*ihram*) of the pilgrim, worn on the occasion of the great pilgrimage (*al-hajj*) to the interior of the sacred territory
that includes Mecca. The pilgrim wears only two pieces of cloth without a
seam, tied round the shoulders and the hip, and sandals on his feet. Thus
attired he is exposed to the intense heat of the sun, conscious of his poverty
before God.

The noblest of the visual arts in the world of Islam is calligraphy, and it is
the writing of the Qur'an that is sacred art *par excellence;* it plays a part
more or less analogous to that of the icon in Christian art, for it represents
the visible body of the Divine Word.[18]

In sacred inscriptions the Arabic letters combine fluently with arabesques,
especially with plant motifs, which are thus brought into closer relationship
with the Asiatic symbolism of the tree of the world; the leaves of this tree correspond to the words of the Sacred Book. Arabic calligraphy contains within
itself decorative possibilities of inexhaustible richness; its modalities vary
between the monumental Kufic script with its rectilinear form and vertical
breaks, and the *naskhi* with its line as fluid and as serpentine as it could be.
The richness of the Arabic script comes from the fact that it has fully

developed its two "dimensions": the vertical, which confers on the letters their hieratic dignity, and the horizontal, which links them together in a continuous flow. As in the symbolism of weaving, the vertical lines, analogous to the "warp" of the fabric, correspond to the permanent essences of things—it is by the vertical that the unalterable character of each letter is affirmed—whereas the horizontal, analogous to the "weft," expresses becoming or the matter that links one thing to another. A significance of this kind is particularly evident in Arab calligraphy, where the vertical strokes transcend and regulate the undulating flow of the connecting strokes.

Arabic is written from right to left; this is as much as to say that the writing runs back from the field of action toward the heart. Among all the phonetic scripts of Semitic origin, Arabic writing has the least visual resemblance to Hebrew writing; Hebrew is static like the stone of the Tables of the Law, while at the same time it is full of the latent fire of the Divine Presence, whereas Arabic manifests Unity by the breadth of its rhythm: the broader the rhythm the more its unity becomes evident.

The friezes of inscriptions crowning the inner wall of a hall of prayer, or surmounting the *mihrab,* recall to the believer, as much by their rhythm and their hieratic form as by their meaning, the majestic and forceful current of the Qur'anic language.

This plastic reflection of a Divine incantation traverses the whole of Islamic life; its expressive richness, its upsurge endlessly renewed and its inimitable rhythms compensate the elusive simplicity of its content, which is Unity; it is immutability of idea and inexhaustible flow of utterance, architectural geometry, and indefinite rhythm of ornament.

The *mihrab* is the niche oriented toward Mecca and is the place where the *imam* who recites the ritual prayer stands in front of the rows of believers who repeat his gestures. The primary function of this niche is acoustic, to reecho the words directed toward it; but at the same time its form is reminiscent of that of a choir or an apse, the "holy of holies," the general shape of which it reproduces on a smaller scale. This analogy is confirmed in the field of symbolism by the presence of the lamp hung in front of the niche of prayer.[19] The lamp recalls the "niche of light" of which it is said in the Qur'an: "God is the light of the heavens and of the earth. His light is like a niche in which there is a lamp; the lamp is in a glass, which is like a shining star...." (Qur'an 24:35).

Here is something like a meeting-point between the symbolism of the mosque and the Christian temple, as well as of the Jewish temple and perhaps of the Parsee temple. To return, however, to the acoustic function of the prayer-niche: it is by virtue of its reverberation of the Divine Word during the prayer that the *mihrab* is a symbol of the Presence of God, and for that reason the symbolism of the lamp becomes purely accessory, or one might say "liturgical";[20] the miracle of Islam is the Divine Word directly revealed in the Qur'an and "actualized" by ritual recitation. This makes it possible to situate Islamic iconoclasm very precisely: the Divine Word must remain a verbal expression, and as such instantaneous and immaterial, in the likeness of the act of creation; thus alone will it keep its evocative power pure, without being subject to that attrition which the use of tangible materials instills, so to speak, into the very nature of the plastic arts, and into the forms handed on through them from generation to generation. Being manifested in time but not in space, speech is outside the ambit of the changes brought about by time in spatial things; nomads know this well, living, as they do, not by images but by speech This is the point of view and the manner of its expression natural to peoples in migration and particularly to Semitic nomads; Islam transposes it into the spiritual order[21] conferring in return on the human environment, particularly on architecture, an aspect of sobriety and intellectual transparency, as a reminder that everything is an expression of the Divine Truth.

NOTES

This chapter first appeared in Titus Burckhardt, *Sacred Art in East and West,* trans. by Lord Northbourne (Bedfont, U.K.: Perennial Books, 1967; Louisville, Kentucky and Bloomington, Indiana: Fons Vitae and World Wisdom Inc., 2001). The general editor of this set thanks the editors of World Wisdom Books for permission to reproduce this chapter.

1.   When Mecca was conquered by the Muslims, the Prophet first ordered the destruction of all the idols which the pagan Arabs had set up on the court of the Ka'ba; then he entered the sanctuary. Its wall had been ornamented by a Byzantine painter, among other figures were one of Abraham throwing divinatory arrows and another of the Virgin and Child. The Prophet covered the last named with his two hands and ordered the removal of all the others.

2.   An artist newly converted to Islam complained to Abbas, uncle of the Prophet, that he no longer knew what to paint (or carve). The patriarch advised him to attempt nothing but plants and fantastic animals, such as those that do not exist in nature.

3.   It can be said that Alexander was the artisan of the world that was destined for Islam, in the same way that Caesar was the artisan of the world that was to welcome Christianity.

4.   One of the reasons for the decadence of Muslim countries in modern times is the progressive suppression of the nomadic element.

5.   The famous black stone is set in a corner of the Ka'ba. It does not mark the center toward which the believers turn in their prayers, and besides, it has no "sacramental" function.

6.   From its inception, Islamic architecture integrated into itself certain elements of Hindu and Buddhist architecture, but these elements had come to it through the arts of Persia and Byzantium; it was only later on that Islamic civilization directly encountered that of India.

7.   The analogy between the nature of crystal and spiritual perfection is implicitly expressed in the following formula which emanates from the Caliph Ali: "Muhammad

is a man, not like other men, but like a precious stone among stones." This formula also indicates the point of junction between architecture and alchemy.

8.   *Turkische Moscheen* (Zurich: Origo-Verlag, 1953).

9.   René Guenon, *Cain et Abel* in *Le Regne de la Quantité et Les Signes des Temps,* Paris, NRF, 1945, English translation (London, U.K.:Luzac, 1953).

10.   See Titus Burckhardt, *Introduction aux doctrines esoteriques de l'Islam* (Lyon: Derain, 1955).

11.   Analogous symbols are found in the ritual costume of the North American Indians: the headdress with bison horns, and the fringes of the garment as an image of rain of grace. The headdress of eagle's feathers recalls the "Thunder Bird" which rules from on high, also the radiant sun, both being symbols of the Universal Spirit.

12.   See Simeon of Thessalonica, *De divino Templo.*

13.   Nudity can also have a sacred character, because it recalls the primordial state of man and because it abolishes the separation between man and Universe. The Hindu ascetic is "clothed in space."

14.   Heraldry has probably a dual origin. In part it is derived form the emblems of nomadic tribes—from "totems," and in part from Hermetism. The two currents mingled in the Near East under the Empire of the Seljuks.

15.   Modern masculine attire, which has its origin partly in the French Revolution and partly in English Puritanism, represents an almost perfect synthesis of antispiritual and antiaristocratic tendencies. It affirms the forms of the body, while "correcting" them to fit in with a conception that is inept as well as being hostile to nature and to the intrinsically divine beauty of man.

16.   The turban is called "the crown (or the diadem) of Islam."

17.   It is not a question of canonical interdiction but of a reprobation, applied more strictly to gold than to silk.

18.   The disputes among Islamic theological schools about the created or uncreated nature of the Qur'an are analogous to the disputes among Christian theologians about the two natures of the Christ.

19.   This is the motif reproduced in a more or less stylized form on many prayer-rugs. It may be mentioned that the prayer niche is not always furnished with a lamp, no such symbol being obligatory.

20.   The conch, which adorns a few of the most ancient prayer niches, is in fact derived as an architectural feature from Hellenic art. However, it scorns to be connected with the very ancient symbolism in which the conch is compared to the ear and the pearl to the Divine Word.

21.   Islamic iconoclasm has another side to it: man being created in the image of God, to imitate his form is regarded as blasphemy. But this point of view is a consequence of the prohibition of images rather than a main reason for it.

3

The Common Language of Islamic Art

Titus Burckhardt

ARAB ART, ISLAMIC ART

One may well ask whether the term "Arab art" corresponds to a well-defined reality since Arab art before Islam does not in practice exist for us because of the scarcity of its remains, and Arab art born under the sky of Islam is confused—and one wonders to what degree—with Islamic art itself. Art historians never fail to stress that the first Muslim monuments were not built by the Arabs, who lacked adequate technical means, but by levies of Syrian, Persian, and Greek craftsmen, and that Muslim art was gradually enriched by the artistic heritage of the sedentary populations of the Near East as these were taken into Islam. Despite this, it is still legitimate to speak of Arab art, for the simple reason that Islam itself, if it is not limited to a "racial phenomenon"—and history is there to prove the point—does nonetheless comprise Arab elements in its formal expression, the foremost of which is the Arabic language; in becoming the sacred language of Islam, Arabic determined to a greater or lesser degree the "style of thinking" of all the Muslim peoples.[1] Certain typically Arab attitudes of soul, spiritually enhanced by the *Sunna* (customary usage) of the Prophet, entered into the psychic economy of the entire Muslim world and are reflected in its art. It would, indeed, be impossible to confine the manifestations of Islam to Arabism; on the contrary, it is Arabism that is expanded and, as it were, transfigured by Islam.

In order to grasp the nature of Islamic-Arab art—the Muslim will naturally stress the first part of this term, and the non-Muslim the second—it is always necessary to take account of this marriage between a spiritual message with an absolute content and a certain cultural inheritance which, for that very reason, no longer belongs to a culturally defined collectivity but becomes a "mode of expression" which can, in principle, be used universally. Moreover, Islamic-Arab art is not the only great religious art to be born from such a marriage; Buddhist art, for example, whose area of expression is chiefly confined to Mongol nations, nevertheless preserves certain typically Indian traits, particularly in its iconography, which is of the greatest importance to it. In a far more restricted context, Gothic art of German-Latin lineage provides an example of a "style" so widespread that it became identified, from a certain moment on, with the Christian art of the West.

Without Islam, the Arab thrust of the seventh century—even supposing it to have been possible without the religious impulse—would have been no more than an episode in the history of the Middle East; decadent as they may have been, the great sedentary civilizations would have made short work of absorbing these hordes of Bedouin Arabs, and the nomadic invaders of the cultivated lands would have finished, as is generally the case, by accepting the customs and forms of expression of the sedentaries. But it was exactly the opposite that happened in the case of Islam, at least in a certain regard: it was the Arabs, nomads for the most part, who imposed on the sedentary peoples they conquered their forms of thought and expression by imposing their language on them.[2] In fact, the outstanding, and somehow refulgent, manifestation of the Arab genius is language, including writing. It was this language which not only preserved the ethnic heritage of the Arabs outside Arabia but also caused it to radiate far beyond its cultural homeland. It was by the mediation of the Arabic language that the essential Arab genius was effectively communicated to Muslim civilization as a whole.

The extraordinary normative power of the Arabic language derives from its role as a sacred language as well as from its archaic nature, both factors being, in any case, connected. It is its archaic quality that predestined Arabic for its role as a sacred language, and it was the Qur'anic revelation that, as it were, actualized its primordial substance. Archaism, in the linguistic order, is not, in any event, synonymous with simplicity of structure—very much to the contrary. Languages generally grow poorer with the passing of time by gradually losing the richness of their vocabulary; the ease with which they can diversify various aspects of one and the same idea; and their power of synthesis, which is the ability to express many things with few words. In order to make up for this impoverishment, modern languages have become more complicated on the rhetorical level; while perhaps gaining in surface precision, they have not done so as regards content. Language historians are astonished by the fact that Arabic was able to retain a morphology attested to as early as the Code of Hammurabi,[3] from the nineteenth to the eighteenth century before the Christian era, and to retain a phonetic system which preserves, with the exception of a single sound, the extremely rich sound range disclosed by the most ancient Semitic alphabets discovered,[4] although there was no "literary tradition" to bridge the gap between the far-off age of the Patriarchs and the time when the Qur'anic revelation would establish the language for all time.

The explanation of this perennial quality of Arabic is to be found simply in the conserving role of nomadism. It is in towns that languages decay, by becoming worn out, like the things and institutions they designate. Nomads, who live to some extent outside time, conserve their language better; it is, moreover, the only treasure they can carry around with them in their pastoral existence; the nomad is a jealous guardian of his linguistic heritage, his poetry, and his rhetorical art. On the other hand, his inheritance in the way of visual art cannot be rich; architecture presupposes stability, and the same is broadly true of sculpture and painting. Nomadic art, in general, is limited to simple, yet striking, graphic formulas, ornamental motifs, heraldic emblems, and symbols. In the situation we are studying, the existence of these formulas is by no means a negligible factor, for they carry creative potentialities that will blossom forth when they meet the artistic techniques belonging to the sedentary civilizations. It is true that the presence of these model formulas among the pre-Islamic Arabs is not generally apparent except retrospectively, by analogy with what we find with other nomads and in consideration of the sudden flowering in the Muslim art of the first centuries of ornamental motifs which are vastly different in their modes from anything coming from the sedentary civilizations and which are, in some way, parallel to the figurative "devices" of the Arab language.

In order to explain in a few words, and without recourse to specialized linguistic knowledge, the specific nature of the Arabic language, let us first of all recall that every language has at its beginnings two poles, as it were, one of which comes to predominate without excluding the other. These two poles can be described by the terms "auditive intuition" and "imaginative intuition." Auditive intuition essentially identifies the meaning of a word with its quality as sound; this presents itself as the development of a simple phonetic formula which expresses a fundamental action such as "to unite," "to sepa-rate," "to penetrate," "to emerge," and so on, with all the physical, psycho-logical, and intellectual polyvalence of which a type-action of this kind is capable. This has, moreover, nothing to do with semantic convention or ono-matopoeia; the identification of sound and act is immediate and spontaneous, and in this regard, speech conceives everything it names as being basically an act or as the object of an act. Imaginative intuition, on the contrary, manifests itself in speech by the semantic associations of analogous images; every word pronounced evokes inwardly a corresponding image, which calls up other images, with the type-images dominating the more particular ones, according to a hierarchy that stamps itself, in its turn, on the structure of speech. The Latin languages are examples of this latter type, whereas Arabic discloses an almost untrammelled auditive intuition or phonetic logic, in which the identity of sound and act, as well as the primacy of action, is affirmed across the entire rich tissue of this language. In principle, every Arabic word is derived from a verb consisting of three invariable consonants, something like an aural ideogram, from which are derived as many as 12 different verbal modes—simple, causative, intensive, reciprocal, and so on—and each of these modes produces in its turn a plethora of nouns and adjectives whose first meaning is always linked, in a more or less direct way, to that of the fundamen-tal action depicted by the trilateral root[5] of the entire verbal "tree."

This semantic transparency of the language, the fact that in its symbolism it flows wholly from the phonetic character of the verb, is a clear proof of its relative primordiality. In the beginning, and in the very seat of our consciousness, things are spontaneously conceived as determinations of the primordial sound which resounds in the heart, this sound being none other than the first, non-individualized, act of consciousness; at this level, or in this state, to "name" a thing is to identify oneself with the action or the sound which bring it forth.[6] The symbolism inherent in speech—and obscured or deformed to a greater or lesser extent by acquired habits—seizes on the nature of things not in a static fashion, as an image is seized, but, as it were, *in statu nasciendi*, in the act of becoming. This aspect of language in general, and of the Arabic language in particular, is moreover, in the Muslim world, the object of a whole gamut of sciences, some philosophical and others esoteric. Muslim scholars can be said not only to have conserved this structure of Arabic but also to have contributed to its precise definition.

In Arabic, the "tree" of verbal forms, of derivations from certain "roots" is quite inexhaustible; it can always bring forth new leaves, new expressions to represent hitherto dormant variations of the basic idea—or action. This explains why this Bedouin tongue was able to become the linguistic vehicle of an entire civilization intellectually very rich and differentiated.

Let us point out, nevertheless, that the logical link between a form of expression and its verbal root is not always easy to grasp, because of the occasionally conventionalized meaning given to that particular form and the extremely complex significance of the root idea. One orientalist has gone so far as to say that "the structure of the Arabic language would be of incomparable transparency were the meanings of the verbal roots not arbitrary"; but it is actually hardly possible for the basis of a language to be arbitrary. The truth is that the verbal roots constitute a threshold between discursive thought and a kind of synthetic perception.[7] The Arabic language is, as it were, dependent upon auditive intuition and we shall see, in what follows, what this signifies for art.

It would be tempting to say that the Arab does not so much see things as hear them, but that would be a false generalization. It is true, nevertheless, that the need for artistic exteriorization is, in the Arab, largely absorbed by the cultivation of his language with its fascinating phonetic range and almost unlimited possibilities of expression. If the term contemplative be taken to describe the type of man who contemplates rather than acts and whose mind loves to repose in the being of things, then the Arab, who possesses a dynamic mentality and an analytical intelligence, is no contemplative. But that he is nevertheless contemplative is proved by Islam and confirmed by Arab art. Contemplation is not, in any case, limited to simply static modes; it can pursue unity through rhythm, which is like a reflection of the eternal present in the flow of time.

Plastic examples illustrating these tendencies leap to the eye. The arabesque in particular, with its both regular and indefinite unfolding, is the most direct expression of rhythm in the visual order. It is true that its most perfect forms are inconceivable without the artistic contribution of the nomads of Central Asia; it was, however, in an Arab *milieu* that it flowered most resplendently. Another element which is typical of Muslim art, and whose development goes side by side with Arab domination, is interlacement. It first appears in all its perfection in the form of sculptured trellis-work on the windows of mosques and palaces.[8] In order to appreciate the geometrical play of interlacement, it is not enough simply to look at it head on; it must be "read," by letting the eye follow the flow of intertwining and compensating forces. Interlacement exists already in the pavement mosaics of late antiquity, but it is rudimentary and naturalistic in conception, without any of the complexity and rhythmic precision of Arab-Muslim interlacing work. These examples belong to abstract art, which is itself a characteristic of the Arab genius. Contrary to what is customarily believed, the average Arab does not by any means possess an "extravagant imagination." Whenever such imagination is found in Arab literature, in the *Tales of the Thousand and One Nights* for example, it comes from some non-Arab source, Persian and Indian in this case; only the art of storytelling is Arab. The creative spirit of the Arabs is *a priori* logical and rhetorical, then rhythmic and incantational. The luxuriance of typically Arab poetry lies in mental and verbal arabesque and not in the profusion of images evoked.

Islam rejects portraiture for theological reasons. Now it is a fact that the Semitic nomads had no figurative tradition—the pre-Islamic Arabs imported most of their idols from abroad—and the image never became a natural and transparent means of expression for the Arabs. Verbal reality eclipsed the reality of static vision: compared with the word for ever "in act," whose root is anchored in the primordiality of sound, a painted or a carved image seemed like a disquieting congealment of the spirit. For the pagan Arabs, it smacked of magic.

The Arabic language is not wholly dynamic; true, its base is the action-verb, but it possesses likewise a static, or more exactly a timeless, ground which corresponds with "being," and which reveals itself particularly in the so-called nominal sentence, where the noun and its predicates are juxtaposed without a copula, thereby permitting a thought to be expressed in a lapidary fashion and without any consideration of time. The Arabic language is such that a whole doctrine can be condensed into a short and concise formula of diamantine clarity. This means of expression is realized in all its fullness only in the Qur'an, yet it is part of the Arab genius nonetheless and is reflected in Arab-Muslim art, for this art is not only rhythmical but also crystalline.

The conciseness of the Arabic sentence does not, quite clearly, limit the profundity of the meaning, but neither does it facilitate synthesis on the descriptive level: an Arab will rarely assemble a number of conditions or circumstances in a single sentence; he prefers to string together a series of brief phrases. In this respect, an agglutinative language like Turkish, which belongs to the family of Mongol languages, is less austere and more flexible than Arabic; when it comes to describing a situation or a landscape, Turkish is frankly superior to Arabic, and the same applies to Persian which is an Indo-European language close to Gothic; however, both languages have borrowed not only their theological terminologies but also their philosophical and scientific terms, from Arabic.

The opposite extreme to Arabic is a language like Chinese, which is ruled by a static vision of things and which groups the elements of a thought around generic images, as is shown by the ideographic nature of Chinese script.

The Turks, like the Arabs, were originally nomads, but their languages reveal vastly different mental types; the Arab is incisive and dynamic in his thought processes; the Turk, for his part, is all-embracing and circumspect. In the general framework of Muslim art, the Turkish genius reveals itself by a certain power of synthesis—one might almost say, by a totalitarian spirit. The Turk has a plastic or sculptural gift which the Arab does not have; his works always proceed out of an all-enveloping concept; they are as if hewn from a single block.

As for Persian art, it is distinguished by its sense of hierarchical gradations; Persian architecture is perfectly articulated, without ever being "functional" in the modern sense of the term. For the Persian, Unity manifests itself above all as harmony. Moreover, Persians are, by nature and by culture, people who see things, but see with lyrical eyes; their artistic activity is as if animated by an inner melody. It is said proverbially in the East that "Arabic is the language of God, but Persian is the language of paradise," and this describes very well the difference that exists, for example, between a distinctively Arab type of architecture, like that of the Maghrib, where crystalline geometry of forms proclaims the unitary principle, and Persian architecture, with its blue domes and floral decoration.

The Arab architect is not afraid of monotony; he will build pillar upon pillar and arcade upon arcade, and dominate repetition by rhythmic alternation and the qualitative perfection of each element.

The language of the Qur'an is omnipresent in the world of Islam; the entire life of a Muslim is filled with Qur'anic formulas, prayers, litanies, and invocations in Arabic, the elements of which are drawn from the Sacred Book; innumerable inscriptions bear witness to this. It could be said that this ubiquity of the Qur'an works like a spiritual vibration—there is no better term to describe an influence which is both spiritual and sonorous—and this vibration necessarily determines the modes and measures of Muslim art; the plastic art of Islam is therefore, in a certain way, the reflection of the word of the Qur'an. It is assuredly very difficult to grasp the principle by which this art is linked to the text of the Qur'an, not on the narrative plane, which plays no part in the customary art of Islam, but on the level of formal structures, since the Qur'an obeys no laws of composition, neither in the strangely disconnected linking together of its themes nor in its verbal presentation, which evades all the rules of meter. Its rhythm, powerful and penetrating as it is, follows no fixed measure; entirely unpredictable, it maintains at times an insistent rhyme like the beat of a drum and will then suddenly modify its breadth and pace, shifting its cadences in a manner as unexpected as it is striking. To affirm that the Qur'an is Arabic verse, because it includes passages with a uniform rhyme like the Bedouin *rajaz,* would be mistaken; but to deny that these uniformities and abrupt breaks correspond to profound realities in the Arab soul would be equally so. Arab art—poetry and music as well as the plastic arts—loves to repeat certain forms and to introduce sudden and unforeseen variants against this repetitive background. But, whereas art is played out in accordance with easily fathomable rules, the waves of sacred speech may sometimes fall in regular patterns, but they arise out of a whole formless ocean. In the same way, the state of inner harmony engendered by the words and sonorous enchantment of the Qur'an is situated on quite another plane than, for example, perfect poetry. The Qur'an does not satisfy, it gives and at the same time takes away; it expands the soul by lending it wings, then lays it low and leaves it naked; for the believer, it is both comforting and purifying, like a rainstorm. Purely human art does not possess this virtue. That is to say, there is no such thing as a Qur'anic style which can simply be transposed into art; but there does exist a state of soul which is sustained by the recitation of the Qur'an and which favours certain formal manifestations while precluding others. The diapason of the Qur'an never fails to join intoxicating nostalgia to extreme sobriety: it is a radiation of the divine Sun on the human desert. It is to these poles that the fluid and flamboyant rhythm of the arabesque, and the abstract and crystalline character of architecture, in some way correspond.

But the most profound link between Islamic art and the Qur'an is of another kind: it lies not in the form of the Qur'an but in its *haqiqa,* its formless essence, and more particularly in the notion of *tawhid,* unity or union, with its contemplative implications; Islamic art—by which we mean the entirety of plastic arts in Islam—is essentially the projection into the visual order of certain aspects or dimensions of Divine Unity.

NOTES

This chapter first appeared in Titus Burckhardt, *Art of Islam: Language and Meaning,* translated by J. Peter Hobson (London, U.K.: World of Islam Festival Trust, 1976; Bloomington, Indiana: World Wisdom, forthcoming in 2008), 39–46. It is reprinted here with minor modifications with the permission of the editors of World Wisdom Books and the Burckhardt estate.

1. The great Muslim scholar Abu Rayhan al-Biruni, born in 973 CE at Khiva, wrote on this subject: "Our religion and our empire are Arab...subject tribes have

often joined together to give the state a non-Arab character. But they have not been able to achieve their aim, and as long as the call to prayer continues to echo in their ears five times a day, and the Qur'an in lucid Arabic is recited among the worshippers standing in rows behind the Imam, and its refreshing message is preached in the mosques, the will needs submit, the bond of Islam will not be broken, nor its fortresses vanquished. Branches of knowledge from all countries in the world have been translated into the tongue of the Arabs, embellished and made seductive, and the beauties of languages have infused their veins and arteries, despite the fact that each people considers its own language beautiful, since it is accustomed to it and employs it in its daily offices. I speak from experience, for I was reared in a language in which it would be strange to see a branch of knowledge enshrined. Thence I passed to Arabic and Persian, and I am a guest in both languages, having made an effort to acquire them, but I would rather be reproved in Arabic than complimented in Persian."

2.   Certain people will raise the objection that not all Arabs were nomads and that there were cities in Arabia like Mecca and Yathrib (Medina) before Islam. The answer is that in Central Arabia, where Islam had its birth, nomadism was broadly predominant; even the aristocracy of the Quraysh, formed of caravan merchants, is inconceivable without a nomadic background. It is true that Mecca already constituted a spiritual center and, therefore, a factor making for stability in the midst of tribal fluctuations. But Mecca is precisely the anchor that Islam used to transform the ethnic substance represented by the nomadic Arabs into a religious community.

3.   See Edouard Dorme, "L'Arabe littéral et la langue de Hammourabi," in *Mélanges Louis Massignon* (Damascus: Institut français de Damas, 1957).

4.   The most ancient Semitic alphabets have a total of 29 sounds or letters, 28 of which are retained by Arabic, the "missing" sound being a variant of "S." It is possible that the reduction of the alphabet to 28 letters conveys a symbolic purpose, for certain Arab authors see a correspondence between these sounds and the 28 stations of the moon. The phonetic cycle progressing from gutturals to palatals, dentals, and labials retraces the "lunary" phases of primordial sound emanating from the sun.

5.   There do exist verbs composed of four- or five-root consonants, but in such cases, consonantal groups such as *ts* or *br* play the role of single sounds.

6.   According to Qur'an 2:31–33, it was Adam who was able to "name" all beings, whereas the angels could not.

7.   The phonetic symbolism that inheres in Arabic is revealed in particular by the permutation of radical consonants; for example, the root RHM signifies "to be merciful" or "to have pity on," whereas the root HRM has the sense of "to forbid," "to make inaccessible," *sacrum facere;* similarly, the root QBL has the sense of "to face" or "to receive" (whence the Hebrew word *Qabbalah*), while the root QLB has the sense of "to return" or "to reverse" (whence the term *qalb* meaning "matrix" and "heart"). A further example is the root FRQ, meaning "to separate" or "to divide" (the Latin word *furca* seems to be derived from an analogous root), and its permutation RFQ has the sense of "to accompany" or "to join," whereas the group FQR means "to be poor, in want."

8.   In the Umayyad mosque at Damascus, for example, or the palace of Khirbat al-Mafjar.

4

The Art and Ambience of Islamic Dress

Frithjof Schuon

When the arts are enumerated, the art of dress is too often forgotten, although it has an importance as great, or almost as great, as architecture. Doubtless, no civilization has ever produced summits in every field. Thus, the Arab genius, made up of virility and resignation, has produced a masculine dress of unsurpassed nobility and sobriety, whereas it has neglected feminine dress, which is destined in Islam, not to express the "eternal feminine" as does the Hindu dress, but to hide a woman's seductive charms. The Hindu genius, which in a certain sense divinizes the "wife-mother," has on the other hand created a feminine dress unsurpassable in its beauty, its dignity, and its femininity. The art of dress of every civilization, and even of every people, embraces many varying forms in time and space, but the spirit always remains the same, though it does not always reach the same heights of direct expression and immediate intelligibility.

The Maghribi garb of North Africa, like other nonworldly Muslim garbs, suggests resignation to the Will of God, and more profoundly the mystery of the House of Peace, *Dar al-Salam*. This calls for another comment: If it is true that Maghribi garb, or any other analogous Muslim garb, manifests a *de facto* religious perspective, exclusivistic by definition, along with the specific blessing (*baraka*) that it contains, it is no less true—and necessarily so—that this garb manifests at the same time attitudes and mysteries appertaining to esoterism. In this sense, it suggests no confessional limitation. Each civilization produces, by heavenly inspiration, several paradigmatic phenomena. The representative dress of Islam is an example of this, as are the arabesques, the prayer niche, and the call to prayer.

The association of ideas between the turban and Islam is far from fortuitous. "The turban," said the Prophet, "is a frontier between faith and unbelief." He also said, "My community shall not decline so long as they wear the turban." The following traditions are also quoted in this context: "On the Day of Judgment a man shall receive a light for each turn of the turban around his head." "Wear turbans, for thus you will gain in generosity." The point we wish to make is that the turban is deemed to give the male believer a sort of gravity, consecration, and majestic humility.[1] It sets him apart from chaotic and dissipated creatures, fixing him on a divine axis and thus destines him for contemplation. In brief, the turban is like a celestial counterpoise to all that is profane and empty. Since it is the head, the brain, which is for us the plane of our choice between true and false, durable and ephemeral, real and illusory, and serious and futile, the head should also bear the mark of this choice. The material symbol is deemed to reinforce the spiritual consciousness, and this is true of every religious headdress and even of every liturgical vestment or merely traditional dress. The turban, so to speak, envelops man's thinking, always so prone to dissipation, forgetfulness, and infidelity. It recalls the sacred imprisoning of his passional nature prone to fleeing from God.[2] The function of the Qur'anic Law is to reestablish a primordial equilibrium that was lost. Hence, the *hadith:* "Wear turbans and thus distinguish yourselves from the peoples (lacking in equilibrium) who came before you."

Hatred of the turban, like hatred of the romantic or the picturesque, or what belongs to folklore, is explained by the fact that the romantic worlds are precisely those in which God is still plausible. When people want to abolish Heaven, it is logical to start by creating an atmosphere that makes spiritual things appear out of place. In order to be able to declare successfully that God is unreal, they have to construct around man a false reality, one that is inevitably inhuman because only the inhuman can exclude God. What is involved is a falsification of the imagination and so its destruction. Modern mentality implies the most prodigious lack of imagination possible.

Overall, the dress of the Muslim indicates a spiritual retreat (*khalwa*), an "interiorization" of the spirit made of holy poverty and divine Peace.

NOTES

The above chapter is excerpted from the article, "The Art of Dress and Ambience," which will appear in the forthcoming volume, *Frithjof Schuon on Universal Art: Principles and Criteria,* edited by Catherine Schuon (Bloomington, Indiana: World Wisdom, 2007). Slight editorial changes have been made to the original for consistency of style and for purposes of clarification. Portions of the chapter have also been abridged. The general editor of this set thanks the editors of World Wisdom Books for permission to reproduce this work.

1.   In Islam, all Prophets are represented as wearing turbans, sometimes of differing colors, according to the appropriate symbolism.

2.   When Saint Vincent de Paul designed the headdress of the Sisters of Charity, he intended to impose on their gaze a kind of reminiscence of monastic isolation.

5

THE QUESTION OF IMAGES

—————————— • ——————————

Titus Burckhardt

ANICONISM

The prohibition of images in Islam applies, strictly speaking, only to the image of the Divinity; it stands, therefore, in the perspective of the decalogue, or more exactly of Abrahamic monotheism, which Islam sees itself as renewing. In its last manifestation as in its first—in the time of Muhammad as in the age of Abraham—monotheism directly opposes idolatrous polytheism,[1] so that any plastic representation of the divinity is for Islam, according to a "dialectic" that is both historical and divine, the distinctive mark of the error which "associates" the relative with the Absolute, or the created with the Uncreated, by reducing the one to the level of the other. To deny idols, or still better to destroy them, is like translating into concrete terms the fundamental testimony of Islam, the formula *La ilaha illa 'Llah* ("there is no divinity save God"), and just as this testimony in Islam dominates or consumes everything in the manner of a purifying fire, so also does the denial of idols, whether actual or virtual, tend to become generalized. Thus it is that portraiture of the divine messengers (*rusul*), prophets (*anbiya'*), and saints (*awliya'*) is avoided, not only because their images could become the object of idolatrous worship but also because of the respect inspired by their inimitability; they are the viceregents of God on earth; "God created Adam in His form" (a saying of the Prophet), and this resemblance of man to God becomes somehow manifest in prophets and saints, without it being possible, even so, to grasp this on the purely corporeal level; the stiff, inanimate image of a divine man could not be other than an empty shell, an imposture, an idol.

In Sunni Arab circles, the representation of any living being is frowned upon, because of respect for the divine secret contained within every creature,[2] and if the prohibition of images is not observed with equal rigor in all ethnic groups, it is nonetheless strict for everything that falls within the liturgical framework of Islam. Aniconism—which is the appropriate term here, and not iconoclasm[3]—became somehow an inseparable concomitant of the sacred; it is even one of the foundations, if not the main foundation, of the sacred art of Islam.

This may appear paradoxical, for the normal foundation of a sacred art is symbolism, and in a religion expressing itself in anthropomorphic symbols—the Qur'an speaks of God's "face," His "hands" and the throne He sits upon—the rejection of images seems to strike at the very roots of a visual art dealing with things divine. But there is a whole array of subtle compensations that need to be borne in mind, and in particular the following: a sacred art is not necessarily made of images, even in the broadest sense of the term; it may be no more than the quite silent exteriorization, as it were, of a contemplative state, and in this case—or in this respect—it reflects no ideas but transforms the surroundings qualitatively, by having them share in an equilibrium whose centre of gravity is the unseen. That such is the nature of Islamic art is easily verified. Its object is, above all, man's environment—hence the dominant role of architecture—and its quality is essentially contemplative. Aniconism does not detract from this quality; very much to the contrary, for, by precluding every image inviting man to fix his mind on something outside himself and to project his soul onto an "individualizing" form, it creates a void. In this respect, the function of Islamic art is analogous to that of virgin nature, especially the desert, which is likewise favorable to contemplation, although in another respect the order created by art opposes the chaos of the desert landscape.

The proliferation of decoration in Muslim art does not contradict this quality of contemplative emptiness; on the contrary, ornamentation with abstract forms enhances it through its unbroken rhythm and its endless interweaving. Instead of ensnaring the mind and leading it into some imaginary world, it dissolves mental "fixations," just as contemplation of a running stream, a flame, or leaves quivering in the wind can detach consciousness from its inward "idols."

It is instructive to compare Islam's attitude to images with that of the Greek Orthodox Church. The Byzantine Church is known to have gone through an iconoclast crisis, perhaps not uninfluenced by the example of Islam. Certainly, the church was moved to reconsider defining the role of the sacred image, the icon; and the Seventh Ecumenical Council, in confirming the victory of the adorers of images, justified its decision in the following words: "God Himself is beyond all possible description or representation, but since the Divine Word took human nature upon itself, which it 'reintegrated into its original form by infusing it with divine beauty', God can and must be adored through the human image of Christ." This is no more than an application of the dogma of divine incarnation, and it shows how far this way of seeing things is from the viewpoint of Islam. Nevertheless, the two perspectives have a common basis in the notion of man's theomorphic nature.

The declaration of the Seventh Ecumenical Council took the form of a prayer addressed to the Holy Virgin, for it is the Virgin who lent the Divine Child her human substance, thus making Him accessible to the senses. This act of veneration recalls incidentally the gesture of the Prophet in placing both hands in protection on the icon of the Virgin and Child painted on the inner wall of the Ka'ba.

It might well be thought that this gesture ought to have led to a concession in Islamic law permitting representation of the Holy Virgin. But this would be to misconstrue the spiritual economy of Islam, which puts aside every superfluous or equivocal element, although this does not prevent Muslim masters of the "inward science" (*al-'ilm al-batin*) from acknowledging the meaning and legitimacy of icons in their proper context. We actually have a particularly profound vindication of the Christian veneration of icons in the words of one of the greatest masters of Muslim esoterism, the Sufi Muhyi al-Din Ibn al-'Arabi who wrote in his *Meccan Revelations* (*al-Futuhat al-Makkiyya*). "The Byzantines developed the art of painting to perfection because, for them, the singular nature (*al-fardaniyya*) of our Lord Jesus is the supreme support of concentration upon Divine Unity." It will be seen that this interpretation of the icon, although it is far removed from Muslim theology as generally accepted, is nevertheless at home in the perspective of *tawhid,* the doctrine of Divine Unity.

Apart from this, the words of the Prophet condemning those who aspire to imitate the work of the Creator have not always been interpreted as a rejection pure and simple of all figurative art; many have taken them only as condemning Promethean or idolatrous intent.

For Aryan peoples like the Persians, as well as for the Mongols, the representational image is far too natural a mode of expression for them to be able to pass it over. But the anathema against artists seeking to imitate the work of the Creator remains nonetheless effective, for figurative Muslim art has always avoided naturalism; it is not simply ingenuousness or ignorance of visual means that causes Persian miniatures not to use perspective giving the illusion of three-dimensional space or not to model the human body in light and shade. In the same way, the zoomorphic sculpture occasionally met with in the world of Islam never exceeds the bounds of a kind of heraldic stylization; its products could not possibly be mistaken for living and breathing creatures.

To recapitulate the question whether figurative art is prohibited or tolerated in Islam, we conclude that figurative art can perfectly well be integrated into the universe of Islam provided it does not forget its proper limits, but it will still play only a peripheral role; it will not participate directly in the spiritual economy of Islam.

As for Islamic aniconism, two aspects in all are involved. On the one hand, it safeguards the primordial dignity of man, whose form, made "in the image of God,"[4] shall be neither imitated nor usurped by a work of art that is necessarily limited and one-sided; on the other hand, nothing capable of becoming an "idol," if only in a relative and quite provisional manner, must interpose between man and the invisible presence of God. What utterly outweighs everything else is the testimony that there is "no divinity save God"; this melts away every objectivization of the Divine before it is even able to come forth.

NOTES

This chapter first appeared in Titus Burckhardt, *Art of Islam: Language and Meaning,* translated by J. Peter Hobson (London, U.K.: World of Islam Festival Trust, 1976; Bloomington, Indiana: World Wisdom, forthcoming in 2008), 27–30. It is reprinted here with the permission of the editors of World Wisdom Books and the Burckhardt estate.

1.   It is no pleonasm to speak of "idolatrous polytheism," as is shown by Hinduism, which is polytheist but in no way idolatrous because it recognizes the provisional and symbolic nature of idols and the relative nature of the "gods" (*devas*) as "aspects" of the Absolute. The esoteric Muslims, the Sufis, occasionally compare idols to Divine Names whose significance has been forgotten by the pagans.

2.   According to a saying of the Prophet, artists who seek to imitate the work of the Creator will be condemned in the hereafter to give life to their creations, and their inability to do so will cause them to be cast into the worst torments. This saying can clearly be understood in several ways; it has, in fact, never prevented the growth, in certain Muslim circles, of a figurative art free from any claims to naturalism.

3.   "Aniconism" can have a spiritually positive character, whereas "iconoclasm" has only a negative sense.

4.   From the Islamic point of view, the "divine form" of Adam consists essentially of the seven universal faculties that are likewise attributed to God, namely: life, knowledge, will, power, hearing, seeing, and speech; in man they have limits, but in God none. Even as attributed to man, they cannot be seen and go beyond his bodily form, which alone can be the object of any art.

6

THE ART OF QUR'AN CALLIGRAPHY

Martin Lings

The need to record and hand down to succeeding generations every syllable of the Qur'an with exactitude made it impossible to rely on anything so fallible as human memory, even though the memories in question were outstanding. But the point to be made here is not that people ungiven to writing and building should have come to be, through the force of circumstances, both writers and builders. The analogy we are drawing is based on the change from almost nothing to almost everything; and in the case of calligraphy, the change is perhaps even more striking than in that of architecture. It might even be said not only that the Arabs have never been surpassed as calligraphers[1] but also that they have only been equaled by one other people, namely the Chinese, whose art has, however, developed along very different lines.

It cannot, however, be considered a paradox that the civilization of the Unlettered Prophet[2] should have been destined to excel in the art of lettering. Even apart from the probable advantages of starting an enterprise uncluttered by previous experiences, the Arabs' disinclination to write down precious words had no doubt a very positive part to play in the genesis of Arabic calligraphy. These people were in love with the beauty of their language and with the beauty of the human voice. There was absolutely no common measure between these two summits on the one hand and the ungainliness of the only available script on the other. Their disdain for writing showed a sense of values; and in light of final results it is legitimate to suppose that it was the reverse side of an openness to calligraphic inspiration, as much as to say, "Since we have no choice but to write down the Revelation, then let that written record be as powerful an experience for the eye as the memorised record is for the ear when the verses are spoken or chanted."

The most usual explanation of the phenomenon we are now considering is that of human genius having been curbed from the art of sculpture, and from that of painting in most of its aspects, and made to flow with all its force into a relatively narrow channel. But this explanation, despite its elements of truth, is really more of a question than an answer, for it impels us to ask,

"Where did that force come from? What was it doing before the outset of Islam? Was it a dormant potentiality that the new Revelation awoke?"

It is impossible to deny that human genius has a vital part to play in sacred art; but there is genius and genius. In art that is related to religion, a distinction has to be made between sacred art in the strict sense and art that is religious without being sacred; and this means making a distinction between a genius which is dominated and penetrated by its own transcendent archetype, and a genius which is more or less cut off from that archetype and free to follow its own devices.

This distinction is one which Western Christendom has been trying not to see for almost the last 500 years. It is nonetheless fundamental and becomes immediately clear in light of a wider context. For if a sensitive and intelligent Christian be confronted with an ancient Egyptian wall-painting of Osiris, for example, or a sacramental statue of Buddha, and if he be asked, "What has your religion produced that can measure up to these?" it is then that he is compelled to see the limitations of humanism, and to return, for an answer, to the theomorphic art of the Middle Ages. The Islamic answer to the same question would be in an altogether different mode—a prayer niche in one of the great mosques or perhaps, despite the smaller dimensions, something within the scope of a book on Islamic calligraphy. Miniature painting, in which the Persians excelled, is only on the periphery of Islamic art and does not come near to the central and sacred domain.[3]

In his concise yet far-reaching definition of what may be said to constitute a religion, Frithjof Schuon includes the presence of sacred art as one of the criteria of authenticity.[4] This will not seem surprising to anyone who bears in mind that the function of sacred art, always in the strictest sense of the term, is parallel to that of the Revelation itself as a means of causing repercussions in the human soul in the direction of the Transcendent. It is seldom, however, contemporary with the initial impact of a religion, and it is thus able to compensate for certain losses, above all as a means of expressing to later generations something of what the presence of the Messenger expressed to the first generation. The Qur'an makes it clear that a Prophet must be considered as a Divine Masterpiece. In one passage, God says to Moses what could be translated: "I have fashioned thee as a work of art for Myself" (Qur'an 20:41); and in another, Muhammad is told: "Verily of an immense magnitude is thy nature" (Qur'an 68:4).

To compensate for an absence is to be a prolongation of a presence; and this function is at once apparent in Christian sacred art, of which the icon is as it were the cornerstone. But it also becomes apparent as regards Qur'an calligraphy and illumination when we remember that to be the vehicle of the Revelation was the primary function of the Prophet of Islam.

If sacred art comes as a half-miraculous sign that Providence has not abandoned the religion since its foundation, and if it therefore comes implicitly as a guarantee of that religion's Divine Origin, it is also a criterion of authenticity in the way that a result is a criterion of its cause. To see this we have to simply remember that the function of religion is to bring about a restoration, if only a virtual one, of man's primordial state. Each new Revelation, whatever form it may take, is destined to precipitate a renewal of consciousness, in a particular people or group of people, that man was made in the image of God and that as His representative he is the mediator between Heaven and Earth. The difference between man and all other creatures is that the latter merely reflect various Divine Qualities, whereas man reflects the Divine Essence, which comprises all the Qualities. The difference between man and man is that though each reflects the Totality, one individual will have certain qualities as it were in the foreground of his nature, whereas another will have others in the foreground and so on, with a never exactly repeated variation. Each soul thus offers a differently ordered receptivity to the imprint of the Divine Nature, so that when that imprint is renewed by the pressure of the Revelation, the general excelling of oneself which results from it will be in different directions. As we learn from the Islamic litanies of the 99 Divine Names, God is not only the King, the Just, the Wise, the Omniscient, the Almighty, the Victorious, and the Irresistible, but He is also the Beautiful, the Creator, the Former, the Marvelously Original, and the All-Holy, and here lies the metaphysical inevitability of sacred art as a result of the Revelation. Here also lie the roots of all artistic genius, and it is only from these roots that a tradition of sacred art can spring; a tradition which will eventually enable less-gifted artists to participate in the consecrated genius of others and to excel themselves beyond all measure, whence the connection between sacred art and the traditional arts and crafts.

In other words, sacred art presupposes, somewhere, inspiration in the fullest sense. But the word "somewhere" is significant, for even where a definite name is attached to a masterpiece, there is always the possibility that the known artist worked under the influence of an unknown visionary, and there may be more than one generation between the perfector of any given style and the man who received the initial spiritual impetus. This possibility, which is in the nature of things, is nowhere more widely recognized than in the civilization of Islam. Thus, for example, when a celebrated fifteenth-century grammarian of Egypt, Khalid al-Azhari, is quoted as saying that he had been prompted to write one of his most important works by a great Sufi Sheikh of his day, the quoter adds the following note, "The good done by most of those who are famous for their outward science has been achieved through their frequenting the company of a saint, that is a man of inward science;" and he goes on to mention the founder of the Shadhili order of Sufis and his successor as eminent personifications of an outward-radiating inward science.[5]

Moreover, apart from such possibilities, it must be remembered that sacred art is always strikingly impersonal[6] through its transcendence of the individual. All the more fitting therefore that it should be anonymous, as in fact so much of it is, and there can be no doubt that a large part of its anonymity has been deliberate, resulting from the consciousness of this or that artist that the work in question is not, ultimately speaking, "his."

To have one of its poles in Heaven and to have come into existence by a path that is something of a parallel to the process of creation are essential conditions without which sacred art could never fulfill its ritual or liturgical function as a "Jacob's Ladder" of return. It is in virtue of its parallel "descent" that a great cathedral or mosque or other monument of sacred art has the privilege of being able to stand amidst the wilds of nature without the eye condemning it as an alien presence, and the rungs of these ladders of return offer the worshipper the relatively effortless means of taking a higher standpoint, which, by repetition and by combination with other means, can even become more or less permanent. The way of creation is also the way of revelation, and in the particular art which is our theme the connection with revelation is very direct. Calligraphy and illumination are as it were compensations for such contingencies as ink and paper, a "step up" that makes it possible, in a flash of wonderment, to approach more nearly and penetrate more deeply the Divine Substance of the Qur'anic text, and thus to receive a "taste," each soul according to its capacity, of the Infinite and the Eternal. The use here of the Sufi term "taste"—in Arabic *dhawq*—may be taken as a reminder of the close connection, in all traditions, between sacred art and mysticism.

As regards the earthly pole of sacred art, it is normal that a certain technical development should need to take place. It cannot be expected that Heaven should always dictate to man the details, as it did, exceptionally, in the case of Solomon's Temple, and the delay caused by the interval of man's apprenticeship is, as we have seen, in perfect harmony with the Providential function of a spiritual support that is needed far less at the outset of a new religion than in subsequent generations. Meantime the Revelation makes it clear that the Archetype of Qur'an calligraphy already exists in Heaven, "in a hidden book" (Qur'an 56:78), accessible only to angels. Nor can it be in the spiritual nature of things that its earthly manifestation should depend mainly on human initiative.

NOTES

This chapter is taken from *Splendours of Qur'an Calligraphy and Illumination* (© 2005 Thesaurus Islamicus Foundation, all rights reserved). It is reproduced with permission from the Thesaurus Islamicus Foundation and the Lings estate.

1. With the Arabs must be included certain others of those people—preeminently the Persians and the Turks—for whom Arabic is the liturgical language, but the Arabs themselves were the pioneers.

2. So Muhammad is named in the Qur'an (7:157–158) and, by extension, in many Islamic litanies.

3.   For one remarkable exception however, which is truly a work of sacred art, though it could never have a central place in the civilization of Islam, see Titus Burckhardt, *Art of Islam: Language and Meaning* (London, U.K.: World of Islam Festival Publishing Company, 1976), plate 13. The miniature in question depicts the Night Journey of the Prophet and a postcard of it is sometimes available at the British Library where the manuscript in question is (Or. 2265.f.195a).

4.   See the opening of Chapter 2 in Frithjof Schuon, *Islam and the Perennial Philosophy* (London, U.K.: World of Islam Festival Publishing Company, 1976).

5.   Ibn Hamdun, *Sharh al-Ajurrumiyya.*

6.   See Frithjof Schuon, *Spiritual Perspectives and Human Facts* (Ghent: Sophia Perennis, 1969), 29–33. See also, in general, Titus Burckhardt, *Sacred Art in East and West* (Ghent: Sophia Perennis, 1967).

7

THE ART OF QUR'AN ILLUMINATION

Martin Lings

The art of Qur'an illumination was bound to develop more slowly than that of calligraphy because it was not directly called for by the text. It was furthermore held in check by the fear of allowing anything to intrude upon that text. More positively, we can be certain that it was this same reverential awe, *hayba,* which guaranteed exactly the right channels for the flow of this development toward a result which is, by general agreement, marvellously right. "Fear of the Lord is the beginning of wisdom." This saying of Solomon, continually quoted in Islam, is itself a synthesis of wisdom which has its application at all levels. Sacred art is "wise," and from what has already been said about its anonymity, it follows that the art of Qur'an calligraphy itself, let alone that of illumination, was bound to start on a note of "reserve," a pious courtesy related to awe and to the artist's consciousness of the Divine Majesty.

The main features of Qur'an illumination have been outlined more than once;[1] but to understand the significance of these features we have no alternative but to consult what was, beyond any doubt, the source of inspiration. Moreover, this source will give us a profound insight into the outlook, we might even say the psychic substance, of the artist himself. It is difficult for Christians, whose primary access to the Divine Presence is not through words, to imagine how deeply a book can penetrate a soul which deliberately invites such penetration. Many of the calligraphers and not a few of the illuminators would have known the Qur'an by heart from beginning to end. But even when they did not know it all, the passages quoted in this and other chapters would have been so familiar as to be almost an organic part of their nature. "The verses of the Qur'an are not only utterances which transmit thoughts; they are also, in a sense, beings, powers, talismans. The soul of the Muslim is as it were woven out of sacred formulae; in these he works, in these he rests, in these he lives, in these he dies."[2]

The Qur'an itself may be said to hold out certain opportunities, as it were, in invitation to the illuminator. The most obvious of these are the *Sura* headings, and the divisions between the verses. In addition, indications that five or ten verses have passed give an opportunity for a regularly repeated ornament in the margin, and the reader will find it helpful to know at what points in the text he is required to make a prostration, which can also be indicated ornamentally. It is, moreover, in the nature of things that if the opening of a *Sura* admits of illumination, the opening of the first *Sura* and therefore of the whole book should be treated with a particularly striking display of art.

Such arguments as these, however, would hardly have been able to overcome the calligraphers' scruples except on the understanding that ornamentation could, in fact, be a very positive means of heightening the effects they aimed at producing by the script. We have already seen that these effects are directly related to the nature of the Revelation itself, and it must be remembered in this connection that according to a fundamental point of doctrine, "the Qur'an is uncreated," which means, however these words be interpreted, that the revealed book constitutes no less than a Divine Presence. How does this affect Qur'an illumination? The answer is bound up with certain aspects of the Islamic perspective.

It has been said that the ancient Greeks were dominated by the idea of perfection which, with the onset of that decadence from which no civilization can escape, tended more and more to exclude other aspects of transcendence, with the eventual result that it took on the limitations of the untranscendent and finite. Now Islam is also dominated by the idea of perfection. To see this, one has only to stand in the courtyard of one of the great mosques, or in front of a prayer niche or an old city gate, not to mention examples which are closer to our theme. But Islam is also dominated by the idea of Infinitude. Perfection, *kamal,* is here imbued with the idea of Totality. "He is the First and the Last and the Outward and the Inward" (Qur'an 58:3).

One of the last *Sura*s of the Qur'an (Qur'an 112) is a definition of the Divinity, revealed in answer to a question about the nature of God. The two key Names with which it opens, *al-Ahad* and *al-Samad,* could be translated, respectively, "the Indivisible One-and-Only" and "the Totally Sufficing unto Himself in His Infinite Perfection." It is true that the definition implied by these Names is nothing other than sound metaphysics with regard to the Absolute. It is therefore universal and belongs as such to all religions. But what characterises Islam is an unwillingness to leave this highest metaphysical plane except in passing and on condition of reverting, as soon as possible, from the relative to the Absolute. The differences between religions are always on the surface and never at the roots. In other words, one religion is implicit where another is explicit, and inversely, and it is these differences of emphasis which explain the immense variety of sacred art from one orthodoxy to another.

It is well known that Islam is a monotheistic religion. Less well known are some of the corollaries of this, and for understanding Islamic art it is essential not to forget the explicitness of Islam that the Absolute One defies not only addition and multiplication but also subtraction and division. Art in a sense depends on the Name the Outward (*al-Zahir*), yet since the One is Indivisible, the Outwardness is always one with the Inwardness. In other words, when the Qur'an says: "Wheresoever ye turn, there is the Face of God" (Qur'an 2:115), no commentator can rightly say that this verse concerns only the Outward, for it also concerns, inseparably and mysteriously, the Inward and the First and the Last.

It is the function of sacred art, in general, to be a vehicle for the Divine Presence, and it follows from what has been said that the Islamic artist will conceive this function not as a "capturing" of the Presence but rather as a "liberation"[3] of its mysterious Totality from the deceptive prison of appearances. Islam is particularly averse to any idea of circumscribing or localizing the Divine, or limiting it in any way. But totality is wholeness, and wholeness means perfection, and on the visual plane perfection cannot be reconciled with formlessness, which leaves us no alternative but contour and therefore limitation. What then is the answer? How can an art conform to a presence that is explicitly conceived as a union of qualities, when on the plane of forms these qualities are scarcely compatible?

The answer partly lies in the domain of what might be called the first sacred art of all, inasmuch as it was, for man, the first earthly vehicle of the Divine Presence, namely nature itself, and it is, moreover, the Qur'an which draws the artist's attention to this primordial "solution." There are few things that evoke more immediately the idea of perfection than a tree which has had time and space to achieve fullness of growth; and in virtue of the outward and upward pointing of its branches, it is not a closed perfection but an open one. The Qur'an uses this very symbol of itself; that is, of the "good word," being itself the best of good words: "Hast thou not seen how God coineth a similitude? A good word is as a good tree, its root firm, its branches in heaven, giving its fruits at every due season by the leave of its Lord. And God coineth similitudes for men that they may remember" (Qur'an 14:24–25). These last words bring us straight to our theme, for the truth to be remembered here, with the help of the tree as a reminder, is precisely the nonfinite nature of the Qur'an. A Qur'an recitation must not be thought of as limited to this world for it has repercussions up to the Heavens, where its "fruits" await the believer. Otherwise expressed, the Qur'an uses the symbol of the tree so that it may liberate itself from being subject, in the awareness or in the subconsciousness of the believer, to the illusion that it is just one book among other books. It may thus be said to point a way for the illuminator,[4] telling him how to set free from the finite its Infinite Presence. We need not therefore be surprised that one of the most fundamental ornaments of Qur'an illumination should be arboreal, namely the palmette, *shujayra* or "little tree,"[5] nor need we doubt that it is meant to stand for the good word. The *Sura* heading consists of the title of the *Sura*, the number of its verses, and the word *makkiyya* or *madaniyya* to show whether it was revealed in

Mecca or Medina. Written in a script deliberately different from that of the Qur'an itself, it is usually set in a wide rectangular panel, often richly framed with gold and other colors, and with an arabesque as background to the letters. This heading is prolonged into the outer margin by means of a palmette which points horizontally toward the paper's edge and which achieves for the eye the effect of a liberation of incalculable scope.[6]

The above-quoted verse of the tree is immediately concerned with man's final ends, with the celestial "fruits" of the earthly action of reciting the holy book, which is considered here above all as a power of reintegration. This aspect of the *Sura* palmette is often confirmed by an upward pointing marginal palmette which corresponds to the marginal "tree of life" in the Qur'an manuscripts of Andalusia and Northwest Africa. But the ascending movements of return cannot be considered independently of the original descent. The Qur'anic text is equally insistent upon both movements. In Arabic the word for revelation, *tanzil,* means literally "a sending down," and the reader is again and again reminded that what he is reading is no less than a Divine Message sent down directly to the Prophet.

There are three main aspects which the artist has an obligation to convey if his art is to be relevant: the Qur'an as a descending power of revelation; the Qur'an as a mysterious presence of the Infinite in the finite; and the Qur'an as an ascending power of reintegration. The tree as we experience it on earth is a symbol of the last two of these aspects, but there is one verse in which the tree may be said to point in the direction of descent: "If all the trees in the earth were pens, and if the sea eked out by seven seas more were ink, the Words of God could not be written out to the end" (Qur'an 31:27). Here the tree plays a negative part, but to be chosen for mention in this context has its positive aspect. The verse tells us, generally speaking, that earthly things are as nothing compared with what they symbolize, but at the same time it implies inescapably that the tree, for the purpose of representing heavenly implements of transcription, is a supreme symbol. One of the chapters of the Qur'an, *Surat al-Qalam* (Qur'an 68), is named after the Celestial Pen, which is also mentioned, in the very first verses revealed to the Prophet (Qur'an 96:1–5), as the instrument through which the Revelation was made.

The Prophet himself said, "The first thing God created was the pen. He created the tablet and said to the pen, 'Write !' And the pen replied, 'What shall I write?' He said, 'Write My knowledge of My creation till the day of resurrection.' Then the pen traced what had been ordained." There are thus three levels to be considered. The Qur'an as men know it is an adapted form, reduced beyond all measure, of what is written on the Tablet, which itself only refers to creation and not to God's Self-Knowledge. It is to this highest level, that of the Divine Omniscience, that "the Words of God" refer in the above-quoted Qur'anic verse. It is nonetheless an essential point of doctrine that the Qur'an as revealed to men, not to speak of the Tablet, contains mysteriously everything, being no less than the Uncreated Word of God. We will come back later to this apparent contradiction.

From the point of view of descent, it is this instrument that the *Sura* palmette may be said to portray. Nor does this constitute a change of meaning inasmuch as the Pen, no less than its "consort" the "Guarded Tablet," is in the direct line of the descent of the Revelation and therefore virtually identical with it. It is simply a question of two directions, and the "neutral" horizontality of the palmette allows for its application to both.

The verse of the tree speaks of "its branches in Heaven." The palmette in the margin is as near to a direct illustration as this art will allow. In other words, it is a reminder that the reading or chanting of the Qur'an is the virtual starting point of a limitless vibration, a wave that ultimately breaks on the shore of Eternity, and it is above all that shore that is signified by the margin, toward which all the movement of the painting, in palmette, finial, crenellation and flow of arabesque is directed.

Another symbol which expresses both perfection and infinitude, and which is intimately, though not apparently, related to the "tree,"[7] is the rayed sun. Again and again the Qur'an refers to itself as light[8] or as being radiant with light, and many periods of Qur'an illumination can give us examples of marginal verse counts inscribed in circles whose circumferences are rayed or scalloped. The solar roundels, *shamsa* or "little sun" is used also of stellar ornaments, and occasionally replace the rosettes which divide the verses, and the rosettes themselves are often made luminous with gold. Sometimes the symbolism of light is directly combined with that of the tree, as when a solar roundel appears inside the *Sura* palmette,[9] or when the palmette itself is rounded and rayed, with its lobe replaced by an outward pointing finial. There are other variants of the same combination, and what has already been said about the two directions applies equally here, for the Revelation is not only a shining of light from the next world, but it also throws its light toward the next world by way of guidance; nor can this reversed reintegrating light be separated from the soul's spiritual aspiration, which is likewise figured by everything that points to the beyond.

Related in more ways than one to the tree are the arabesques with which the palmettes, the roundels and other marginal ornaments are filled, and which often serve as a surrounding frame for the main part of the page. Being vineal rather than arboreal, the arabesque does not by its nature point out a way, though it can give a clear indication of tendency,[10] and that is certainly one of its main functions in Qur'an illumination. At the same time, in virtue of its elusiveness, it constitutes in itself a mysterious and supraformal presence. It is also, like the tree, a vital presence and, where it is a background for the script, it serves to heighten the effect of the letters as vehicles of the Living Word. Moreover, as a portrayal of rhythm, by its constant repetition of the same motifs, in particular the small palmette, at regular intervals, it suggests rhythmic Qur'an recitations, which take place, we are told, not only on earth but throughout all the degrees of the universe.[11]

In this context, mention must also be made of the symbolism of certain numbers and their geometrical equivalents. Nine and three, like the circle and the triangle, are worldwide symbols of Heaven, their earthly complements being the number four and the square or the rectangle. The rectangular setting of the Qur'anic text thus signifies the terrestrial state which has been penetrated by the Revelation, and in most periods we find examples of a semicircular or triangular anse attached to the outer or "beyond" side of the rectangle, or to its summit. In either case it can only be the celestial dimension of the text which is indicated. The exact architectural equivalents are in the two varieties of *qubba*, the hemispherical dome of the Eastern mosque and its pyramidal equivalent in the Maghrib.

It may be asked why, if the founders of the tradition desired certain effects, they did not use more directly imperative means. To give the impression of light, for example, why did they not surround their ornaments and the text itself with broad golden rays, instead of the delicate antenna-like finials which, though occasionally red, are more often black or brown or blue? The answer is not only that the illuminator does not wish to "raise his voice" above that of the Qur'an but also that he particularly wishes to avoid any such obviousness as might cause a premature crystallizing of the imagination and thus fatally arrest the soul from continuing to penetrate more deeply in the required direction. Inevitably, the more obvious impression of light has been attempted; analogously, there is a tenth/sixteenth-century Western Qur'an[12] in which the illuminator has replaced the palmettes by naturalistic tree branches. But such experiments merely serve to make one appreciate all the more the subtle and incalculable power of the traditional stylised symbol, which the craftsman has only to follow, "blindly" or not, as the case may be.

It must also be remembered that the whole purpose of illumination is to recall the higher or deeper dimension of the text. The relationship between the "hidden book" and the fully revealed Qur'an is one of majesty to beauty, of contraction, or reserve, to expansion, and, however, paradoxical it may seem, illumination, being there to remind us of the "hidden book," has an overall function of majesty in relation to the beauty of the text. This holds true[13] even when the illumination is at its most beautiful and when the text is written in a particularly majestic style.

Color is used toward the same ends as form. Gold was the initial element, and after a short period of fluctuation, that is, by the middle of the tenth century CE, blue had been given a marked precedence over both green and red, and it was soon raised to the level of parity with gold in the East, whereas in the West, gold retained its original supremacy with blue as secondary. The importance of these two colors can be gauged by the fact that whatever extra pigments might be added, it was nearly always in a subordinate capacity. Moreover, in almost every style and age, one is likely to find a Qur'an in which the illuminations consist exclusively of blue and gold, and this same exclusiveness is liable to be a feature of certain pages in any Qur'an even where polychrome illuminations are to be found on other pages.

Blue is the color of the Infinite, which is identical with Mercy, for "My Mercy embraceth all things" (Qur'an 7:156). The great symbol of this Infinitude is the all-surrounding sky. The relevant Divine Name, *al-Rahman*, the first of the two Names of Mercy, has been well translated "the Infinitely Good," for it expresses the essential "roots" of Mercy. At this level, mercy, revelation, and religion are one. We have here what might be called the "feminine" aspect of Providence[14] or more precisely the "maternal" aspect. Thus the supreme archetype of Revelation is termed the "Mother of the Book" (Qur'an 13:39) and in this connection it may be noted that the most simple word formed from those letters which have the basic meaning of mercy, *ra', ha', mim*, is *rahim*, "womb."[15] Closely related to *al-Rahman* is the Name *al-Muhit*, the All-Embracing, and by extension, the word *muhit* also means "ocean."[16]

As a symbol of Infinite Mercy, the sea is, in fact, second only to the sky itself, whose color it takes and assimilates, and in particular connection with the All-Embracing, another feature of Qur'an illumination must be mentioned; so prevalent that many have suspected a "superstition," namely the use of blue for the outermost edge, both in individual ornaments and where there is a border to the text. One has the impression of an unwritten law that blue must have the last word, and enough has been said to make it clear why such a circumscription is no limitation.

If blue liberates by Infinitude, gold liberates because, like the sun, it is a symbol of the Spirit and therefore virtually transcends the whole world of forms. Gold, by its very nature, "escapes" from form to the point that a calligrapher writing in gold has to outline his letters with black in order to make them formally effective. As the color of light, gold is, like yellow, intrinsically a symbol of knowledge. Extrinsically, it means teaching or manifestation. Blue in the presence of gold is therefore Mercy inclined to reveal itself.

This brings us to the second Name of Mercy, *al-Rahim*, which signifies Mercy manifested and which we translate "the All-Merciful" since linguistically it is an intensive form of *rahim*, merciful, though less intensive than the name which precedes it. If it be asked why the illuminators did not revert from blue to green,[17] which is the color of Mercy manifested (being the result of the mixture of the colors of intrinsic mercy and of light), it might be answered that the Qur'anic text itself takes the place of green. This is no reason why green should not make a parallel appearance. But in his overall fidelity to blue, which takes religion back to its first origins, the illuminator assents to a typically Islamic ellipsis whereby the whole process of revelation is as it were folded back into its principle, with nothing between primary cause and ultimate effect. Islam loves to dwell on the roots of things; the chapter that is named after the "cause" in question, *Surat al-Rahman*, begins with an ellipsis in the opposite direction: "The Infinitely Good taught the Qur'an" (Qur'an 55:1–2). To say that blue and gold are the equivalents of the subject and the verb of this sentence is to sum up all that has so far been said about color in Qur'an illumination.

Blue and gold are opposite enough to enhance each other greatly. But in the triple domain of primary color, perfect balance cannot come by two, but only by three. To take two of the colors and to leave out the third or to reduce it to being a mere auxiliary means that the scales will necessarily be tipped one way or another, but this can be a way of gaining or heightening a required effect. Gold has the exaltation to balance the depth of blue, but not being a hot color, its mere warmth does not level out the coldness of blue. The resulting overall coolness does much to contribute to the total effect of holiness.[18]

Of all the features of illumination so far touched on, fine examples are to be found considerably before the close of the thirteenth century. That date is mentioned here chiefly because it marks the end of an era, or more precisely because the end which had in fact taken place some 50 years previously had time by the turn of the century to make itself felt in the domain of art. Moreover, for reasons not unconnected with what brought the era to a close, the year 700/1300 or thereabouts forms a kind of barrier on the far side of which Qur'an manuscripts are relatively rare. Inestimable treasures must have been destroyed by the Mongol invaders who sacked Baghdad[19] in 1258, perhaps even more than had already been destroyed in the course of the Crusades. But, as if by compensation, the new era seems to have brought with it a fresh impetus, which had its effect on Qur'an calligraphy.

NOTES

This chapter is taken from *Splendours of Qur'an Calligraphy and Illumination* (© 2005 Thesaurus Islamicus Foundation, all rights reserved). It is reproduced with minor modifications with permission from the Thesaurus Islamicus Foundation and the Lings estate.

1. Particularly important is Richard Ettinghausen's "Manuscript Illumination" in *A Survey of Persian Art,* vol. III (London, U.K.: Oxford University Press, 1939), 1937–1974.

2. Frithjof Schuon, *Understanding Islam* (Bloomington, Indiana: World Wisdom Books, 1998), 60.

3. We are here at the very roots of the question, and it may be inferred from this that the relative absence of the "living" figural element in all the central arts of Islam has causes which are far more profound and more positive than is generally supposed.

4. It goes without saying that this reference here is not to every artist or craftsman but to the small minority of "founder-artists" whoever they may have been. Once the tradition had been established it would simply have been followed, with more or less

understanding but without question, by generation after generation. Nor does this chapter claim, by putting certain trains of thought into the minds of its readers, to reproduce the mental processes of the pioneers themselves. Inspiration tends to fold up thought, and all that the following paragraphs can presume to do is to note some of the more obvious relevancies of Qur'an illumination to the Book it illuminates, in the knowledge that sacred art is providentially, by definition, the most strictly relevant art in the world. It would be beside the point and void of interest to say that such and such an artisan may well not have had some particular intention or other. At this artistic level, any correspondence that strikes the intelligence of one who contemplates the work in question is the proof of an intention *in divinis*.

5.   There are two main varieties of this symbol; the heavier and more complicated form with its cumbersome protruding petals or wings had a period of ascendancy, fortunately never exclusive, from the ninth to the eleventh centuries CE. But it was eventually superseded altogether by the simpler and more stylised palmette which is incomparably the more effective, and which itself may be subdivided into two varieties according to whether its roundness be suddenly or gradually tapered to its lobe.

6.   The importance of this ornament is tragically demonstrated whenever, as is all too often the case, a binder in trimming the pages of an old manuscript has trimmed away the lobes of the palmettes. How little has been lost, and yet how much!

7.   For this relationship, see René Guénon, *The Symbolism of the Cross* (London, U.K.: Luzac, 1958), 52; and Martin Lings, *Symbol and Archetype* (Cambridge, U.K.: Quinta Essentia, 1997), 90–94.

8.   For example, "We have sent down to you a clear light" (Qur'an 4:174) and "We have made it a light whereby We guide whom We will" (Qur'an 42:52).

9.   These luminous palmettes are suggestive of another Qur'anic tree, the one that feeds the lamp that is the symbol of the Divine Light of which the Qur'an itself is an aspect: "a sacred olive tree that is neither of the East nor of the West; its oil well-nigh blazeth in splendour though the fire hath not touched it" (Qur'an 24:35).

10.   As is found in the powerfully extroverted arabesque.

11.   The Qur'an mentions the angels as reciting its verses (Qur'an 37:3). For a profound and relevant comment on this passage, see René Guénon, "The Language of the Birds," in *Fundamental Symbols* (Cambridge, U.K.: Quinta Essentia, 1995), 39.

12.   1522 in the Chester Beatty Library, Dublin. See A. J. Arberry, *The Koran Illuminated* (Dublin: Hodges Figgis, 1967), plate 47.

13.   It could almost be said that when it ceases to hold true, this is the beginning of decadence.

14.   This manner of speaking must not be taken too exclusively since truth and wisdom belong to this aspect and blue is one of their symbols, but they cannot be called specifically "feminine." See also the author's chapter on "The Symbolism of the Triad of Primary Colours," in *Symbol and Archetype* (Cambridge, U.K.: Quinta Essentia, 1997).

15.   Not unanalogous is the iconographical connection in Christianity between the color blue and the Virgin Mary, who may be considered as the supreme human manifestation of the principle in question.

16.   Also relevant is the connection, we might almost say symbolic identity in certain respects, between Mary and the sea.

17.   Astrologically, the color blue corresponds to the planet Jupiter, "the greater benefic," and green to Venus, "the lesser benefic," and there is a certain analogy between these two principles and the two Names of Mercy *al-Rahman* and *al-Rahim*.

18.   The phrase "coolness of the eyes" means "delight" in Arabic and is especially connected with the joys of Paradise. But needless to say, red is also related to spiritual joy, and sometimes, especially in the Islamic West, the illumination on a page is almost entirely red and gold, but here also the outermost edges are blue.

19.   For just over 500 years, since 750 CE, Baghdad had been the cultural and administrative center of the Islamic world, but after 34 days of destruction it never reached this status again. Nonetheless, Islam was able to absorb its conquerors.

8

ART AND LITURGY

Titus Burckhardt

THE NATURE AND ROLE OF SACRED ART

In speaking of Islamic worship in relation to art, we used the term "liturgy," and this needs further definition because it evokes *a priori* the Christian pattern of worship, which developed gradually on the basis of an apostolic tradition and by the work of the Church Fathers. In this context, the liturgy is distinguished from the sacrament, the divinely instituted rite which, in a way, the liturgy enfolds, protecting it and at the same time manifesting it, while being itself protected and unfolded by sacred art which transposes its themes into architecture and iconography, to mention only the two most important visual arts in the *milieu* of Christianity. Things present themselves quite differently in Islam, where the forms of worship are fixed, down to the smallest detail, by the Qur'an and the Prophet's example. There is practically no liturgical borderline, so that one can say equally that the liturgy is comprised within the rite itself, that is, in the form of worship divinely instituted or, again, that sacred art assumes the role of the liturgy, and that this role consists of creating a framework to suit the rite, open to "angelic blessings" and closed to dark psychic influences. We shall see that such is indeed the role and position of art in Islam, and it immediately explains the importance assumed in this context by religious architecture and even by architecture in general—since every dwelling is in principle a place of worship—as well as by every other art that serves to shape the environment, such as decoration, epigraphy, and the art of carpets, not forgetting the liturgical role of clothing.

Sacred art therefore fulfills two mutually complementary functions: it radiates the beauty of the rite and, at the same time, protects it. The first of these functions is legitimized in Islam by the fact that the Prophet advised his companions to chant the Qur'an, that is, to recite it in rhythmic and melodious fashion. Thus, the revealed word reverberates in the musical order, and this is assuredly the firmest possible link between rite and art.

The notion that worship should be accompanied by beauty and, as it were, enwrapped in it is also confirmed by these passages from the Qur'an: "Oh sons of Adam! wear your comely garments in every place of prayer...who then has declared unlawful the comely garb that God has brought forth for His servants...?" (Qur'an 7:31–32). We shall return later to the liturgical role of clothing.

The complementary function of sacred art, that of protection, is illustrated by the traditional story (*hadith*) in which the Prophet is said to have had a cloth or curtain, which was decorated with figured designs, removed from his room because, he said, these figures disturbed his prayers. Now the Prophet certainly did not lack the power of abstract concentration, but he wished thereby to show that certain forms of art are incompatible with Islamic worship. It must not be said that he was condemning art as such, as if the rejection of certain forms did not necessarily call forth others, for we live in a world woven out of forms and we cannot avoid choosing among them.

In a certain sense, a rite is a divine art. For those who balk at this way of expressing things, let us make clear that we mean by this a manifestation, on the level of forms and according to a specifically human mode, of a reality that itself goes beyond all forms or limitations. This art cannot therefore be imitated, but it radiates; we could also say that it reverberates and needs surroundings to echo in.

The term "mosque," which applies to every Muslim place of prayer, comes from the Arabic *masjid* which means a "place of prostration," and this shows implicitly that canonical prayer in Islam involves certain bodily gestures or positions.

There is nothing surprising in the body's being required to share in the act of adoration, when it is remembered that this act engages man in his totality—he must pray with his whole being and his whole awareness—and that this totality is conceived empirically only from the starting point of the body. The body's integration into prayer demands its sacralization, and this is effected in the ablution preceding the prayer; to bring the limbs into contact with water, an image of primordial in-differentiation, serves moreover, by analogy and according to intention, as a kind of restoration to the state of innocence.

Let us note parenthetically that there is a link between the sacralization of the body, as realized by ritual purifications, and the Islamic conception of sexuality.

The chief positions or attitudes of prayer are the following: the upright position facing the *qibla*, in which the worshipper recites the words of prayer revealed in the Qur'an; then bowing and prostration. The significance of these three attitudes, which are linked in a sequence of movements and repose to the accompaniment of sacred utterances, is clear: it is in the upright position, which distinguishes man from all other animals, that the believer speaks to God, or that God speaks through him; bowing is an act of homage by the servant to what surpasses him, while prostration is the abandonment of oneself to the will of an all-powerful Lord. These three attitudes describe in space the directional segments of a cross, which esoteric science identifies with what might be termed the "existential dimensions" of man, namely, active and "upright" participation in the spirit which transcends the natural world, the unfolding of consciousness into the "horizontal" of existence, and, finally, the creature's movement away from its divine source, a downward fall for which submission to the Divine Will compensates.

The actualization of these dimensions is equivalent to reintegrating them into "Adamic" equilibrium. And it is this equilibrium, by virtue of which man is all and nothing before God, which confers on Islamic art its plentitude, sobriety, and serenity.

THE *MIHRAB*

The prayer niche, or *mihrab,* is indisputably a creation of sacred art and has become in practice a regular element in the liturgy, though not an indispensable one. Art historians believe that this element was introduced into mosque architecture in the time of the Umayyad Caliph al-Walid and, more exactly, when this caliph rebuilt the mosque of the Prophet at Medina. But it is extremely probable that the niche replaced a more simple form, such as a false door, which showed the direction of Mecca in primitive mosques. If the *mihrab* in the cave beneath the rock of the Dome of the Rock (*Qubbat al-Sakhra*) at Jerusalem goes back to the years during which this sanctuary was built (691–692 CE), it is an example of this. This *mihrab* consists of an arch on small columns, carved in relief on a slab of marble. At the level of the capitals, there is a very simple inscription in Kūfi script across the back: the two Muslim declarations of faith. In the center of the background is a rosette with eight petals. An even simpler indication of the *qibla* must have existed in the ancient mosque at Medina; according to certain accounts, a stone slab marked the spot where the Prophet stood to lead the communal prayers.

The form of the niche may well have been suggested by the example of the apse in Coptic churches, or even by that of the liturgical niches in certain synagogues,[1] but these are no more than "incidental causes"; what matters is that the sacred niche derives from a worldwide symbolism, and that this symbolism is implicitly confirmed by the Qur'an.

Its very shape, with its vault corresponding to heaven and its piedroit to the earth, makes the niche a consistent image of the "cave of the world." The cave of the world is the "place of appearance" (*mazhar*) of the Divinity, whether it be a case of the outward world as a whole or the inner world, the sacred cave of the heart. All oriental traditions recognize the significance of this, and the exedra of Roman basilicas is simply a worldly version of it, with the emperor replacing the Divinity.[2]

To establish the symbolism of the *mihrab* in its Islamic perspective, it must be related to its Qur'anic context. The word literally means, "refuge"; the Qur'an in particular uses this word to describe a secret place in the Temple at Jerusalem where the Holy Virgin entered into a spiritual retreat and was nourished by angels. It is identified by certain Arab commentators with the Holy of Holies, the *debir* of the Temple at Jerusalem, and this interpretation, which does not appear to take into account the Judaic laws governing access to the *debir*, accords in fact with the Patristic tradition and the liturgy of the Greek Orthodox Church.[3] The inscriptions round the arch of the *mihrab* are frequently such as to recall the Qur'anic story in question, especially in Turkish mosques, starting with the *mihrab* of the Hagia Sophia, thereby confirming its dedication to the Holy Virgin. The link between the *mihrab* and Sayyidatna Maryam (Our Lady Mary) leads us again to the analogy between the prayer niche and the heart: it is in the heart that the virgin-soul takes refuge to invoke God; as for the nourishment miraculously bestowed there, it corresponds to grace.

The form of the *mihrab*—discounting its name—calls to mind another passage from the Qur'an, the "Verse of Light," where the Divine Presence in the world or in the heart of man is compared to a light from a lamp placed in a niche (*mishkat*): "God is the light of the heavens and the earth. The symbol of His light is a niche wherein is a lamp; the lamp is in a glass, and this glass is as a radiant star. [The light] is nourished by a blessed olive tree, which is neither of the east nor of the west, whose oil would all but glow though fire touch it not. Light upon light. God guideth to His Light whom He will, and God striketh symbols for man, and God knoweth all things" (Qur'an 24:35). The analogy between the *mihrab* and the *mishkat* is clear; it is emphasized, moreover, by hanging a lamp before the prayer niche.

Many of the oldest prayer niches are adorned with a canopy in the form of a seashell. This motif is already found in Hellenistic art, but it would not have been incorporated into the art of Islam unless it had a spiritual significance; the shell is associated with the pearl, which is one of the Islamic symbols of the Divine Word, according to a saying of the Prophet, the world was created from a white pearl. The seashell enclosing the pearl is like the "ear" of the heart receiving the Divine Utterance; it is, in fact, in the *mihrab* that this utterance is made.

It may seem surprising that a form such as the *mihrab*, which is, after all, simply an accessory to the liturgy, should be the focus of a particularly rich and profound symbolism. But this is implicit proof of the link between sacred art and esoterism, the "science of the inward" (*'ilm al-batin*). It is on this same plane that the somewhat Christian typology of the prayer niche is situated; it is in Islamic esoterism that certain Christly themes reappear, not in their historical or dogmatic content, but as patterns of the contemplative life.

THE *MINBAR*

The Arabic term *al-jami'*, which means literally "what brings together," refers to a mosque where the Friday prayers are celebrated together. The term has sometimes been translated "cathedral mosque," since, as a general rule, it is only mosques of this order which have a *cathedra,* a pulpit, called *minbar* in Arabic. The question remains to what extent the *minbar* corresponds to a bishop's chair, or even to a king's throne. Actually, it is neither the one nor the other, or it is both at the same time, since it is in some way an image of the Prophet's function and then of the function of his Caliphs, and thus unites in itself both spiritual authority and temporal power.

The prototype of the *minbar* is a sort of stepped stool which the Prophet used in his mosque at Medina to talk to the assembled faithful. According to certain traditional authorities, this stool had three levels. The Prophet sat on the third level and rested his feet on the second. After him, Abu Bakr, the first caliph, sat on the second level and rested his feet on the first. 'Umar, the second caliph, took his seat on the first level and placed his feet on the ground. The hierarchical sense of the levels is clear.

According to other sources, the original *minbar* at Medina had six steps. The oldest surviving *manabir* (plural of *minbar*) have from seven to eleven steps, and this multiplication of levels is easily explained by the custom which requires the *imam* to preach his Friday sermon from one of the *minbar's* lower levels. He stands up to speak, head and shoulders covered in a white cloth and a staff in his hand. Between the two canonical sections of the sermon, exhortation of the faithful and praise of the Prophet, he sits briefly on the nearest step. The upper steps of the *minbar,* and in particular the top one, which is adorned with a headboard in the manner of a throne, are left empty; they recall the preeminent function of the Prophet.

The overall shape of the *minbar* bespeaks the continuity of tradition; it always takes the form of a staircase, fairly narrow and nearly always enclosed by handrails. Since the Seljuk period, this simple structure has been supplemented by a canopy sheltering the topmost level and by a doorway at the foot of the stairs. These additions have simply accentuated the *minbar's* symbolism, which corresponds to the ladder of the worlds—the most broadly spaced levels are the corporeal world, the psychic world, and the world of pure spirit—and to the throne as a "polar" station. None of these points of significance was added later; they result logically from the first action of the Prophet in choosing a stool with three steps to preside over the assembled believers.

The fact that the uppermost level of the *minbar,* the throne sheltered by its canopy, remains empty, is strangely reminiscent of the awaiting throne that, in both Buddhism and Christianity, represents the unseen presence of the *Logos* or of the *Tathagatha* or, in other terms, the unseen presence of the Divine Messenger. But this is certainly not a case of an influence coming from outside Islam, but of a coincidence due to the universal character of symbolism.

TOMBS

That a great many mausoleums are found in Islamic lands is something of a paradox, for the glorification of the dead is foreign to the spirit of Islam. "The most beautiful tomb," said the Prophet, "is one that vanishes from the face of the earth"; and the Qur'an says "All who are upon it [the earth] are fleeting, and there abides only the face of thy Lord full of majesty and generosity" (Qur'an 55:26–27). This paradox is explicable by two factors that are in a way ineluctable, the first of which is the ambition of sovereigns to perpetuate their names; implying as it does a wish for personal glory, this ambition is perhaps not altogether Islamic but it is, after all, fairly natural and it is made legitimate by the hope that the soul of the deceased shall benefit from the prayers offered up for it by the visitors to the tomb. The second factor closely follows the first and consists of the wish of the community of believers to honor the saints, whom they see as the true kings of the earth as much as, or more than, princes. The proliferation of princely mausoleums coincides historically with the coming to power of the Seljuks who, perhaps, retained and transposed the funeral customs of their Central Asian ancestors, for their tombs greatly resemble ceremonial *yourts*. In the same period, that is, from the twelfth to the fourteenth century, the general veneration of saints, among both people and sovereigns, reached its definitive form with the organization of Sufism—the mysticism of Islam—into orders or brotherhoods, each with its chain of founding or renovating masters. The Muslim saint (*wali*) is nearly always a contemplative whose state of spiritual perfection finds permanent expression in the teaching bequeathed to his disciples. To this bequest, to a greater or lesser degree esoteric, there is generally superadded the spontaneous veneration of the people, and it is this that affects his "canonization," and not some ecclesiastical institution. We have no hesitation in translating the Arabic term *wali Allah*, literally "friend of God," by the word "saint," for what is understood by the one term as much as by the other is a man who has become the object and instrument of a divine grace. What is sought at the tomb of a *wali* is his *baraka*, his "blessing" or spiritual influence, which remains active and is in a way linked with the corporeal remains of a man who was in life a recipient, as it were, of the Divine Presence. Moreover, the saint is not thought of as being dead, but as mysteriously alive, according to this passage from the Qur'an: "Say not of them that were killed in the path of God that they are dead; they are alive, but ye perceive not" (Qur'an 2:154). This verse refers in its most immediate sense to those who fall in the holy war, and many of the tombs venerated are in fact *martyria* (*mashahid*), burial places of those who fought against the enemies of Islam. But since the Prophet described the struggle against the passions of the soul as "the greatest holy war" (*al-jihad al-akbar*), this verse applies *a priori* to all those who have sacrificed their lives to the contemplation of God. The veneration of saints is, moreover, a kind of reflection of the veneration accorded to the Prophet, whose tomb at Medina is second as a place of pilgrimage only to the sanctuary of Mecca.

Whereas the mausoleums of princes were usually built by the persons who expected to repose in them, those of saints were the gift either of their disciples or of sovereigns, like the famous tomb of Salim Chishti at Fatehpur Sikri built by the Emperor Akbar, or of the nameless common people.

Besides the mausoleums of princes and the tombs of saints, there are the funerary monuments dedicated to descendants of the Prophet. Their architectural forms give all these monuments an equal dignity; the mausoleum of a great conqueror like Tamerlane is simply a glorification of God, and the tomb of one of "God's poor" often stands as a token of homage to his spiritual kingship.

The interior of a mausoleum generally contains a cenotaph indicating the spot where the deceased is buried, or laid to rest, in a crypt of indeterminate depth. There is also a *mihrab* showing the direction of Mecca, but so placed that persons at prayer shall not face the tomb.

Mausoleums of princes are occasionally grouped around the tomb of a saint in such a way as to constitute, together with all the more humble graves that come to be placed near by, veritable "cities of the dead" like the necropolis of Shah-i-Zindah ("The Living King") at Samarqand or that of the Mamluk tombs at Cairo. These "cities of the dead" have nothing mournful or sad about them; as in all Muslim cemeteries, the dominant note is serenity.

There is one architectural formula that has come to be most prevalently used for relatively simple mausoleums, namely, the cube crowned with a cupola, the transition between the two usually being mediated by a polygon. Funerary buildings of this sober form predominate in Muslim cemeteries and rise as landmarks on the edges of the desert and the seacoasts from the Atlantic to India. Often whitened with lime, they attract the eye from afar and hold it by their image of an equilibrium that reconciles heaven with earth.

THE ART OF APPAREL

We have alluded to the liturgical role of clothing. Let us make clear that there are no priestly vestments in Islam because, properly speaking, there is no priesthood; but neither is there any clothing that is Muslim and profane. What determines Muslim costume in general is first of all the *Sunna*, the example given by the Prophet, and second, the fact that clothing must suit the movements and positions of the prescribed prayers. It is in this latter respect that Imam Malik condemns clothing that clings to the body; in fact the traditional clothing of all Muslim peoples is distinguished by its ample cut; it conceals the body, or part of the body, at the same time as adapting itself to the body's movements.

The example given by the Prophet amounts to no more than a few guidelines that permit a great deal of liberty in the art of dress, while indicating the limits set, on the one hand, by spiritual poverty and, on the other, by the dignity of the *Imam,* which pertains in principle to every Muslim of male sex and mature years. It is known that the Prophet took the occasion to wear clothes of various colors and various places of origin as if to demonstrate that Islam would spread to different ethnic surroundings; however, he preferred white and rejected excessively sumptuous materials, while insisting on the need for certain of his Companions to mark their rank and standing in the community. He forbade men to wear gold ornaments or silken robes, reserving these for women. Gold is by its nature sacred, and Islam reserves it for the domain which is, for Islam, *sacratum (haram) par excellence,* that of woman, conjugal love, and family life sheltered from all public gaze.

It is fashionable to question the authenticity of traditions extolling the wearing of the turban. Now whether the saying "the turban is the crown of Islam" is the word of the Prophet or not, this saying is, in any case, expressive of the inherent significance of this item of manly apparel, which proclaims both the majesty of the believer who is "God's representative on earth" and his submission (*islam*) to God's will. In the Semitic environment, it is always a token of reverential fear to keep the head covered, no doubt because to expose it to the sun is symbolically equivalent to exposing it to the divine rigor. It may well be suggested that the turban became an integral part of Muslim costume because it was worn by the Arabian Bedouins, but this is not proved nor, for that matter, does it disprove our point. It was only natural that Arab costume should have been spread by the Islamic conquests, but the positive value of this phenomenon lies in the simple fact that the Prophet had taken over certain Arabian and Bedouin customs, rectifying them and transposing them into a spiritual ordinance. It is extremely probable that loosely cut garments, which are eminently suitable for the desert climate with its extremes of temperature, are of Arab origin, and one can be certain that garments of very simple cut like the *'aba'a,* or the seamless *ha'ik* that covers the head and shoulders, are of nomadic origin. It is perhaps the Maghribi costume—a long tunic, a rectangular robe with or without sleeves, burnous, and turban wrapped in a *litham*—that constitutes the most typically Arab and Muslim style, for it sits equally well on the scholar of Islamic sciences, the warrior chief, and the man of the people. Its beauty and dignity are at one with its simplicity. In the Islamic East, Turkish and Mongol influences are responsible for a greater diversity in forms of dress, which, however, are never incompatible with the general Islamic style of apparel; a host of Muslim pilgrims from the most diverse countries is always recognizably a host of Muslims.

We are considering masculine garb in particular, for women's dress has far less unity since it is made for life at home, and women go veiled in the streets. Feminine garb is happy to hold on to certain items of a regional character and to retain occasional forms of apparel of great antiquity, such as the robe made from a single piece of unstitched cloth, draped around the body and held together by two clasps at the shoulders, which is found in particular among certain tribes in the Sahara.

Men's garb in Islamic countries makes for the effacement of social differences, with the exception of certain extravagances of dress deriving either from princely courts or, again, from groups of ascetics who have cut themselves off from the world. These latter may well follow the example of the Prophet, who occasionally wore a robe made up of pieces of cloth stitched together.

The art of apparel is made all the more important in Islamic countries by the absence of any human image; it is the art of clothing that in a way conveys the Muslim's ideal image of himself as a Muslim. There is, moreover, no art that has a more telling effect on a man's soul than that of clothing, for a man instinctively identifies himself with the clothes he wears. It is vain to say that "the habit does not make the monk"; in a certain sense there is no monk without an appropriate habit.

The art of clothing is an essentially collective one; it is therefore subject to fluctuations and obeys, to some degree or other, the psychological law referred to by Ibn Khaldun, according to which conquered people imitate the manners and clothing of their conquerors. Despite this, Muslim dress shows such historical and geographical continuity that one can attribute it only to that positive quality of the *Umma,* the religious collectivity, which moved the Prophet to say "my community will never be single-minded in error."

The gradual disappearance of traditional Muslim costume in favor of modern European dress can be only partly explained by the law of psychology referred to above. This form of "acculturation" does amount to imitating the man who holds in his hands the means of power and success, and modern European clothing has become the emblem of material efficiency. At the same time, a more acute change of direction in the soul is involved. There is a turning away from a way of life entirely dominated by contemplative values with its bearings fixed on the hereafter; the aim is to be in the "here and now," on the level of newspaper events. Modern European dress is welcome in such a perspective, because it expresses individualism, an attitude that stands outside all that is sacred, in the same way as egalitarianism has nothing in common with the self-effacement of the Muslim within the *Umma,* but represents a leveling down, a negation of any *élite,* whether of nobility or saints.

One could well believe that modern European dress had been expressly invented to destroy the patterns of Muslim life; it makes the ablutions prescribed by the Qur'an difficult and directly impedes the movements and positions of the canonical prayer by its stiff folds. If it is not within its power to destroy the inner value of these rites, it detracts nonetheless from the radiation of their value by the unavoidable triviality of its associations.

The teaching that inheres in the traditional apparel of Islam is, in sum, that the human body, created "according to the form" of God, is a kind of revelation. This is true of man as he was before the Fall, and still is in virtuality, although he bears the marks of his decadence upon him, which love alone forgives. Thus, it is fitting that the body should be veiled at least in part, but not that it should have forms imposed on it that are not its own. To veil the body is not to deny it, but to withdraw it like gold, into the domain of things concealed from the eyes of the crowd.

NOTES

This chapter first appeared in Titus Burckhardt, *Art of Islam: Language and Meaning,* translated by J. Peter Hobson (London, U.K.: World of Islam Festival Trust, 1976; Bloomington, Indiana: World Wisdom, forthcoming in 2008), 83–100. It is reprinted here with minor modifications with the permission of the editors of World Wisdom Books and the Burckhardt estate.

1. For example, a sacred niche in the underground necropolis of Mea Shearim, which is very like a *mihrab.*

2. In Hindu iconography also, divine appearances are usually surrounded by an arch representing the cosmos.

3. According to this tradition, Zacharias took Mary as a child into the Holy of Holies because he recognized that she was herself the holy tabernacle.

9

MUSIC AND SPIRITUALITY IN ISLAM

———————————— • ————————————

Jean-Louis Michon

A CONTROVERSIAL QUESTION

"Oh Lord, Show us things as they are!" asked the Prophet Muhammad when addressing himself to his Lord.[1] The same prayer was to be repeated over and over by devout Muslims desiring to objectively judge a more or less ambiguous situation. It is therefore well placed at the beginning of a chapter on the art of music, as it was understood and is still understood in the countries of *Dar al-Islam*. Few subjects have been as debated or have raised as many contradictory emotions and opinions as the status (*hukm*) of music *vis-à-vis* the religious Law at the heart of Muslim society. In fact, the debate is not yet over and, no doubt, never will be because it concerns a domain in which it seems that Providence wanted to give Muslims the greatest possible freedom of choice and appreciation. No Qur'anic prescription explicitly aims at music. The *Sunna*, the Tradition of the Prophet Muhammad, cites only anecdotal elements, none of which constitutes a peremptory argument either for or against musical practice. The third source of Islamic law, the opinions of the doctors of the law (*ulama*), spokesmen recognized by social consensus, varies widely, ranging from the categorical condemnation of music to its panegyric, while passing through various degrees of acceptance and reservation.

To understand how such divergent positions could have arisen and been expressed on this subject in Islamic thought and ethics, it is useful to refer to those interpreters who knew how to take into consideration ideas that were at once metaphysical, philosophical, or theosophical, as well as the imperatives of Muslim ethics, both individual and social. To this category belong the "Brethren of Purity" (*Ikhwan al-Safa'*), whose vast encyclopedia of philosophy, science, and art, compiled in the tenth century CE, contains a precious "Epistle on Music."[2]

Like the Greek philosophers, the Ikhwan al-Safa' recognized in terrestrial music the echo of the music of the spheres, "inhabited by the angels of

God and by the elite of his servants." "The rhythm produced by the motion of the musician evokes for certain souls residing in the world of generation and corruption the felicity of the world of the spheres, in the same way that the rhythms produced by the motion of the spheres and the stars evoke for souls, who are the beatitude of the world of the spirit." By reason of the law of harmony, which reigns over all the planes of existence, linking them according to an order at once hierarchical and analogical, "the caused beings belonging to secondary reactions imitate in their modalities the first beings, which are their causes...from which it must be deduced that the notes of terrestrial music necessarily imitate those of celestial music." Like [the Greek philosopher] Pythagoras, who "heard, thanks to the purity of the substance of his soul and the wisdom of his heart, the music produced by the rotation of the spheres and the stars," and who "was the first to have spoken of this science," other philosophers such as Nichomus, Ptolemy, and Euclid had "the habit of singing, with percussive sounds produced by chords, words and measured verses that were composed for exhortation to the spiritual life and described the delights of the world of the spirit, the pleasure and the happiness of its inhabitants." Later came the Muslim conquerors who, when given the signal to attack, recited verses of the Qur'an or declaimed Arabic or Persian poems describing the paradisal delights reserved for those who died while fighting on the path of God. When resorting to music, when inventing the principles of its melodies and the constitution of its rhythms, the sages had no other goal than "to soften hardened hearts, to wake the negligent souls from their sleep of forgetfulness and the misguided spirits from their slumber of ignorance, to make them desire the spiritual world, their luminous place and their journey of life, to make them leave the world of generation and corruption, to save them from submersion in the ocean of the material world and to deliver them from the prison of nature."

How, under such circumstances, can it be explained that music could become an object of reprobation? Because, explain the Ikhwan, even if music is good in itself, it can be turned aside from its natural and legitimate ends: "As for the reason for the interdiction of music in certain laws of the prophets...it relates to the fact that people do not use music for the purpose assigned to it by the philosophers, but for the purpose of diversion, for sport, for the incitement to enjoy the pleasures of this lower world." Thus, that which can become reprehensible is not music itself but the use to which certain people put it. "Be watchful while listening to music, so that the appetites of the animal soul do not push you toward the splendor of nature. Nature will lead you astray from the paths of salvation and prevent you from discourse with the Superior Soul."[3] This warning issued by the Ikhwan goes along with the teaching given a century earlier by the Sufi Dhu'l-Nun the Egyptian (d. 861 CE): "Listening (*sama*) is a divine influence that stirs the heart to see Allah; those who listen to music spiritually attain to Allah, whereas those who listen to it sensually fall into heresy."[4] In the same way, the Sufi 'Ali Hujwiri (d. 1071 CE) wrote in his *Kashf al-mahjub* (The Lifting of the Veil), "Listening to sweet sounds produces an effervescence of the substance molded in man; true, if the substance be true, false, if the substance be false."[5]

Such was, generally speaking, the attitude of the philosophers and theoreticians of music, as well as that of the majority of Sufis and a good number of canonists. Aware of the benefits of the art of music, they did not show themselves less circumspect as to its utilization, distinguishing between noble and vulgar genres, and between sensual melodies, "useful" melodies, and the like.[6]

However, numerous jurists went much further and, seeing the sensual usage that could be made of the practice of music, concluded that music itself was evil or at least that it involved more disadvantages than advantages and had, therefore, to be banned from society. Poetry that was sung and the use of instruments gave rise, they said, to corrupting excitations of the soul, which turned the individual aside from his religious duties, encouraged one to seek out sensual satisfactions and bad company, and pushed one into drunkenness and debauchery. Such jurists went so far as to say that the public singer, even if he or she sings the Qur'an to arouse pleasure in his listeners, could not be heard as a legal witness. They also maintained that it was lawful to break musical instruments.

For the jurist and moralist Ibn Abi al-Dunya (d. 894 CE), who wrote a short treatise on the "Censure of Instruments of Diversion" (*dhamm al-malahi*), singing and music were condemnable distractions of the same type as the games of chess and backgammon.[7] Later, the Hanbalite jurist Ibn al-Jawzi (d. 1201 CE) was to show himself to be just as severe *vis-à-vis* music, which evil human nature, "the soul which incites to evil" (*al-nafs al-ammara bi al-su'),* according to the Qur'an (Qur'an 12:53), has a tendency to seize upon in order to anchor man in sensuality. "The spiritual concert (*sama'*) includes two things," he wrote in *Talbis Iblis* (The Dissimulation of the Devil). "In the first place, it leads the heart away from reflection upon the power of God and from assiduity in His service. In the second place, it encourages enjoyment of the pleasures of this world." Furthermore, "Music makes man forget moderation and it troubles his mind. This implies that man, when he is excited, commits acts that he judges reprehensible in others when he is in his normal state. He makes movements with his head, claps his hands, strikes the ground with his feet, and commits acts similar to those of the insane. Music leads one to this; its action appears to be like that of wine, because it clouds the mind. This is why it is necessary to prohibit it."[8]

Ibn al-Jawzi admits, however, that there are certain musical genres in which the emotional element does not enter and that, therefore, are legal, such as the songs of pilgrims traveling to Mecca, the songs of fighters for the faith, and the songs of camel drivers. He also recognized that in the previous epoch in which the jurist Ibn Hanbal lived (ninth century CE), poems were sung that exalted only religious feeling and that, consequently, escaped interdiction. But such times, according to him, are over and the innovations introduced since then in music and poetry are such that these arts can only have a deleterious influence.

THE PHILOSOPHER-MUSICOLOGISTS

Although they must be regarded as admissible on the part of jurists concerned above all with the moral health of the common man and the collectivity, arguments of the sort made by Ibn al-Jawzi cannot be held as applying to those seekers of Truth who have sufficiently refined themselves so as not to fall into the trap of sensuality. These are people for whom music occupies an important place in the hierarchy of the arts and the sciences, and who consider and practice it as a discipline capable of elevating the human being above the gross world, of making one participate in the universal harmony. Such seekers have been numerous from early times in the Islamic world, which, thanks to them, can pride itself on an extremely fecund tradition of musical theory as well as of the practice of vocal and instrumental music. Among the theoreticians who thought and wrote about music, two clearly distinguishable schools can be recognized which sometimes converged, but more often, went along their separate paths, drawing on their own sources and applying different methods of investigation. They are, on the one side, the philosophers—*falasifa* or *hukama'* (the plural of *hakim,* "sage")—and, on the other side, the mystics—*sufiyya* (the plural of *sufi)* and the *'arifun* or *'urafa'* (alternative plurals of *'arif,* "gnostic").

To the philosopher-sages are linked the great thinkers whose names are forever inseparable from the history of Islamic philosophy: Ya'qub al-Kindi (d. 866 CE); Abu Bakr al-Razi (Rhazes, d. 923 CE); Abu Nasr al-Farabi (d. 950 CE); whose *Great Book on Music* (*Kitab al-Musiqa al-Kabir*) achieved considerable fame; Abu 'Ali ibn Sina (Avicenna, d. 1037 CE); Ibn Bajja (Avempace, d. 1138 CE) and Safi al-Din (d. 1293 CE). Although they inherited the legacy of ancient Greece and resumed the Pythagorean, Aristotelian, Platonic, and Neo-Platonic philosophical discourses, they imprinted on them a unique and profoundly original mark, thus enriching the Greek tradition not only with numerous scientific developments but also with a whole school of thought based on the Qur'anic Revelation.[9] The previously mentioned Ikhwan al-Safa' also belonged to this group. Their "Epistle on Music" opens as follows: "After having completed the study of the theoretical spiritual arts, which are the *genera* of the sciences, and the study of the corporeal practical arts, which are the *genera* of the arts,...we propose in the present epistle entitled 'Music' to study the art which is made up of both the corporeal and the spiritual. It is the art of harmony (*ta'lif*), which can be defined as the function of proportions."[10]

Two ideas, therefore, impose themselves at the outset, the first being that music is composed of corporeal and spiritual elements, the second that it is based on proportions. Because of its dual composition, the art of music possesses the special power of freeing matter in order to spiritualize it, and of materializing the spiritual in order to render it perceptible. This power comes also from the fact that music is a science of proportions, as the Ikhwan explain in another epistle (the sixth). After having shown by example how number, proportion, and numerical relationship are applied to all phenomena, they add, "All of these examples demonstrate the nobility of the science of proportion, which is music. This science is necessary for all the arts. Nevertheless, if it was connected with the name of music it is because music offers the best illustration of harmony."[11]

According to the Ikhwan, that which characterizes music and distinguishes it from other arts is that the substance upon which it works (the soul of the listener), like the elements that it employs (notes and rhythms), are of a subtle nature and not corporeal. "Music leaves in the souls of those who listen to it diverse impressions similar to those left by the work of the artisan in the matter that is the substratum of his art." The Ikhwan cite many examples of emotional states that melodies are capable of inspiring in man, such as regret and repentance for past mistakes, courage in battle, relief from suffering, and joyful excitation. Animals themselves are roused by hearing music; the camel quickens his step upon hearing the song of the camel-driver, the horse drinks more willingly when his master whistles a tune, and the gazelle allows herself to be approached at night by the hunter who hums a melody. Ibn Khurdadhbih (d. 912 CE), who was educated in Baghdad by the inspired Ishaq al-Mawsili (d. 850 CE),[12] made the following statement about music in a speech delivered at the court of the Abbasid Caliph al-Mu'tamid, his protector and friend: "Music sharpens the intellect, softens the disposition, and agitates the soul. It gives cheer and courage to the heart, and high-mindedness to the debased.... It is to be preferred to speech, as health would be to sickness."[13]

Not only does music stir the soul and the emotions, but it also "descends" into the body. From there comes its power to move the body and make it dance, and from there also come the therapeutic applications to which the classical treatises refer, notably those of al-Kindi and Ibn Sina. Besides this, music "rises" as far as the Spirit because it is itself a vibration of supernatural origin like the *kun* (the Arabic command, "Be!"), the primordial *fiat lux,* which from nothingness, from silence, and from darkness, existence was brought forth. Thus, the remark of Ibn Zayla (d. 1048 CE), a disciple of Ibn Sina: "Sound produces an influence on the soul in two directions. One is on account of its special composition, i.e. its physical content, the other is on account of its being similar to the soul, i.e. its spiritual content."[14]

Because of the power of its effects (*ta'thir*), the theosophical Ikhwan and most Sufis gave music the highest rank, for music sets souls in flights that are determined in measured proportion by the human receptacle in which souls are contained: "Know, my brethren, that the effects imprinted by the rhythms and melodies (*naghamat*) of the musician in the souls of listeners are of different types. In the same way, the pleasure that souls draw from these rhythms and the melodies and the manner in which they enjoy them are variable and diverse. All of this depends on the rank that each soul occupies in the domains of knowledge (*al-ma'arif*) and on the nature of the good actions that make up the permanent object of one's love. Therefore, each soul, while listening to descriptions that correspond to the object of one's desires, and to melodies which are in accord with the object of one's delight, rejoices, is exalted, and delights in the image that music makes of the beloved."[15]

The Ikhwan al-Safa' conclude their epistle on music with a justification of the most beautiful and the most perfect music, which is none other than the psalmody of sacred texts: "Tradition teaches that the sweetest melody that the inhabitants of Paradise have at their disposal and the most beautiful song they hear is the discourse of God, great be His praise." It is thus that the word of God Most High states, "The greeting that will welcome them there will be, 'Salvation!' And the end of their invocation will be, 'Praise to Allah, Lord of the worlds' (Qur'an 10:10–11). It is said that Moses (may peace be upon him) was overcome with joy upon hearing the words of his Lord, and was overcome with happiness and rapture to the point of being unable to contain himself. He was overwhelmed by emotion and transported while listening to this serene melody. From that point on, he regarded all rhythms, all melodies, and all songs as insignificant."

SUFIS AND THE SPIRITUAL AUDITION (*AL-SAMA'*)

To listen to music is, in the final analysis, to open oneself to an influence, to a vibration of supra-human origin that is "made sound" in order to awaken in us the echoes of a primordial state and to arouse in the heart a longing for union with its Essence. At the beginning of a long chapter in *Ihya' 'ulum al-din* (The Revival of the Sciences of Religion) that he consecrates to the laws governing the spiritual concert of song and ecstasy (*al-sama'*), Abu Hamid al-Ghazali (d. 1111 CE) writes:

Hearts and inmost selves are treasuries of secrets and mines of jewels. Infolded in them are their jewels like as fire is infolded in iron and stone, and concealed like as water is concealed under dust and loam. There is no way to the extracting of their hidden things save by the flint and steel of listening to music and singing, and there is no entrance to the heart save by the antechamber of the ears. So musical tones, measured and pleasing, bring forth what is in it and make evident its beauties and defects. For when the heart is moved, there is made evident only that which it contains like a vessel drips only what is in it. And listening to music and singing is for the heart a true touchstone and a speaking standard; whenever the soul of the music and singing reaches the heart, then there stirs in the heart that which preponderates in it.[16]

For the person in whom the desire for the good and the beautiful predominates, and who has an ear for music, music is a privileged tool for self-knowledge and inward improvement. Manifesting the latent possibilities of the individual, it permits one to observe, by its movements and reciprocal tonal interactions, potentialities of which one has not been aware until that moment. A sense of discrimination operates in the listener, which makes one perceive in the inmost heart, with an acuity in proportion to the quality of the music and to one's own receptive capacity, zones of aspiration toward the Absolute, often in alternation with emotional attractions. This age-old doctrine, taught by the sages of Antiquity and elevated by generations of Sufis to the rank of a veritable alchemy of the soul, has been transmitted and maintained down to the present time. It is summarized by a sentence that the father of a contemporary Turkish musician who specializes in the songs of the Sufi brotherhoods inscribed on his tambourine: "This instrument increases both the love of the lover and the hypocrisy of the hypocrite."

The use of the spiritual concert (*sama*ʿ) as a technique for spiritual realization must necessarily surround itself with conditions and precautions that will guarantee its efficacy and that will overcome the wandering and misguidance of the passional soul (*nafs*). These conditions are generally the same as those demanded of candidates for the initiatic path (*al-tariqa*): moral and spiritual qualifications for the disciple, obedience to the spiritual master (*shaykh* or *pir*), service to one's fellow adepts (*fuqara*ʾ), and the strict observance of ritual practices particular to the order, as well as those of the Shariʿa. Most important, at the time of participation in sessions of spiritual concert, dervishes are enjoined to remain as sober as possible and to exteriorize their emotions only when they undergo an ecstatic rapture so great that it exceeds all control. Referring to the example of the Prophet Muhammad who, at the time of the first appearance of the Archangel of Revelation, could not master his emotions, Hujwiri excuses those beginners who show excitement in *sama*ʿ: "You must not exceed the proper bounds until audition manifests its power. [However,] when it has become powerful you must not repel it but must follow it as it requires: if it agitates, you must be agitated, and if it calms, you must be calm.... The auditor must have enough perception to be capable of receiving the Divine influence and of doing justice to it. When its might is manifested on his heart he must not endeavor to repel it, and when its force is broken he must not endeavour to attract it."[17]

Al-Ghazali expresses a similar opinion in the *Ihya*ʾ: "The participant should remain seated, his head lowered as if he were deep in meditation, and avoid clapping his hands, dancing, or making any other movement designed to artificially induce ecstasy or to make a display of it. . . . But when ecstasy takes hold of him and causes him to make movements independent of his will, he is to be excused and must not be blamed."

However, the same master admits that it is certainly not blameworthy to imitate the attitudes and movements of an ecstatic if the intention is not to make a display of a state that one has not attained, but rather to put oneself into a frame of mind receptive to grace: "Know that ecstasy (*wajd*) *is* divided into that which attacks and that which is forced, and that which is called 'the affectation of ecstasy' (*tawajud*). Of this forced affectation of ecstasy there is that which is blameworthy, which is what aims at hypocrisy and at the manifestation of the Glorious States despite being destitute of them. And of it there is that which is praiseworthy, which leads to the invoking of the Glorious States and the gaining of them for oneself and bringing them to oneself by device. Therefore, the Apostle of God commanded him who did not weep at the reading of the Qur'an that he should force weeping and mourning; for the beginning of these States is sometimes forced while their ends thereafter are true."[18]

Summarizing the teachings of numerous masters of Sufism in his glossary of Sufi technical terms, the Moroccan Sufi Ahmad ibn 'Ajiba (d. 1809 CE) describes four successive degrees of approach toward ecstasy:

First, the "seeking out of ecstasy" (*tawajud*), in which one affects the appearances of ecstatic emotion (*wajd*) and one uses them methodically; thus, one employs dance (*raqs*), rhythmic movements, etc. This seeking out is only admissible among the *fuqara'* [Sufi adepts] who have made vows of total renunciation. For them, there is nothing wrong in simulating ecstasy and in repeating its gestures in order to respond to an inner call (*hal*). . . . It is, certainly, the station of the weak, but the strong practice it nevertheless, either in order to sustain and encourage the weaker ones, or because they find a sweetness in it. . . . Myself, when I participated in a session of spiritual concert with our Shaykh al-Buzidi, I saw him sway from right to left. One of the disciples of Mawlay al-'Arabi al-Darqawi told me that his master would not stop dancing until the end of the concert.[19]

In the second place comes "ecstatic emotion" (*wajd*), through which must be heard "that which befalls the heart" and takes hold of it unexpectedly, without the person having any part in it. It can be an ardent and anxious desire or a troubling fear. . . .

Thirdly, one speaks of "ecstatic meting" (*wijdan*), when the sweetness of the presence is prolonged, accompanied most frequently by intoxication and stupor.

Finally, if the meeting lasts until the stupor and hindrances dissipate and the faculties of meditation and insight are purified, it becomes ecstasy (*wujud*), the station to which Junayd (d. 911 CE)[20] alluded in this verse: "My ecstasy is that I disappear from existence, by the grace of what appears to me of the Presence."[21]

ELEMENTS OF MUSICAL EXPRESSION

The animating power of music comes, as we have seen, from what music is in essence—a manifestation of the Divine Word, a language that reminds the human being of the state in which, before creation, one was still united with the Universal Soul, radiated from the original Light, which reminds the person of the instant in preeternity when, according to a Qur'anic verse frequently cited by the Sufis, the Lord asked souls before their manifestation: "Am I not your Lord?" and they answered, "Indeed, we do so testify" (Qur'an 7:172). It is the memory of this primordial covenant and the nostalgia for it that music evokes in hearts trapped within their earthly attachments.

There is in music an interpenetration of two aspects inherent in Allah, the Supreme Being. One is the aspect of Majesty (*jalal*), which translates into rhythm, and the other is the aspect of Beauty (*jamal*), which melody renders. The drum, which is beaten rhythmically, announces the arrival and the presence of the all-powerful King. It is a symbol of transcendence, of the discontinuity that separates us, impoverished and dependent, from God, the Highest, who subsists in Himself. Conversely, the human voice and the flute, which express melody, sing of the Immanence, of the inexhaustible Wealth (*ghina'*) that no human imagination will ever comprehend, but whose every manifestation, mode, or station (*maqam*) is capable of becoming a grace and a blessing for the believer.

Musical Instruments

Each of the elements of the spiritual concert is invested with a symbolic value and becomes an aid for recollection or remembrance (*dhikr*) for those who are attentive to the language of signs. According to Ahmad Ghazali (d. 1126 CE), who taught the elements of a whirling Sufi dance approximately a century and a half before Mevlana Jalaluddin Rumi made the whirling dance of the Sufis famous:

The saints of Allah apply the forms to the realities (*ma'ani*) on account of their abandoning the ranks of the forms and their moving in the ranks of the branches of gnosis. So among them the tambourine is a reference to the cycle of existing things (*da'irat al-akwan*); the skin which is fitted on to it is a reference to Absolute Being, the striking which takes place on the tambourine is a reference to the descent of the divine visitations from the innermost arcana within the Absolute Being to bring forth the things pertaining to the essence from the interior to the exterior.... And the breath of the musician is the form of the rank of the Truth (Exalted and holy is He!), since it is He who sets them in motion, brings them into existence, and enriches them. And the voice of the singer is a reference to the divine life, which comes down from the innermost arcana to the levels of the spirits, the hearts, and the consciences (*asrar*). The [reed] flute (*qasab*) is a reference to the human essence, and the nine holes [in the flute] are a reference to the openings in the outer frame (*zahir*), which are nine, viz. the ears, the nostrils, the eyes, the mouth, and the private parts. And the breath which penetrates the flute is a reference to the light of Allah penetrating the reed of man's essence. And the dancing is a reference to the circling of the spirit round the cycle of existing things in order to receive the effects of the unveilings and revelations; and this is the state of the gnostic. The whirling is a reference to the spirit's standing with Allah in its inner nature (*sirr*) and being (*wujud*), the circling of its look and thought, and its penetrating the ranks of existing things; and this is the state of the assured one. And his leaping up is a reference to his being drawn from the human station to the station of unity and to existing things acquiring from him spiritual effects and illuminative aids.[22]

It will be noted that in this passage Ahmad Ghazali makes no mention of stringed instruments. That is because he, like his more famous brother Abu Hamid al-Ghazali, considered stringed instruments forbidden "by general consensus" (*ijmaʿ*). This was because, during the first centuries of Islam, frequent use of stringed instruments was made by effeminates (*mukhannathun*) for evenings of entertainment that were hardly compatible with the concerns of the men of God. Their disapproval of stringed instruments, however, was not universal and only reflected the uncertainties that, even in mystical circles, existed on the subject of musical practice. It did not prevent the lute, the *tanbur* (pandore), the *rabab* (rebec), and the *qanun* (zither) from finding their place next to the drums and the reed flute (*nay*) in the oratorios of several Sufi orders, such as the Mevlevis ("Whirling Dervishes") and the Bektashis of Turkey, the Chistis of India, and much later (mid-nineteenth century), the Shadhilis-Harraqis of Morocco, who adopted for their sessions of remembrance the instruments of the classical Andalusian musical session, the *nawba*.

Musical instruments were held in the highest esteem by the philosopher-musicologists of Islam, who based scholarly studies concerning the groupings and divisions of notes on them. It must be remembered that the philosopher Farabi, among others, was himself such a marvelous lute player that he was able, according to his contemporaries, to hold his listeners in rapt attention, to put them to sleep, to make them laugh or cry, and to inspire in them feelings that matched his own spiritual "moments." Although such accounts may seem exaggerated today, they are consistent with the theory of the tuning of the lute, formulated by the Arab philosopher al-Kindi among others, according to which the four strings of the instrument corresponded to fundamental micro- and macrocosmic quaternaries, such as the Animal Tendencies (gentleness, cowardice, intelligence, and courage), the Faculties of the Soul (mnemonic, attentive, imaginative, and cognitive), and the Elements (water, earth, air, and fire).[23]

Melodic Modes

The effect that Islamic music, whether vocal or instrumental, has on the soul is directly connected with its modal structure, which, technically speaking, is without doubt its fundamental characteristic. In contrast to Western music, which has only two modes, the major and the minor, Oriental modes are quite numerous. Contemporary Arab, Turkish, and Persian musicians list them most often as numbering either 32 or 24. Of these modes, 12 are very commonly used, but in the classical epoch, more than a hundred modes were used.[24]

A "mode" (Arabic *maqam,* Turkish *makam,* Persian *dastgah* or *avaz*) is a type of melody that is expressed by a series of well-defined sounds.[25] It is a series (*sullam,* literally, "ladder") of sounds, corresponding approximately to a Western scale, that does not have to use the same notes for ascending and descending to the octave. Each mode carries a specific name that may denote, for example, its geographic origin (*Hijaz, Nahawand,* or *'Iraqi*), the position of its dominant note on the lute—*Dugah* (second position, or A), *Sikah* (third position, or B)—or suggests the state of the soul or the phenomenon that the mode is supposed to translate into music (*Farahfaza,* "joyous," *Nasim,* "breeze;" *Saba,* "morning wind" the bringer of longing; or *Zamzama,* "murmur"). It is said that musicians in former times had a precise knowledge of the virtues of the modes and performed them in accordance with this knowledge. This still occurs in Pakistan and northern India, where the system of *ragas* obeys rules very similar to those of Persian, Turkish, and Arabic modes. Thus, medieval Muslim musicians played certain melodies only during certain seasons, at certain hours of the day, or on special occasions in conjunction with the places and the ceremonies for which they wished to create a propitious ambience, a spiritual or emotional aura. In the opinion of specialists of Turkish music: "The emancipation of music, its detachment from the complex base of human activities, has certainly taken from the *makam* much of its original character, but a portion remains alive, even if it is unconscious. Musicians recognize a *makam* right from the first notes.... Therefore, the *makam* always exerts an influence, but only long practice permits one to feel it."[26]

From the mystical perspective, the exploration of a mode by a performer who on the one hand, humbly adapts himself to the preexisting pattern that makes up the mode and, on the other hand, improvises a series of melodic passages and vocalizations around the essential notes, constitutes a true spiritual discipline. It demands as its basic condition a sort of poverty (*faqr*) through a sense of detachment or interior emptiness, and in compensation brings about the unveiling of a state (*hal*) or contemplative station, which, in Sufi terminology, is also called a *maqam.* This terminological correspondence is not accidental. Lifted up on the wings of the melody, the musician progresses from *maqam* to *maqam,* up to the extreme limits of joy and plenitude, carrying along in his wake those listeners whose hearts have been opened.

Rhythm

The rhythmic structures of Arabo-Islamic music (*usul,* from *asl,* "root," or *iqa'at,* singular *iqa,* "beat") serve the function of sustaining the melody while providing it with conceptual divisions, a temporal framework, and sometimes also a profound and majestic sonorous base. They produce periods of equal duration, which, like the meters of prosody, are composed of beats that are at times regular or uneven, broken, and precipitous. The beats themselves are of two kinds: muffled and clear. Their varied combinations evoke the alternation of complementary principles—such as heat and cold, dry and humid, active and passive—in the sustenance and renewal of cosmic harmony. The effect of rhythm on the human soul is described in the following way by Seyyed Hossein Nasr, a contemporary scholar of the science and sacred art of Islam: "The rhythm, the meter of the music changes the relation of man with ordinary time which is the most important characteristic of the life of this world. Persian music possesses extremely fast and regular rhythms in which there are no beats or any form of temporal determination. In the first instance man is united with the pulsation of cosmic life, which in the human individual is always present in the form of the beating of the heart. Man's life and the life of the cosmos become one, the microcosm is united to the macrocosm.... In the second case, which transcends all rhythm and temporal distinction, man is suddenly cut off from the world of time; he feels himself situated face to face with eternity and for a moment benefits from the joy of extinction (*fana'*) and permanence (*baqa'*)."[27]

The Human Voice

Among the Arabs as among the ancient Semites, music was primarily a vocal art, designated by the word *ghina',* "song," which for a long time served to signify music, before it was supplanted by the term *musiqa,* derived from the Greek. In pre-Islamic Arabia, music was sung in verses, which the soothsayers and magicians used to render their oracles and utter their incantations. And even if bards and professional singers (*qa'inat*) played instruments, these served above all to introduce or to accompany the sung poems.

The advent of Islam did not change the attraction exercised by vocal music, and song and poetry remained respected arts during the lifetime of the Prophet Muhammad as well as after it. It is told, for example, how Muhammad admitted the presence of singers among his wives or how, while traveling, he asked some of his companions to sing the *huda',* poems that punctuated the march of the caravans.[28] When the chronicler Isfahani reports, in the 20 volumes of his *Book of Songs* (*Kitab al-aghani*) composed in the tenth century CE, the acts and gestures of the successive generations of musicians up to the Abbassid Caliphate, it is the cultural life of Arabia and the Near East, both before and after Islamization, that he brings before our eyes.

For the philosopher and musicologist Farabi, only the human voice was capable of attaining to perfect music, that is, to that which unites the three virtues of the art of music: the ability to bring pleasure and calm, the ability to provoke certain emotions and sentiments, and the ability to speak to the imagination and inspire ideas. "Instrumental music sometimes possesses certain of these qualities," concludes Farabi, implying by this statement that instrumental music never possesses them all.[29] He thus expresses a consensus of opinion that has always prevailed in the world of Islam, that what makes the human voice the most appropriate instrument for perfect music is above all its aptitude to convey the Divine Word. When, in a rare exception, an instrument such as the *nay*, the reed flute of the Mevlevi dervishes, also attains to the perfect music, this is because the *nay* is itself a voice, the breath of the human soul that traverses the body, a microcosm purified by love.

MUSICAL GENRES

In each of the great ethno-linguistic sectors of the Muslim world—the Arab, the Persian, the Turkish, and the South Asian (without mentioning here the Malays and Chinese who, because of their distance, have been less permeated by the classical artistic models of Islam except as it concerns the liturgical arts, the recitation of the Qur'an, and calligraphy)—three musical genres coexist:

   a. *Liturgical and devotional music:* In addition to Qur'anic psalmody, whose exceptional importance has already been underlined, Islamic liturgical music includes the call to prayer, songs dedicated to the praise of the Prophet, and those that, among the Shiites, commemorate the martyred Imams, and the multiple forms of the spiritual concert (*sama'*), with or without dance, practiced by the Sufis.

   b. *Classical music of an intellectual nature:* This is primarily the music of the cities, of princely courts, and of men of letters and dignitaries. Although this music is intended to give birth to diverse nuances of aesthetic emotion (*tarab*), because it rests on the same technical base as liturgical music, it can show itself capable, if played with the desired intention and in the proper context, of opening the doors of mystical experience to the listeners.

   c. *Popular music:* If in general this music only aims at marking the seasonal rhythms and at celebrating occasions for rejoicing or mourning, it nonetheless allows itself in many instances to be penetrated by Islam and thus opens to the common person exceptional possibilities for going beyond oneself.

Strictly speaking, only the first of these categories, liturgical music, relates directly to the sacred domain; thus, it is this music in particular that will be discussed in the following sections. Among the classical and popular musical styles of the Islamic world, only those that, adopted by the mystics, found their way into the *zawiyas, tekkes,* and *sama'-khanehs* will be examined. By so doing, we will perhaps succeed in evoking the immense richness of the sonorous heritage of Islam and inspire the reader to seek out musical experiences that no description is capable of replacing.

The Call to Prayer (adhan)

Instituted by the Prophet Muhammad soon after the hijra from Mecca to Medina, the call to prayer has been, among the exterior signs of Islam, the most powerful symbol of the influence of the realm of the Divine upon the world of the human being. Chanted five times each day, every day of the year, the *adhan* marks time and fills it. Issued from the tops of minarets toward the four cardinal points, it traverses and fills space, thus affirming the sacred character of these two dimensions in which human existence unfolds. By the proclamation of the *takbir,* the formula *Allahu akbar,* "God is infinitely great," and of the *Shahada,* the Islamic testimony of faith, it places the entire universe under the sign of transcendence. The words of the call to prayer also liken prayer to joy (*falah*), enjoining the faithful to interrupt their ordinary chores or pleasures for a moment of consecration, a veritable preparation and prelude to the beatitude that awaits the believers in the Hereafter.

Like psalmody, the *adhan* uses modes of cancellation that can vary according to region; however, in all of these variations, under a diversity of styles, the same homogeneous structure appears. The one who is charged with giving the call to prayer, the muezzin (*mu'adhdhin*), is chosen not only for his beautiful voice (the muezzin is invariably a man) but also for his human qualities and piety. Sometimes the muezzin also performs the functions of the Imam of a mosque, and many of them participate as singers (*munshid*) at religious festivals and spiritual gatherings.

Music in Praise of the Prophet (amdah nabawiyya)

The second great source of knowledge in Islam after the Qur'an is the Prophet Muhammad, whose teachings, transmitted in the collections of Hadith, and whose deeds, related in biographical accounts of his life (*Sira*), make up the prophetic example, the Sunna. If Qur'anic psalmody was able to give birth to different forms of modulated recitation, the love of the Prophet, for its part, has given rise to a great wealth of literary compositions and devotional songs.

The importance of these litanies is linked in Islamic mysticism to the doctrine of the Perfect Man (*al-insan al-kamil*). Although Muhammad was a man who lived and died like other men, he was certainly not an ordinary man. He was, according to the Sufi saying, "like a ruby among stones." He is also called "The Best of God's Creation" (*khayr khalq Allah*) and in the Qur'an, "a fine example" (*uswa hasana*, Qur'an 33:61) for the believers, meaning by this that he is the summation of the entire creation, a universal model. To offer prayers on behalf of the Prophet is thus to pray for the salvation of all believers. It is also to pray for the rediscovery of one's own primordial nature and for one's own deliverance. Mystical gatherings in the Islamic world almost always begin with praise of the Prophet. In the Syrian *zawiyas* of the Qadiri or Shadhili Sufi orders, for example, the gatherings open with a song, performed as a solo, of the *Mawludiyya* ("Birthday Song") of Shaykh Barzanji (d. 1765 CE). The words of this song are as follows: "Our Lord Muhammad was always smiling and affable. He never showed the least brutality or the least violence in his words or in his criticisms. He never made a show of his desires and he abstained from judging others and speaking ill of them. When he spoke, his companions kept silent, as if a bird had perched on their heads. Never did they raise their voices in argument, and when they spoke, it was he who was silent."

Another poem that is also very popular among the Sufis of North Africa and the Middle East is the *Burda*, the "Cloak," composed by Muhammad al-Busiri (d. 1296 CE), who is buried in the Egyptian city of Alexandria. The title of this poem recalls a miraculous healing. Having been stricken with paralysis, Shaykh Busiri in a dream saw the Prophet, who enveloped him in his cloak. Upon awakening, he found himself cured and able to move. He also found that the poem of the *Burda* was carried within him and that it only needed to be transcribed. For more than seven centuries, this poem has been recited in choruses by generations of Sufis. As a poem of 162 verses, and rhyming in the Arabic letter *mim* (*qasida mimiyya*), it lends itself admirably to quick rhythmic variations and possesses a great emotional charge when it is sung in unison.

In Turkey, the meetings of the Mevlevis, the "Whirling Dervishes," also open with a song in praise of the Prophet Muhammad. This is the *Naat i-Sherif* ("The Noble Praise-Song"), whose words were composed by the great Sufi master Rumi (d. 1273 CE), and whose music is attributed to the Mevlevi Sufi composer Itri (d. 1711 CE). The solemnity of this song, which is reminiscent of Byzantine psalmody, plunges those who hear it into a state of remembrance and recollection (*dhikr*), which prepares them to perform the whirling dance. Its words go like this:

Oh Beloved of God, oh incomparable Messenger,
Preferred among all Creatures, the Light of Our Eyes,
You know the weakness of nations,
You are the guide for the infirm,
The Guardian of the Garden of Prophecy,
The springtime of Gnosis.
You are the rose garden of the Law and its most beautiful flower.

Examples such as these could be multiplied. They illustrate the ways in which Muslims—while keeping themselves away from the deification of the Prophet—revered the Prophet Muhammad as an ever-present spiritual guide, who is able to help the seeker through his influence and intercession to approach the Lord of the Worlds. In Sufism, this role was not only reserved for the Prophet but also included several categories of saints, both living and dead, who were seen as living embodiments of the Prophetic example. In Shiite Islam, devotion to the Prophet was complemented by devotion to the Imams and their representatives.

Devotional Music of Shiite Islam

Among the genres of music that are practiced in contemporary Iran, certain ones show a devotional efficacy and an incontestable mystical resonance. These are first of all the ceremonial musical styles associated with the great Shiite mourning period of *Azadari,* which commemorates the Karbala' massacre in which Imam Husayn and many members of his family were martyred in 680 CE. These events are recalled in the singing of poems, especially those composed at the beginning of the seventeenth century by Husayn Wa'iz Kashifi in his *Garden of the Martyrs.* This collection of poems has become so popular that the first word of its title, *rozeh* (from the Arabic *rawda,* "garden"), now designates all gatherings, whether they are held in a mosque or in a private home, during which the martyrdom of the Shiite Imams is evoked. The *rozeh khans,* the singers who specialize in the recitation of these poems, are held in high esteem by the people of Iran.

The mourning period of *Azadari* takes place between the first and the tenth day of Muharram, the first month of the Islamic year. Its highlight is a procession of penitents and flagellants, who ritually express remorse for the failure of Imam Husayn's followers to come to his aid. The procession is accompanied by songs and exclamations that are modulated to the rhythm of the march, and that are used by the penitents to punctuate the blows of their fists to their chests and backs.

Theatrical presentations also retrace the same tragic events. These are the *ta'ziyas,* sacred dramas that have been enacted, at least since the eighteenth century, in the open air in a location that has been specially arranged (*takyeh*). The *takyeh* includes an elevated stage surrounded by an open space for the actors and their mounts. The performance lasts well into the night and includes processions accompanied by songs and the sounds of trumpets, with rhythms maintained by drums and cymbals. The actors' cries of "Hassan, Husayn," the names of the martyred grandsons of the Prophet Muhammad, return again and again, arousing echoes and tears in the crowd. Each sequence of the *ta'ziya* drama is sung in a mode (*dastgah*), that corresponds to the nature of the scene and the character of the person represented.[30] One finds in this singing an example of classical Islamic music that was popularized and later became a source of inspiration for numerous court musicians, particularly during the Qajar period of Iranian history (eighteenth and nineteenth centuries CE).

Also specific to Iran is the music of the *zurkhaneh,* centers of martial training where the participants wield clubs and heavy chains, spurred on by lyrical songs and powerful rhythms. The *zurkhaneh* is a school in which corporal discipline serves the ideal of chivalry. In Persian culture, chivalry was first incarnated in the figure of Rustam, the mythical hero of the "Book of Kings" (*Shah-Nameh*). This Persian cultural tradition was assimilated to Islam by including with Rustam 'Ali, the son-in-law of the Prophet Muhammad and the first of the Shiite Imams, whose courage earned him the nickname "Lion of God."

The Qawwalis of South Asia

The mystical songs known as *Qawwali* (from the Arabic root *qul,* "to say") were popularized in India by the Chishtiyya Sufi order during the thirteenth and fourteenth centuries CE. This is attributed sometimes to the patronage of Shaykh Mu'in al-Din Chishti (d. 1236 CE), the founder of the order, and sometimes to that of the Sufi poet Amir Khusraw (d. 1326 CE), whose tomb in Delhi adjoins that of Nizam al-Din Awliya' (d. 1325 CE), the fourth great master of the Chishti order. The tomb of Nizam al-Din remains to this day one of the preferred meeting places of the *qawwal,* that is, the singers of *Qawwali* music. In this sanctuary throughout the year one can hear dervishes singing their religious hymns and poems while accompanying themselves on drums. On holidays, concerts are organized in which eight to ten singers accompanied by various instruments participate. These instruments include the Japanese zither, the clarinet, a drum shaped like a cask (*dholak*), the violin (*sarangi*), and a small manual harmonium, which was imported from Europe in the nineteenth century.

The lyrics of *Qawwali* songs, sometimes in Urdu and sometimes in Persian, are borrowed from the repertoire of the figurative type of Sufi poetry. This poetry is noted for evocations of terrestrial beauty, such as the garden, with its flowers and perfumes, wine, taverns and cupbearers, and the face of the beloved and the sighs of the lover. These evocations are

believed to elevate the soul toward contemplation of celestial realities and to
lead it back to its true existence. Repetitive formulas drawn from the Qur'an
such, as *Huwa Allah*, "He is God," often separate the stanzas of the songs
and are taken up as a refrain by the audience. As in the Shadhili or Mevlevi
sama' sessions, certain songs are praises of the Prophet Muhammad or
his Companions and the saints who came after them. Others are connected
with the Arabic poetic tradition, especially the Persian love song (*ghazal*).
Here in the ambience of the Sufi brotherhoods is a musical art, which,
while expressing itself at a popular level, remains spiritually rich through its
permeation by the rhythms and melodic modes (*ragas*) of Hindustani music.

The Music of the Kurdish "People of the Truth" (Ahl-i Haqq)

In Iranian Kurdistan (especially in the province of Kirmanshah), and
in other regions where Kurdish communities are numerous such as Iraq,
Turkey, and Azerbaijan, there exists a Shiite sect of an esoteric nature, the
Ahl-i Haqq or "People of the Truth," for whom music plays an important
role during their ritual assemblies.[31] The importance given to music by
this sect rests in doctrinal and theosophical considerations that are heavily
influenced by Ismailism and are close to Sufism. Central to these considerations is the notion that music awakens the aspiration of the believer and links
him once again to the God the Beloved (*Yar*), with whom a covenant was
sealed in Pre-Eternity.

Technically speaking, the principal characteristic of Ahl-i Haqq music is the
almost exclusive use that it makes of the *tanbur*, a type of long-necked man-
dolin having two, sometimes three, metallic strings and sixteen frets, which,
when touched with the fingertips, produce one low sound and one high-
pitched sound. The high-pitched sound is used especially for performing
solos, while the low sound is used for accompanying singers. Each spiritual
guide (*pir*) of the Ahl-i Haqq is a musician who, while playing the melodies
transmitted by the tradition (certain among them dating from the eleventh
century CE), renews the primordial covenant in the manner in which the
Angel Gabriel, *Pir-Binyanun*, celebrated it with the angels and later on the
occasion of his earthly appearances.

The spiritual and musical assembly (*jam'*) of the Ahl-i Haqq includes a
series of chanted recitations, during which the chanter (*kalam-khwan*), who
accompanies himself on the *tanbur*, sings religious poems. Those who are
in attendance take up the refrain in a chorus and at times clap their hands
to mark the rhythm. They often return to the invocation, "My beginning
and my end are the Beloved (*Yar*)," in order, they say, to attract the heart's
attention to the divine Principle. One of the remarkable traits of this music
is that it has kept many of the characteristics of the ancient Iranian tradition
of court music, which, following several periods of persecution, especially in

the late Safavid period (seventeenth to eighteenth centuries CE), were completely lost. This is why both Iranian musicians and Western musicologists are academically interested in the 12 melodic modes (*dastgah*) that are expressed in the sacred songs and hymns that resonate throughout the rural sanctuaries of the Ahl-i-Haqq: "The Eternal Hunter, oh my soul, has cast the net of the Pact, oh my soul."

The Spiritual Audition of Classical Music

Throughout the Muslim world very close threads have been woven between the mystical path and the principal expressions of classical music, this music having shown itself capable, as the Ikhwan al-Safa' affirmed, not only of arousing aesthetic emotion (*tarab*) but also of putting the soul in communication with spiritual realities. The distinction between sacred music, devoted to worship, and profane music was often abolished, and music "for entertainment," with its inseparable constituent of sung poetry, was retained in literary and artistic circles as well as in mystical gatherings. Because of the diverse levels of interpretation to which the majority of Muslim poetic compositions lent themselves, with their metaphorical and allegorical language, Sufi musicians did not hesitate, following the example of the *Qawwal* of India in the singing of *ghazals,* to introduce into their concerts "profane" poems that were charged with a supra-terrestrial resonance.

Conversely, musicians without a mystical affiliation appreciated the works of Sufi poets, if not for the profundity of their symbolism, then at least for their evocative power and formal beauty. Sufi poetical works used in musical concerts include the *Great Ta'iyya* (a poem with each verse ending in the Arabic letter *ta'*) and the *Khamriyya* (wine poem) of the Egyptian Sufi 'Umar ibn al-Farid (d. 1234 CE) in Arabic, selections from the poems of Hafiz (d. 1389 CE), Jami (d. 1492 CE), or Rumi in Persian and the poems of Yunus Emre (d. ca. 1321 CE) and Ismail Hakki (d. 1724 CE) in Turkish. Thus, music allowed a breath of spirituality to penetrate as far as the interiors of the princely courts and noble residences of the cities. The association between Sufi groups and classical musicians was a quasi-permanent characteristic of medieval Muslim society and it continues to the present day. The importance of this can be illustrated by some examples taken from the great cultural regions of the Islamic world.

Arabo-Andalusian Music

In the Arabic-speaking world, a constant quest for the perfection of musical knowledge was carried on during the first three or four centuries of Islamic history. From the mid-eighth century CE, at the end of the Umayyad Caliphate of Damascus, there existed a formal Arabic music, which, being an elaborated version of the former popular recital, was enriched by Persian and Hellenistic elements borrowed from the new urban environments of the Islamic empire. To ancient poetic meters there came to be added new rhythmic formulas, including the one furnished by the quatrain. Through the influence of such devices, Arabic music assimilated the modal systems of the Byzantines and Persians. To the traditional reed flute and the single-stringed *rabab,* were added the *'ud* (lute), the *qanun* (zither) and the three-stringed violin (*kamanja*), as well as several percussion instruments such as the frame drum (*daff*). This music reached its full development during the long reign of the Abbassids, from 750 to 1258 CE.

Then came the Mongol invasion, the destruction of Baghdad, and the end of the great epoch of Arabo-Islamic civilization. Some musicians survived this disaster and continued to transmit their art in various Oriental cities. However, it would not be possible today to form any kind of precise notion as to what this music was in its plenitude if a branch of this art had not been transplanted from Baghdad to the land of al-Andalus or Islamic Spain, and if it had not later been taken up in North Africa, where it has been perpetuated to the present day. A major figure in this process of transplantation was Ziryab, a musician of genius, who, after having studied with Ishaq al-Mawsili in Baghdad, found himself forced to immigrate to Cordoba in order to escape the jealousy of his teacher. Received there with full honors at the court of the Umayyad Caliph 'Abd al-Rahman II in 821 CE, Ziryab developed an original musical style, which was based on the canons of classical music as performed in Iraq. Relying on the correspondences established by the philosopher Kindi between the four strings of the lute, the four cosmic qualities (cold-humid and hot-dry), the four basic colors (yellow, red, white, and black), and the four human temperaments (bilious, sanguine, phlegmatic, and melancholic), Ziryab went far in increasing the knowledge and utilization of the psycho-physiological effects of musical modes. He also added a fifth string to the lute, which represented the soul, and elaborated a musical style called the *nawba,* which was thoroughly imbued with these symbolic understandings.[32]

A *nawba,* a word that could be translated approximately as "suite," contains four (five, in Morocco) melodic and rhythmic movements (*dawr*) performed with song and orchestra in an order fixed by Ziryab and that never varied. The order of the movements of the *nawba* is as follows: (1) a free recitative movement (*nashid*), (2) moderato movement (*basit*), (3) rapid passages (*muharrakat*), and (4) a lively finale (*hazajat*). There are currently 11 *nawbas,* each of which is performed in a particular musical mode (*maqam*),[33] which expresses a specific feeling or sentiment: the major mode (*rasd*) expresses pride; the mode of lovers (*'ushshaq*) expresses joy and is played in the morning; the mode of *maya* evokes the sadness of separation and is played in the evening; the mode of *ramelmaya* is reserved for praise of the Prophet Muhammad.

A concert of Andalusian music always has a soothing and purifying effect on the souls of listeners, whether it be in a light style (*kalam al-hazl*) or a serious style (*kalam al-jadd*), or whether its recitatives are borrowed from classical prosody (*kalam mawzun*) or popular poetry (*kalam malhun*), or whether, as often happens, it alternates different styles. All vulgarity is excluded from this music and the numerous allusions and conventional but always efficacious images with which it is punctuated are a constant call to return toward the Source of Beauty. Themes that are evoked in Andalusian music include the divine or earthly beloved; the personified Night (*Layla*), whose presence is awaited with hope and longing; the earthly and paradisal Garden with its flowers, its fruits, and its streams of nectar; the Friend of God (the Prophet Muhammad) and God Himself, named by his "Beautiful Names" (Qur'an 77:180). The continued popularity of these themes is why in the Moroccan city of Fez, for example, the authorities and dignitaries of the city have patronized Andalusian music for over 700 years and still encourage the practice of an art felt to be supremely compatible with their religious sentiments.

This is also why, despite the rule usually followed in the cities of North Africa, where the performance of instrumental music was excluded from the religious context, some forms of *sama'* derived directly from Andalusian music and using its instruments (the lute, the *rabab,* the tambourine, and the flute) found blessings in the eyes of certain Sufi masters. In the northern Moroccan city of Tetouan, which has been a refuge for Andalusian artistic traditions from the time of the exodus of the Muslims from Spain in the fifteenth and sixteenth centuries, an eminently "orthodox" Sufi order can be found—the Harraqiyya founded around 1845 by Muhammad al-Harraq, a disciple of Mawlay al-'Arabi al-Darqawi—which uses the instruments and the melodies of the *nawba*. The spiritual sessions of the Harraqiyya are built around the singing of the poems (*diwan*) of Muhammad al-Harraq, whose name alludes to his having been "burned" or consumed with the fires of divine love. Listening to the Andalusian *nawba* prepares the participants for the performance of the sacred dance (*'imara*) of the Harraqiyya, which is sustained by a chorus of singers (*munshidun*) and by beats of a drum.

Iranian Music

Heir to the rich Sassanian musical tradition, then impregnated by Islamic influences, first Arab and later Turkish and Indian, the music of Iran has managed to preserve its personality and its distinctive characteristics throughout the centuries. The efficacy of music as an agent for the transmutation of the soul has perhaps never been explained as explicitly as by the Sufi Ruzbihan Baqli of Shiraz (d. 1209 CE), a master of theology, music, and poetry, who was "one of the *fideli d'amore* of Islam."[34] All of Ruzbihan's written works—treatises, commentaries, and poems—are exhortations to return to the Divine Source that calls to the human being, issuing from Itself, by means of the voice of the Qur'anic Word and that of spiritual music, the *sama'*: "Sometimes He says, 'You are myself,' and sometimes He says, 'I am you'.... Sometimes, He rejects [the seeker] and sometimes He grants him peace in divine intimacy.... Sometimes He throws him into complete slavery, and sometimes He plunges him into the essence of Lordship. Sometimes He makes him drunken from the Beauty of God, sometimes He belittles him before His Majesty.... All this happens during the *sama'* and still much more."[35]

This is the same message that Rumi delivers in his *Masnavi:* "The believers say that the effects of Paradise will make every voice beautiful. We were all part of Adam and heard those melodies in Paradise. Though water and clay have covered us with doubt, we still remember something of those sounds.... Sounds and songs strengthen the images within the mind, or rather, turn them into forms."[36]

That the Persians were particularly gifted at composing, performing, and listening to music with a spiritual intention is attested to by numerous historical testimonies. In the contemporary period, despite certain signs of degeneration and ruptures that are probably irreparable, there are still musicians to whom it is given to enter into a sublime mystical state (*hal*) and who are able to communicate their state to their listeners. In this state, the artist "plays with an extraordinary facility of performance. His sonority changes. The musical phrase surrenders its secret to him."[37] According to another contemporary observer, even if the hardening of opinion that the official Shiite circles manifested toward the Sufi orders at the end of the Safavid period has more or less discouraged the use of music in mystical gatherings, the content of this music has nonetheless preserved its spiritual efficacy: "There always exists among traditional musicians a certain sense of the sacred."[38] Thus, for the master Davami, the 99-year-old depository of a vast and difficult repertoire, it is indispensable to first have a knowledge of the Hereafter before being able to practice music, this knowledge itself implying a purification of the external senses and the internal faculties which makes a person become like a mirror.

Judging by my personal experience, listening to a concert of Iranian classical music demands of the listener the same meditative disposition and leads him along the same paths and toward the same experiences as an evening of Andalusian music. Even if the resonances of the voices and instruments are different, those of Iran possessing more mildness and femininity, the melodic and rhythmic structures show so many affinities that one feels oneself transported into the same realm. It is a realm of 12 fundamental modes (*avaz*), which subdivide into modal figures (*gusheh*) arranged according to an order (*radif*) established by the greatest masters, and is in part immutable. It is a world where quality does not consist of innovation and of displays of virtuosity, but rather of exposition with fidelity, while embellishing with appropriate ornamentation and improvisation the various sequences or figures of the chosen mode. The concert thus takes on the aspect of a gathering of friends, where a theme is solemnly introduced and developed and then debated during an exchange of questions and responses before being meditated upon in a collective spirit and finally culminating in the exaltation of a discovery that fills all the listeners with joy.

Turkish Music

The same remarks, or very similar ones, could be applied to the classical music of Turkey. Turkish music was not only an heir to the Arab, Byzantine, and Persian melodic modes but was also the bearer of sounds and rhythms that came from the steppes of Asia and that for centuries was strongly permeated with mystical concerns. In Turkey in fact, perhaps more than in any other Islamic region, the great Sufi religious orders—the Mevlevis, the Bektashis, and the Khalwatis—made use of music in their ceremonies. The Mevlevis in particular trained a large number of singers and instrumentalists, who, while remaining affiliated with the order, became musicians attached to the court of the Ottoman Sultans. Such was the *dede* (dervish) Ismail, one of the great masters of classical music, who was much in favor during the reign of the Ottoman Sultan Selim III (r. 1789–1807 CE), and from whom some 150 compositions have been handed down to us.

Performing and listening to *a peshrev* or "prelude," one of the most characteristic forms of Turkish classical music, constitutes an exercise of concentration for the musician and is an invitation to contemplative reflection for the listener. Composed of four parts (*hane*, "house"), each one followed by a refrain (*teslim*), which forms the key to the melodic construction, the *peshrev* is played in one or more modes (*makam*). During its unfolding, which is always slow and restrained, accelerating slightly only at the finale, each musician restricts himself to embellishing the fundamental melody at the appropriate places, adding here and there the conventional grace-notes—the *tashil bezek* or "petrified decoration"—a term that also designates the arabesques of architectural decoration. At the desired moment the musician interrupts the combined movement to perform an improvised solo (*taksim*).

During the sessions of *sama'* of the Mevlevi Whirling Dervishes, the *taksim* solo is always given to the player of the *nay*, the reed flute, which symbolizes the voice of the soul in love with the Absolute: "It is necessary to have heard a *nay* played in a large resonant hall; it is necessary to have seen at the same time the dance of the dervishes, in all its solemnity: to realize the profound inner emotion which is released."[39] However, the use of the *nay* in Turkish music is not restricted to the dervishes. Whether it accompanies vocal ensembles or is integrated into complete instrumental ensembles, which include the zither (*qanun*), the lute, the *tambur* (a lute with a very long neck allowing the division of the octave by 24 frets), the violin (*kemenceh*) of two or three strings, and percussive instruments, it punctuates most classical concerts with its nostalgic voice.

Hindustani Music

In the realm of the art of music, a remarkable synthesis has taken place between Hindus and Muslims in northern India, beginning with the growth of Islam on the Indian subcontinent in the twelfth and thirteenth centuries CE. The first architects of this synthesis were, as we have seen in relation to the singers of *Qawwalis,* the masters and the members of the Chishtiyya Sufi order who, by the radiance of their faith, brought about conversions to Islam by the hundreds of thousands. Mu'in al-Din Chishti, the founder of this order, believed that "song is the sustenance and the support of the soul,"[40] and under his influence the Chishtiyya Sufis contributed a number of Islamic elements into Indian classical music, while themselves borrowing extensively from the very rich melodic and rhythmic repertoire of India.

In order for such a synthesis to be possible, it was necessary that the theoretical and practical foundations of the two musical universes thus brought into contact—the Arabo-Persian and the Indian—be at least compatible, if not identical. To the theory of "influence" (*ta'thir*), that is to say, the *ethos* of the ancient Greeks that was Arabized and applied to the Arabo-Persian musical modes, corresponds that of the Hindu *bhava,* the nature of the emotion connected to the *raga* (the musical mode of India), which engenders *rasa,* the flavor or state of the soul (Arabic *dhawq* or *hal*) that is particular to each mode. As for the classification of the types of the *raga* and its relationship to the macrocosm and microcosm, this aspect of Indian music theory surpassed in subtlety even that of the Muslim musicologists. All of the conditions were therefore present for the fruitful cross-pollination of musical genres, which often occurred in the princely courts. These courts included that of Sultan 'Ala al-Din Khilji of Delhi, where the Sufi poet, musician, and composer of Turkish origin, Amir Khusraw (d. 1325 CE) inaugurated the style of highly modulated "imaginative" song (*khayal*) and popularized the Persian love poem (*ghazal*). They also included the court of the great Moguls, especially of the emperor Akbar (d. 1605 CE), where Hindu and Muslim musicians brought to perfection such noble styles as the *dhrupad,* which is constructed on rhythmic poems of four verses; the *dhamar,* more rhythmic than the *dhrupad,* and the *tappa,* with its delicate ornamentation.[41]

Even today, the performers of Hindustani music are recruited from among both Hindu and Muslim families, the latter being able to take pride in having contributed through generations of musicians to one of the most beautiful musical traditions humanity has ever known. According to Hindu doctrine,

"He who is expert in the science of modal intervals and scales and who knows the rhythms travels easily on the path of Deliverance."[42] When this perception is combined with the belief, stated by Rumi, that "at the time of *sama'*, the Sufis hear another sound, from God's throne," there can be no doubt that the combination of musical traditions in India was an effective means of reaching inner perfection for members of the two religious communities. As Seyyed Hossein Nasr has stated, comparing the Indian and Muslim musical traditions, "Music is not only the first art brought by [the Hindu god] Siva into the world, and the art through which the *asrar-i alast,* the [Qur'anic] mystery of the primordial Covenant between man and God in that pre-eternal dawn of the day of cosmic manifestation is revealed; but it is also the key to the understanding of the harmony that pervades the cosmos. It is the handmaid of wisdom itself."[43]

Popular Music

In all of the regions penetrated by Islam, numerous forms of popular music were allowed to exist or to expand, in addition to the strictly religious music and the great classical currents that we have just outlined. To make an inventory of all types of popular music would not be possible in these pages, but we would like nevertheless to cite by means of illustration some cases in which popular music is used for the mystical quest. Sometimes, it is music with a classical structure that is popularized by adopting the vernacular language and local instruments. Thus, the *griha* of North Africa, sung in various Arabic dialects—Moroccan, Algerian, or Tunisian—continues the tradition of pre-Islamic odes (*qasida*) that in more classical musical genres were based on the airs of the *nawba*, while the Moroccan, Tunisian, and Libyan *malhun* is a dialectized form of Andalusian music. Both the *griha* and the *malhun* were used to perform innumerable pieces of poetry or rhymed prose composed in dialectical Arabic by Sufi masters.

Throughout the expanse of the Islamic world, non-Arab ethnic groups integrated Islamic formulas into their repertoires. This is the case with the Berbers of the Atlas Mountains, who sing the *ahellel* (Arabic *tahlil*), which is none other than the Islamic profession of faith, *la ilaha illa Allah.* The Moorish women of the Western Sahara dance the *guedra,* an ancient rite of communication with the fecundating forces, while a chorus of men introduces the names of the Prophet Muhammad and the One God into its rhythmic breathing.

A final example taken from the folklore of Morocco illustrates the very frequent situations in which the music of a village, connected to the cult of a local saint, regularly animates religious ceremonies and feasts. The village of Jahjuka, located in the region of Jabala, not far from the northeastern Moroccan town of Ksar el-Kebir, possesses a troupe of clarinetists and drummers whose origin goes back to the time when 12 centuries ago the village was founded by the Saint Sidi Ahmad Sharqi and his companion, a musician named Muhammad al-'Attar. Each Friday, the musicians march through the village to the tomb of the saint, where the faithful come to ask for healing of diseases of the body and soul. The high-pitched sound of the *ghita* clarinet and the intense rhythm of the drums puts the listener into a state of trance, which opens the way for the blessed influence (*baraka*) of the saint, and facilitates its therapeutic action.

EPILOGUE

From each of these areas of classical music as well as from popular music flow strong and enduring testimonies, showing that various styles of music in the Islamic world, like those that serve more explicitly as vehicles for the words of the Qur'an or the hymns of mystics, are an echo of the Beyond, an open path to the liberation of the soul and its return to the lost Homeland, toward the infinite Silence that is the origin of all sounds. As a providential instrument for the symbolic unification of multiplicity, the traditional music of Islam aids the human being in realizing, through a path of beauty, that "In truth we belong to God, and to Him we will return" (Qur'an 2:156).

NOTES

This chapter will also appear as, "Music and Spirituality in Islam," in Jean-Louis Michon, *Introduction to Traditional Islam: Illustrated* (Bloomington, Indiana: World Wisdom, forthcoming in 2008). Slight editorial changes and abridgements have been made to the original text for consistency of style and purposes of clarification. The general editor of this set thanks the editors of World Wisdom Books for permission to reproduce this work.

1. *Arina al-ashya' kama hiya:* this hadith was cited by Fakhr al-Din al-Razi in his "Great Commentary" on the Qur'an (*Mafatih al-Ghayb*), with respect to verse 17:85: "They will question you concerning the Spirit." See al-Razi, *al-Tafsir al-Kabir,* 2nd ed. (Tehran, n.d.), vols. 21–22, 37.

2. The complete work of the Brethren of Purity includes 51 (or 52) "Epistles" (*rasa'il*), of which the one treating music is the fifth. See "L'épître sur la musique des Ikhwân al-safâ," translation annotated by A. Shiloah, *Revue des Etudes islamiques,* 1964, 125–162; 1966, 159–193. The passages cited hereafter are found on pages 155–158 (1964).

3. A. Shiloah (1966), 185. In the same way, Frithjof Schuon writes, "While listening to beautiful music, the guilty will feel innocent. But the contemplative, on the contrary, while listening to the same music, will forget himself while fathoming the essences." Schuon, *Sur les traces de la religion pérenne* (Paris, 1982), 66–67.

4. H.G. Farmer, *A History of Arabian Music to the XIIIth Century* (1929; repr., London, U.K., 1973), 36.

5. 'Ali ibn 'Uthman al-Jullabi al-Hujwiri, *The Kashf al-Mahjub: the Oldest Persian Treatise on Sufism,* trans. Reynold A. Nicholson (1911; repr., London, U.K.: Luzac, 1976), 402.

6. As was the case with the philosopher Farabi (d. 950 CE); see A. Shiloah, *La Perfection des connaissances musicales* (Paris, 1972), 65–68.

7. A translation of this work was made by James Robson, *Tracts on Listening to Music* (London, U.K.: Royal Asiatic Society, Oriental Translation Fund, 1938). It is followed by the translation of the treatise entitled *Bawariq al-ilma'* by the Sufi Ahmad al-Ghazali (d. 1126 CE), brother of the celebrated Abu Hamid al-Ghazali (d. 1111 CE). In contrast to Ibn Abi al-Dunya, Ahmad Ghazali supports the legality of music and exalts the virtues of the spiritual concert. In his Introduction to these two treatises (1–13), Robson summarizes the arguments employed by the defenders of these antithetical positions.

8. Cited by M. Molé in "La Danse extatique en Islam," *Les Danses sacrées* (Paris: Le Seuil, 1963), 164. This study contains abundant documentation, drawn from original and often little-known sources, on the arguments for and against the use of music and dance in the mystical path.

9. For a better understanding of the Greco-Islamic affinities and their influence on the theory of music in Islam, one should consult H.G. Farmer, *The Sources of Arabian Music* (Glasgow, 1940), which includes the writings of Arabic authors. See also P. Kraus, *Jabir ibn Hayyan, contribution à l'histoire des idées scientifiques dans l' Islam,* vol. II, *Jabir et la science grecque* (Cairo, 1942); Y. Marquet, *Imamat, résurrection et hiérarchie selon les Ikhwan as-Safa* in *Revue des Études Islamiques,* 1962, 49–142; E. Werner and J. Sonne, *The Philosophy and Theory of Music in Judeo-Arabic Literature,* in *Hebrew Union College Annual,* vols. 16 and 17, wherein three chapters concerning music are translated from the *Kitab adab al falasifa* (Book of the Practice of the Philosophers) by Hunayn ibn Ishaq.

10. Shiloah (1964), 126–127.

11. Ibid.

12. Ishaq al-Mawsili was a singer, composer, theoretician, and historian, as well as a jurist. He played a considerable role in the transmission of a highly refined Arabo-Persian musical tradition under the Abbasid Caliphate. His father Ibrahim (d. 804 CE) was himself a consummate musician. A regular guest of the Caliph Harun al-Rashid, he headed the most richly endowed music school of Baghdad. See Farmer, *History,* 124–126.

13. Farmer, *History,* 156.

14. Cited by G.H. Farmer, "The Religious Music of Islam," *Journal of the Royal Asiatic Society* 1952: 60–65, and also in M.M. Sharif, *A History of Muslim Philosophy,* vol. 2, 1126. Chapter 58 of this latter work contains a good summary of musical theories, which were expressed in different epochs and in different regions of the Muslim world.

15. Shiloah (1966), 192–193.

16. This passage is from the eighth book of the quarter of the *Ihya'* dealing with social customs ('*adat*). It was translated into English by E.B. MacDonald, *Journal of*

the Royal Asiatic Society (1901): 195–252 and 705–746, and (1902), 1–28. This passage appears in (1901), 199.

17. Hujwiri, *Kashf al-Mahjub,* 419.

18. Al-Ghazali in MacDonald trans. (1901), 730–731. The hadith to which al-Ghazali alludes states: "If you do not weep, try to weep," and it is often cited to justify certain Sufi practices, such as the sacred dance. See Martin Lings, *A Sufi Saint of the Twentieth Century: Shaikh Ahmad al-'Alawi, His Spiritual Heritage and Legacy* (Berkeley and Los Angeles: University of California Press, 1973), 92–93.

19. Ahmad ibn 'Ajiba, his master Muhammad al-Buzidi (d. 1814 CE), and the latter's master Mawlay al-'Arabi al-Darqawi (d. 1823 CE), belong to the great initiatic line of the Shadhiiliyya, who, in Morocco, gave rise to numerous ramifications such as the Darqawi order, founded by the last cited of these spiritual masters.

20. Abu al-Qasim al-Junayd (d. 911 CE) is called the "Master of the Circle" of the Sufis or "Master of the Way" (*Shaykh al-Tariqa*). He lived and died in Baghdad and is considered one of the most important teachers of Sufi doctrines.

21. Jean-Louis Michon, *Le Soufi marocain Ahmad Ibn 'Ajiba et son Mi'raj: Glossaire de la mystique musulmane* (Paris: Vrin, 1973), 241–242.

22. Ahmad Ghazali, *Bawariq al-ilma',* in Robson, *Tracts on Listening to Music,* 98–99; and Molé, *Les Danses sacrées,* 205–206

23. On the subject of these quaternary correspondences, which the Arabs systematized from Greek sources, but which also had roots among the ancient Semites, see H.G. Farmer, *Sa'adiyah Gaon on the Influence of Music* (London, U.K., 1943), 9.

24. On the theory of the mode in Arabo-Islamic music, see in particular, R. Erlanger, *La Musique arabe, volume V* (Paris, 1949). On its current practice in diverse areas of the Arabo-Muslim world, see S. Jargy, *Musique arabe* (Paris: Presses Universitaires Françaises, 1971), 49–69.

25. The earliest term used in Arabic for the mode was *sawt,* literally, "voice," a term that clearly marks the principally vocal character of Arabo-Islamic music during its first period. Later, authors spoke of *tariqa,* "way" or "manner of acting," a term that has also fallen into disuse.

26. See K. Reinhard and U. Reinhard, *Les Traditions musicales—Turquie* (Paris, 1969), 69–70.

27. Sayyed Hossein Nasr, "The Influence of Sufism on Traditional Persian Music," in *The Sword of Gnosis,* ed. Jacob Needleman (Baltimore, Maryland: Penguin Books, 1974), 330–343.

28. Farmer, *History,* 25.

29. Erlanger, *La musique arabe,* vol. 1, 14–16.

30. Examples of *ta'ziya* music with transcriptions can be found in N. Caron, "La musique chiite en Iran," in *Encyclopédie des musiques sacrées,* vol. I (Paris, 1968), 430–440.

31. The Ahl-i Haqq sect has been thoroughly studied by Mohammad Mokri, who sets the number of its adherents at approximately 500,000. See Mokri, *L'Ésoterisme kurde* (Paris, 1966) and "La musique sacrée des Kurdes" in *Encyclopédie de musiques sacrées,* vol. 1, 441–453.

32. On the *nawba* and the music of the Western part of the Islamic world (*al-Maghrib*) in general, consult J. Rouanet, "La musique arabe" and "La musique

maghrebine," in *Encyclopédie de la Musique et dictionnaire du Conservatoire,* ed. A. Lavignac and L. de la Laurencie (Paris, 1921–1931); see also, P. Garcia Barriuso, *La Musica Hispano-Musulmana en Marruecos* (Madrid, 1950).

33.   In Morocco, the modes of a *nawba* are called *tuba'* (plural *tubu'*) instead of *maqam.*

34.   Henri Corbin, *En Islam iranien,* cited by Seyyed Hossein Nasr in "L'Islam e la Musica secondo Ruzbahan Baqli, santo patrono di Sciraz," *Sufi, musiche e ceremonie dell'Islam* (Milan: Centro di Ricerca per il Teatro, 1981).

35.   Ruzbihan Baqli, *Risalat al-Quds,* cited by Jean During, "Revelation and Spiritual Audition in Islam," *The World of Music: Sacred Music, Journal of the International Institute for Comparative Music Studies and Documentation* 24, no. 3 (1982): 68–84.

36.   Cited by William Chittick in *The Sufi Path of Love: the Spiritual Teachings of Rumi* (Albany, New York: State University of New York Press, 1983), 326.

37.   N. Caron and D. Safvate, *Iran—les Traditions musicales* (Paris, 1966) 232.

38.   Jean During, "Eléments spirituels dans la musique traditionelle iranienne contemporaine," *Sophia Perennis* 1, no. 2 (Autumn 1975): 129–154.

39.   Reinhard, *Traditions musicales: Turquie,* 105.

40.   Cited by J. Sharif, *Islam in India* (London, U.K., 1975), 289.

41.   Concerning the different styles of Hindustani music, consult A. Daniélou, *Northern Indian Music* (London and Calcutta, 1949–1952). The spiritual value of Indian music and the vigor that the music of Mogul India experienced under the influence of Islam have been analyzed in depth in the article by L. Aubert, "Aperçus sur la signification de la musique indienne," *Revue Musicale de la Suisse romande* no. 2, (May 1981) (34th year): 50–61.

42.   *Yanavalkya Smriti* cited by Whitall N. Perry, *A Treasury of Traditional Wisdom* (London, U.K.: George Allen & Unwin, 1971), 685.

43.   Seyyed Hossein Nasr, "Traditional Art as Fountain of Knowledge and Grace," in *Knowledge and the Sacred* (Edinburgh, U.K.: Edinburgh University Press, 1981), 272.

10

REGAINING THE CENTER: GARDENS AND THRESHOLDS

———————————•———————————

Virginia Gray Henry-Blakemore

It is more than coincidental that many doorways throughout the world exhibit a corresponding set of symbolic motifs that point to the One manifesting itself as duality—a duality and a world that must return to that One. The shape of this is basically a triangle, whose apex is a single point and whose lower angles indicate the masculine and feminine. This is a deeply satisfying shape, full of harmony and balance, which can represent the Divine Source and the manifested world.

This center, or apex, may be represented by a Tree of Life, the Axis Mundi, the Fountain of Immortality, a Throne, a Mountain, Royalty, a sun disc, and so on. Also, the center can refer to the Gardens of Paradise where the Tree and Fountain are located. It is interesting that in sacred structures through-out the world this Garden or sacred grove is recalled in architectural features. A church, for example, will have a cross, which corresponds to the Tree, and a baptismal font, which corresponds to the Fountain. The Sacred Mosque in Mecca has the Ka'ba or Cube, which represents the Divine Center and the well of Zam Zam, the Fountain. Atop the mountainous temple of Angkor Wat in Cambodia are images of Buddha surrounded by four pools with a moat beyond.

Just as the entrance to the Gardens of Paradise is protected by two cherubim, who "keep the way of the Tree of Life" (Genesis 3:24),[1] sacred structures invariably have flanking guardians at their thresholds. One finds paired lions at the door of each Burmese Buddhist temple and sphinxes in Egypt. Over the gates to Christian churches are paired creatures, such as griffins or cherubim, on either side of Jesus or Mary. This configuration continues to be used for secular doorways, which may exhibit palmettes and vases, which again bring to mind the Garden and Fountain. Often public libraries and other institutions have guardian lions at their entranceways. In the steppes of Central Asia, the threshold to the yurt is decorated with the image of the Tree of Life flanked by two mountain sheep, which are represented by their horns. This particular motif, which resembles a fleur-de-lis pattern, is used everywhere in Kazakhstan and Kyrgyzstan, and extends to all items of daily use. According to Ananda Coomaraswamy, the guardians flanking a gateway symbolize the duality we must overcome in ourselves in order to regain the Center, or Paradise, or the Kingdom of Heaven within. This is what these particular symbols of the flanked central principle are there for—to remind us what to do and be. In the words of the German mystic Meister Eckhart, Paradise is a place where "neither virtue nor vice ever entered in."

The image of the Tree and the Fountain participates in an essential and archetypal reality that is part of the primordial makeup of humankind as a whole. Whether the Tree is an ash in the northern climes or a palm in the southern hemisphere is of no consequence. Neither does it matter if the forms attendant upon the threshold are those of sheep horns, split palmettes, or cherubim.

These threshold guardians, in fact, provide the conditions that qualify the aspirant to pass through the Threshold. The price of *theosis*, the attainment of transcendent character, is becoming a "veritable nonentity." The hero must overcome the dragons that guard the Treasure and symbolize our own failures and inadequacies. In the *Mathnawi*, Mevlana Jalaluddin Rumi remarks, "Whoever is uttering 'I' or 'we' is turned back from the Door."

The moment of this Return through the Threshold to the Center is a forever that is now—the Present/Presence that is not bound in the duality of past and future.

> The Saint hath no fear, because fear is the expectation either of some future calamity or of the eventual loss of some object of desire; whereas the Saint is the "Son of His Time" (resides in the Eternal Present/Presence); he has no future from which he should fear anything and, as he hath no fear, so he hath no hope since hope is the expectation either of gaining an object of desire or of being relieved from a misfortune, and this belongs to the future; nor does he grieve because grief arises from the rigor of time, and how should he feel grief who dwells in the Radiance of Satisfaction and the Garden of Concord. [2]

NOTES

Excerpted from Viriginia Gray Henry-Blakemore, *Thy Self, the Logos: Symbolism of the Cherubim from Mesopotamia to Monticello as Understood from the Last Essays of A.K. Coomaraswamy,* forthcoming from Fons Vitae, Louisville, Kentucky. Reproduced by permission of the author and publisher. Sources for the above book include three unpublished manuscripts by Ananda Coomaraswamy: "The Guardians of the Sun Door," "Philo's Doctrine of the Cherubim," and "The Early Iconography of Sagittarius."

1.   Martin Lings describes this Tree as an "outward image of the inward Tree of Immortality, which grows in the garden of the heart, and is on the axis as a gateway to the Spirit." Lings, *The Book of Certainty* (Cambridge, U.K.: Islamic Texts Society, 1992), 28.

2.   Abu al-Qasim al-Junayd, famous Sufi of Baghdad, ninth century CE.

11

THE ISLAMIC GARDEN: HISTORY, SYMBOLISM, AND THE QUR'AN

Emma C. Clark

In Arabia at the time of the coming of Islam in the seventh century CE, a garden was conceived as a walled orchard or vineyard (Ar. *hadiqa, rawda,* or *riyad*), and was irrigated by a channel of water or a well. The pre-Islamic hero and poet 'Antara ibn al-Shaddad recited the following verse: "Every noble virgin bestowed her bounty upon it/and we left every enclosed garden (*hadiqa*) shining like a silver coin."[1] However, in its most basic form, a grove of palm trees (*Phoenix dactilifera*) and a source of water—the oasis—was a garden too. For both the pre-Islamic Arabs and the early Muslims the walled garden, the *hadiqa*, was a gift of Perso-Mesopotamian civilization. Islam absorbed the already well-established Persian tradition of hunting parks and royal pleasure gardens and invested them with a new spiritual vision. It was through this vision, as portrayed in the Qur'an, that the traditional Islamic garden was born.

The first Muslims came from the deserts and towns of Arabia and Syria. The Prophet Muhammad, like most young Arab boys at that time, spent his early childhood brought up by a foster-mother from one of the nomadic desert tribes. It was believed that the demanding desert environment and nomadic way of life would instill the virtues of steadfastness, strength, and courage in boys at an early age and would stand them in good stead in adulthood. "As desert dwellers, the notion of invisible hands that drove the blasts that swept the desert and formed the deceptive mirages that lured the traveler to his destruction was always with [the Arabs]," writes Huston Smith, a noted scholar of comparative religion.[2] For the pre-Islamic Arabs, accustomed as they were to living in a hostile environment, the smallest amount of water or the slightest indication of nature's greenness was considered precious and sacred, its rare appearance the work of "invisible hands." To them, an oasis offered mercy in water and shade. Thus, a lush garden with fountains and shade-giving trees and the gentle green everywhere—as depicted in the descriptions of the gardens of Paradise in the Qur'an—was a symbol of ease and comfort, a veritable abode of bliss.[3] The pre-Islamic Arabs already revered nature as a sign of the life-giving power of Allah, Creator of the Universe. Thus, when the Holy Qur'an was revealed to the Prophet Muhammad with its promise of gardens of Paradise for the faithful and righteous—havens of such beauty and happiness that only a foretaste and reflection of them could be experienced on Earth—it was perfectly natural for them to accept this vision.

A glance at the art and architecture of the Islamic world shows a tremendous diversity of artistic expression: the Qarawiyyin Mosque in Fez, the Al Azhar Mosque in Cairo, and the Friday Mosque in Isfahan, all have rich art and artisanship adorning them. Each geographical location, with its native people, cultural characteristics, and artistic gifts, adapted the Islamic vision and principles to achieve pinnacles of art and beauty that are both reflections of the land in question and also recognizable manifestations of the Islamic spirit and this is no less true with Islamic gardens. Across the Islamic world, these gardens show a great variation of styles, reflecting practical and environmental factors, as well as indigenous cultural factors: factors such as topography, availability of water, and purpose or type of garden. However, like the other Islamic arts and architecture, despite their diversity, Islamic gardens retain the same principles and are quintessentially expressions of the same Islamic spirit.

Some Islamic gardens are vast open spaces, such as the magnificent Shalimar Bagh ("Abode of Love") in Lahore, Pakistan, with its terraces and marble pavilions, or the Shalimar Bagh in Kashmir where water rushes down, channeled from the mountains. Some gardens, like the pre-Islamic *hadiqa*, have the appearance of orchards and are also called *bustan* (the Persian word for "orchard"), for example, the Menara Garden in Marrakech, Morocco, with its olive groves and fruit trees. Then there are the great mausoleum gardens of Mogul India, such as those of Itimad ud-Dawlah or Humayun. However, our main interest in this chapter is the smaller, enclosed garden, the *chahar-bagh*, which is the type of garden that most people associate with Islam.

The classic *chahar-bagh* is a fourfold garden (from the Persian *chahar*, "four," and *bagh*, "garden") that is constructed around a central pool or fountain with four streams flowing from it, symbolizing the four directions of space. Sometimes, the water is engineered to flow from the central fountain outward as well as inward toward the center of the garden from fountains placed at the four corners—as in the Court of Lions at the Alhambra. Often, paths are substituted for channels of water. This basic fourfold pattern is the quintessential plan of the Islamic garden, and there are many interpretations of it across the Islamic world. For example, the garden might be rectangular rather than square, such as the Patio de la Acequia ("Patio of the Water-Channel") of the Generalife in Granada. The plan of the garden may also be repeated on a kind of grid system, following irrigation channels, as in the Agdal gardens near Marrakech. The pattern may also be manifested in the smaller, inward-looking courtyard garden of the traditional Islamic house, which is not always divided into four sections. However, with its central pool or fountain and surrounded by four walls, it still echoes the classic *chahar-bagh,* both in its form and in its symbolism. As we shall see, the fourfold garden is not a symbol particular only to Islam. Rather, it is of a universal nature, and it is founded upon a profound understanding of the cosmos.

PROTOTYPES OF THE ISLAMIC GARDEN

The idea that Paradise is a garden is a very ancient one. It predates Islam, as well as Judaism and Christianity, by centuries, and appears to have its origin as far back as the Sumerian period (around 4000 BCE) in Mesopotamia. Here, a garden for the gods is mentioned in some of the first writings known to humanity. The Babylonians (*c.* 2700 BCE) described their Divine Paradise as a garden in the *Epic of Gilgamesh:* "In this immortal garden stands the Tree... beside a sacred fount the Tree is placed."[4] Thus, in Mesopotamian sources we already have two indispensable elements of the Paradise Garden of Islam: water and shade. In the Qur'an, the Gardens of Paradise are called *jannat al-firdaws: jannat* (plural) meaning "gardens," and *firdaws* (singular) meaning "Paradise."[5] The word *janna* (singular) can also mean "Paradise." Most of the other terms in traditional Islam that describe gardens, such as *bagh* ("garden"), *bustan* ("orchard"), and *gulistan* ("rose-garden"), are Persian words.[6] Thus, they indicate where the developed form of the Islamic garden originated. It was the unique impact of the Qur'anic revelation on the ancient Sassanid and Achaemenian civilizations of Persia with their *pairidaeza*s (walled hunting-parks) and sophisticated irrigation systems, such as those in the gardens of Cyrus the Great at Pasargardae, that ultimately brought the Islamic garden into being. The English word "Paradise" itself comes from the Middle Persian word *pairidaeza, pairi* meaning "around," and *daeza* meaning, "wall."

Persian gardens and hunting-parks were distinct areas, set apart from the surrounding, often inhospitable, landscape and were usually defined by high walls. Thus, we immediately envisage an isolated region, shutting out a difficult environment to protect an area of fertility and ease within. The traditional Islamic fourfold garden is often represented in miniature paintings as surrounded by high walls. It is in the nature of Paradise to be hidden and secret, since it corresponds to the interior world, the innermost soul—the Arabic noun *al-janna* having the sense of "concealment" as well as of a garden.[7] This concept is similar to that of the *hortus conclusus,* the monastic garden of medieval Christendom. The courtyard of a traditional Arab-Islamic house is a kind of *chahar-bagh* in miniature; there may not be room for many plants and flowers but there is always water, usually a small fountain or a small pool in the center with possibly one palm tree or some plants in pots. These houses are often quite high, with four stories or more and a flat roof on which one can sleep on hot summer nights, the windows rarely opening out onto the street. Instead, they look inward, usually with balconies, onto the courtyard and the miniature Paradise Garden within. On entering one of these houses, in order to maintain privacy from the street, the corridor is cleverly constructed so that it bends around, preventing passers-by from peering into the secluded family home.

The plan on which the Arab-Islamic house is based is inherited from an ancient prototype originating in Mesopotamia. Here people made maximum use of what little water was available and built their houses of mud-brick around enclosures or courtyards with water in the center. This kept the adverse conditions outside, while simultaneously creating a cooler, cleaner, and refreshing refuge within. Under Muslim direction, this architecture also reflected the separation between the public and private domains in traditional Islamic society. This distinction between public and private domains was to become one of the hallmarks of traditional Islamic architecture, and incorporated, by extension, the "interior" courtyard garden. The house opens inward toward the heart rather than outward toward the world. The heart, symbolically represented by the courtyard, represents the interior (*batin*), the contemplative aspect of human nature. By contrast, the modern villa-type house represents the opposite, the exterior (*zahir*) or worldly attitude.[8]

The traditional Islamic house may be in the middle of a bustling old city (*madina*)—such as Fez, Tunis, or Damascus—but when the door to the street is shut, the visitor enters a very different world. The contrast is immediate: suddenly peace and quiet descend; the high, thick stone walls keep out the noise and bestow a kind of muffled silence on the interior, not dissimilar to a church. The gentle murmur of a fountain in the center of the house draws the visitor in, contributing to the atmosphere of interiorizing reflection. At night, these small courtyards (often about six meters square or less) are quite magical. Sitting on a rug or a cushion on the stone floor, one's gaze is inevitably drawn upward, toward the stars in the sky. It is a beautiful example of how traditional architecture can not only have an impact upon the individual soul and affect a whole society and way of life, but it is also a mirror of that society's values.[9]

Titus Burckhardt, the great commentator on Islamic art wrote:

If [a Muslim's] house has no windows onto the street and is normally built around an inner court from which the rooms receive light and air, this is not simply in response to the frequently torrid climate of Muslim lands; it is clearly symbolic. In conformity with this symbolism, the inner court of a house is an

image of paradise; when it contains a fountain and water-courses which gush
forth to water trees and flowers, it does in effect recall the descriptions in the
Qur'an of the abode of the blessed.[10]

THE QUR'AN AND THE GARDEN

There are many references to fountains, flowing waters, and perfect
temperate climates in the descriptions of Paradise in the Qur'an, where the
blessed shall be shaded by "thornless lote-trees and serried acacias" and
"palms and vines" (Qur'an 56:28–34; 2:266). In hot and dry environments,
water is understandably viewed as a symbol of God's mercy; rain is referred to
throughout the Qur'an as a mercy and as life-giving. Indeed, there is no
doubt that water in whatever form, whether a still pool, a rushing waterfall,
a murmuring fountain, or a fast-flowing rill, is a key element in a traditional
Islamic garden. To those brought up in countries where rain is frequent
and the climate is temperate, it is all too easy to take water for granted and
to be unaware of how much a lush garden with flowing water and a green
canopy of shade mean to inhabitants of countries with baking-hot desert
climates. It is no accident that green is the color of Islam. It is the color used
repeatedly in the Qur'an to describe Paradise, where the faithful recline on
"green cushions" (Qur'an 55:76) and wear "green robes" (Qur'an 18:31).
Not only is green the color of vegetation, appearing young and fresh and
symbolizing growth and fertility in the spring, but it is also the antithesis of
the monotonous sandy-browns of the stony desert; it offers a longed-for
soothing and gentle relief to the eyes.[11] A famous English gardener writing
at the beginning of the twentieth century gives a very evocative description
of the unavoidable heat and longing for coolness and green foliage that he
experienced while trekking in Iran:

> Imagine you have ridden in summer for four days across a plain; that you have
> then come to a barrier of snow-mountains and ridden up that pass; that from
> the top of the pass you have seen a second plain, with a second barrier of moun-
> tains in the distance, a hundred miles away; that you know that beyond these
> mountains lies yet another plain, and another; and that for days, even weeks,
> you must ride with no shade, and the sun overhead, and nothing but the
> bleached bones of dead animals strewing the track. Then when you come to trees
> and running water, you will call it a garden. It will not be flowers and their
> garishness that your eyes crave for, but a green cavern full of shadows and pools
> where goldfish dart, and the sound of a little stream.[12]

In the approximately 120 references in the Qur'an to the Gardens of
Paradise—the *jannat al-firdaws* that are promised for "those who believe
and do deeds of righteousness" (Qur'an 18:107)—various epithets
are attached to the word *janna* in order to describe the qualities that the

Gardens possess. For example, one finds *jannat al-khuld* (singular), the Garden of Immortality or Eternity (Qur'an 25:15); *jannat al-na'im* (plural), the Gardens of Bliss, Delight, or Felicity (Qur'an 56:12); and *jannat al-ma'wa* (plural), the Gardens of Refuge, Shelter, or Abode (Qur'an 32:19). One also finds *jannat 'Adnin* (Qur'an 18:30)—the Garden of Eden—which suggests the peace and harmony of humanity's primordial state. From these descriptive terms attached to the Arabic word *janna*, we see that the Islamic Gardens of Paradise are not only blissful and eternal, but they are also a refuge or sanctuary, a sheltered and secure retreat far from the disquiet of the world. However, the descriptive phrase most often used for the Gardens of Paradise in the Qur'an (it is used over 30 times) is *jannat tajri min tahtiha al-anhar*, "Gardens Underneath which Rivers Flow" (for example, Qur'an 61:12). Even in translation, the repetition of this phrase has a soothing rhythm to it. Closing one's eyes, it is possible to imagine sitting in a garden under dappled shade, listening to the gentle music of flowing water.

Flowing rivers and the coursing of water and fountains are the most powerful and memorable images one retains after reading the portrayals of the Paradise Gardens in the Qur'an. There is no doubt that the reason water is the essential element in an Islamic garden is both because of the lack of water in the desert lands of Arabia and because of the importance placed upon water in the Qur'an. The Almighty knew that in order to tempt His flock back to the "Straight Path" (*al-sirat al-mustaqim*),[13] He must promise them rewards in the Afterlife—such as water and shade—that they would understand and desire and that they already revered for their life-giving properties. Islam gave the first Muslims the knowledge and faith that these two elements, together with the rest of the natural world, were not to be worshipped for themselves alone but were to be revered for what they represented. Nature and beauty are the outward symbols of inward grace. Throughout the Qur'an, the faithful are exhorted to meditate upon God's signs and symbols, since everything in the created world is a sign or symbol of God. "Thus God makes clear His signs for you so that you may understand" (Qur'an 2:242). The Qur'an also refers to the mediocrity and ephemeral nature of this lower life compared to the happiness of the life everlasting and the Gardens of Paradise: "The present life is naught but a sport and a diversion" (Qur'an 47:36).

Human beings would cease to be truly *muslim*, in submission to God, if they were to revere the created world as an end in itself. The world must instead be seen for what it is—an illusion (*maya* in Hinduism) that both veils and reveals the archetypal heavenly world. When a civilization is centered on the sacred, whether it is Islamic, Native American, or medieval Christian, the practical is always inextricably linked to the spiritual. This is the language of symbolism: linking everyday practical activities back to their heavenly archetypes.[14] However, human beings are forgetful and need to be reminded that the things of this world are not ends in themselves. The importance of sacred art lies in this truth. The Islamic garden is best seen as a kind of open-air sacred art: the content, form, and symbolic language of this art all combine to remind one of the eternal invisible realities that lie beneath outward appearances.

The following are some brief excerpts from the Qur'an that give an indication of the sense of rich abundance and blissful delight that is given by a fuller reading of the Qur'anic descriptions of the Gardens of Paradise:

> In Paradise there is "no vain talk or lies" (Qur'an 78:35); "they hear no idle speech" (Qur'an 88:11); "they hear no vain talk or recrimination, but only the saying, 'Peace, peace'" (Qur'an 56:25).
>
> "We shall strip away all rancor that is in their breasts; as brothers they shall be on couches, set face to face" (Qur'an 15:47).
>
> There is a perfect temperate climate: "Reclining therein on couches, they shall see neither [the heat of the] sun nor bitter cold" (Qur'an 76:13).
>
> There will be cool pavilions, couches, cushions, carpets, and silk attire, "green garments of silk and brocade" (Qur'an 76:21).[15]
>
> Weariness is unknown in this Paradise: "Fatigue will not come unto them there" (Qur'an 15:48).
>
> Fruit will be in abundance; produce will be eternal, "such fruits as they shall choose and such flesh of fowl as they desire" will be provided (Qur'an 56:20–21).
>
> Gold and silver jewelry will be worn and sweet potions will be drunk from "vessels of silver" and "goblets of crystal" (Qur'an 76:15). The potions are of such purity that there are no after-effects, "no brows throbbing, no intoxication" (Qur'an 56:19).
>
> An essential element of the gardens of paradise is that they are eternal, that the righteous will be there forever, "therein to dwell for ever; that is indeed the mighty triumph" (Qur'an 57:12).
>
> Finally, and movingly, the Lord rewards the faithful for remembering Him on earth: "And their Lord shall give them to drink a pure draught. Behold this is recompense for you, and your striving is thanked" (Qur'an 76:22).

The joys and delights of the Gardens of Paradise as depicted in the Qur'an give the faithful a clear idea of the heavenly reward for their striving. These descriptions transport the reader or listener to heavenly realms, to places of infinite and surpassing peace and felicity, which only the most dedicated spiritual seekers on earth may reach. This is only achieved through the constant and sincere remembrance of God (*dhikr Allah*), through nurturing the "garden within," the garden of the heart. This interior garden is the domain of the Sufis, those who concentrate on the inward or mystical aspect of Islam and who understand profoundly that the visible world is a symbol, a transient mirror image of an invisible eternal reality.[16]

SYMBOLIC GARDENS IN THE QUR'AN: *SURAT AL-RAHMAN* (55, "THE ALL-MERCIFUL")

In the Qur'an, not only are there four rivers in the Gardens of Paradise but also, in Sura 55, there are four gardens, which are described as two pairs of gardens. Sura 55 contains one of the most detailed references to the Gardens of Paradise in the Qur'an. According to some commentaries, these four gardens are divided into a lower pair, the "Garden of the Soul" and the "Garden of the Heart," which is reserved for the Righteous (*al-salihun*). The second and higher pair of gardens, the "Garden of the Spirit" and the "Garden of the Essence," is reserved for the Foremost (*al-sabiqun*), those who are closest to the Divine Presence. The first garden is covered by spreading branches and contains two flowing springs (*'aynan*), which water "every kind of fruit in pairs" (Qur'an 55:48–52). Its inhabitants recline on couches of silk brocade, with the fruit of both gardens near at hand (Qur'an 55:54). The second pair of gardens is dark green with foliage, and contains two gushing springs that water orchards of date palms and pomegranates (Qur'an 55:64–68).

Fountains in an Islamic garden are not just for coolness and beauty. They are also reminders of the archetypal springs of water that are described in this Sura. In each of these gardens is a flowing or gushing spring (*'ayn*, "source"), which indicates that Paradise is metaphysically near to the Ultimate Source (*'ayn*)—to God Himself. Elsewhere in the Qur'an, the springs of the Gardens of Paradise are named *Tasnim* (Exaltation), "a spring from which Those Brought Near to God (*al-muqarrabun*) drink" (Qur'an 83:27–28); *Salsabil* (Ever-Flowing), which gives its water mixed with fragrant ginger (Qur'an 76:18); and *Kauthar* (Abundance), which is said to be flavored with musk (Qur'an 108:1–2). The complex and profound symbolism that is contained in *Surat al-Rahman* and other passages of the Qur'an that describe the Gardens of Paradise cannot be described fully in an introductory article such as this.[17] However, the most important point to emphasize is that the fourfold form of the archetypal Islamic garden is not just a whim of design or an interesting horticultural plan, but is fundamentally a reflection of a higher reality and a universal symbol of Divine Unity.

DESIGN AND SYMBOLISM: THE NUMBER FOUR

Although the symbolism of the fourfold garden is used in other religious traditions, notably in the Christian tradition, where the monastic herb garden and the "cloister garth" spring to mind, there is still no doubt that in most people's minds the classic *chahar-bagh* layout is quintessentially Islamic. Inherent in the number four is a universal symbolism based on an understanding of the natural world. The number four encompasses the four cardinal directions, the four elements, and the four seasons. The cube, the three-dimensional form of the number four, represents solidity, the Earth. The word *Ka'ba*, indicating the cube-like structure in the courtyard of the Great Mosque of Mecca to which Muslims orient their prayers, means "cube."[18] The fourfold plan also recalls the fundamental *mandala* of the Vedic tradition, which is divided into nine squares and symbolizes the terrestrial realm. Tibetan Buddhist *tangka*s are also based on a square diagram within a circle, representing the earth encircled by heaven.

The religion of Islam reconfirmed these ancient, widespread, and universal truths, and invested them with a new spiritual understanding. In describing his visionary ascent to heaven (*mi'raj*), the Prophet Muhammad spoke of four rivers: one of water, one of milk, one of honey, and one of wine. These four rivers are also mentioned as part of the Gardens of Paradise described in the Qur'an: "Rivers of unpolluted water, rivers of milk whose flavor does not change, rivers of wine delicious to the drinkers, and rivers of purified honey" (Qur'an 47:15). This description from the Qur'an echoes the Book of Genesis, in which it is written: "And a river went out of Eden to water the garden and from thence it was parted into four heads" (Genesis 2:10).

Burckhardt's description of the Court of Lions at the Alhambra is worth quoting in full here:

> The plan of the heavenly garden always includes the four rivers of Paradise flowing towards the four quarters of Heaven, or from them towards the center. The watercourses of the Court of Lions are fed from the two halls to the north and south and from the two stone canopies at the west and east end. The floor of the halls is set higher than the garden, and so the water, which flows from round basins, runs down over the threshold towards the fountain, where it collects around the lions and soaks away.... The fountain itself, with its twelve lions supporting a basin spewing water, is an ancient symbol which reached the Alhambra from the pre-Christian Orient by way of all kinds of intermediary links. For the water-spewing lion is none other than the sun, from which life gushes forth, and the twelve lions are the twelve suns of the Zodiac, twelve months that are all present concurrently in eternity. They support a 'sea'... and this sea is the reservoir of Heavenly waters.... The stone canopies, too, at opposite ends in the east and west of the garden, are also a part of the picture of the garden of paradise, for in the description of paradise, the Qur'an mentions high canopies or tents.[19]

It is probably the case that only the master-gardeners would have been aware of the profound meanings underlying the plan and construction of the great Islamic gardens, passing on the knowledge gradually to their apprentices as they proved themselves spiritually mature. As with all traditional arts and crafts, including architecture and landscape design, a master-craftsman would have first conceived of the design of a garden and would have overseen the project as it developed. He would have worked in close collaboration with his patron, just as the great architect Sinan did in the sixteenth century CE when designing his masterpieces in Istanbul for Sultan Suleyman the Magnificent. At the Alhambra, Muhammad V was the patron who initiated the Court of the Lions and would have understood much of the profound meaning of the fourfold pattern. Interestingly, the English word "patron" comes from the Latin *patronus* and old French *patron,* meaning, "father." The term implies care and protection as well as support and guidance. The word "pattern," or model upon which a thing is designed, also has its origins in *patron* and *patronus.* This common set of meanings reinforces the idea central to the esoteric perspective (partly inherited from Plato) that everything on Earth is a symbol of its divine model or archetype in Heaven. Indeed, as mentioned earlier, the Islamic gardens on earth are not only a foretaste of where the faithful may hope to go after death, but are also symbolic representations of the divine archetype, the Heavenly Gardens as presented to us in the Qur'an.

MANIFESTATIONS OF THE *CHAHAR-BAGH*

The *chahar-bagh,* based as it is on the number four, has become the principal Islamic symbol of the Qur'anic Gardens of Paradise. This model was taken up and developed all over the Islamic world. For example, in Isfahan there is a road called The Avenue of the *Chahar-Bagh,* which in earlier times was lined with several beautiful fourfold gardens. These gardens were evocatively described by Russell Page, an English gardener in the 1960s: "Perhaps the world's loveliest processional way, and almost every garden is set symmetrically round a central pool whose four subsidiary rills carry water into each quarter of the garden and then to the roots of every tree and plant."[20] Page's description is enough to make one weep, since the present-day traffic-choked street in contemporary Isfahan is very different from the enchanting scene conjured up here.

In India, some of the great mausoleum gardens were built with the tomb placed in the center of the quadripartite plan, as in the mausoleum of Humayun, or with the mausoleum placed at one end, the *chahar-bagh* stretching out in front with a pool in the center, as at the Taj Mahal. The beauty of these mausoleums and their gardens is quite breathtaking. More modest, but still enchanting, examples of *chahar-bagh*s are to be seen across the Islamic world in Morocco, Syria, Persia, and Turkey, where many court-yard gardens integral to houses and public buildings still survive. Moorish Spain saw the construction of some of the most beautiful Islamic gardens in the world. The best known of these are the courtyard gardens of the Alhambra Palace, together with the gardens of the Generalife. The gardens of the Alcazar in Cordoba also deserve special mention since, despite being in Christian hands for many hundreds of years they are still utterly Islamic in their ambience. Clearly, the original intention of echoing the Gardens of Paradise is so closely interwoven with the fourfold geometric design and its inherent symbolic meaning that it is not possible to separate one from the other. As with most of the great Islamic gardens, there is a perfect balance and harmony between the principal elements of geometric formal design, the exuberance of the planting to soften the geometry, and the focal point of the garden: water. An important factor in the planting of the garden, besides shade and the color green, is that the garden should contain scented plants. It is mentioned in the Qur'an that sweet basil (*rayhan,* 55:12) can be found among the flowers growing in the Paradise Gardens.

In Morocco, there is a type of garden called a *riyad* that is related etymologically to the term *rawda,* a word that can mean both "garden" and "cemetery" in Arabic.[21] *Riyad* usually refers to a garden that is walled on three sides, the fourth side being the house of the garden's owner. The term may also refer to the house itself, with a walled garden at the back. In premodern times, a *riyad* more often than not contained an arbor of vines and a vegetable garden, as well as providing shade, solace, and food for the family. The name of Riyadh, the capital city of Saudi Arabia, comes from the same term. In the larger Mogul and Persian gardens, as well as in the Menara Garden in Marrakech, architecture in the form of pavilions or "kiosks" (another Persian word) can be found, which were often placed near the water for a cooling breeze. As Constance Villiers Stuart observed in the early twentieth century CE, "In Persia and India a house or palace is always understood to be included under the name of garden, and the whole composition was closely and beautifully interwoven."[22] This principle of the close interweaving of the house with the garden is crucial to an understanding of the sense of unity fundamental to all Islamic design.

WATER

"Gardens Underneath which Rivers Flow": the idea of water flowing underneath the Gardens of Heaven probably arose from the demands of a desert existence, where the only source of water for most of the year was from oases or underground irrigation systems such as the *qanat*s in Persia.[23] In the gardens themselves, water is to be seen and experienced; in order to irrigate the flower-beds, it has to flow in straight channels and rills, often under the pathways, thereby giving the visitor the impression of actually being in a garden "underneath which rivers flow." On a more profound level, water flowing underneath suggests the nurturing of the "garden within" or the "Garden of the Heart" by the ever-flowing water of the spirit, which serves to purify the souls of those on the spiritual path (*al-tariqa*). Indeed, water is symbolic of the soul in many sacred traditions. Its fluidity and constantly purifying aspect is a reflection of the soul's ability to renew itself, yet always to remain true to its source. The apparently endlessly flowing waters in the gardens of the Alhambra Palace and the nearby Generalife are some of the most evocative representations of the Islamic Gardens of Paradise anywhere in the world. The sound of water not only muffles the voices of the visitors, but it also has the miraculous effect of silencing one's own thoughts and allowing an overwhelming sense of peace to descend.

One glance at traditional Islamic gardens shows that, besides their geometric layout, they all have a fundamental element in common: water. Water, as already observed, is the single most defining element in an Islamic garden. Just as there are rivers and fountains in the Gardens of Paradise, so there are rivers, or rather channels or rills, and at least one fountain, in the earthly gardens. Indeed, in many cases it is true to say that the geometric layout of a garden has been determined by the practical demands of irrigation, by the water-flow itself. In a traditional culture, as pointed out above, there is no clear distinction between what is carried out for practical purposes and its spiritual significance: they go hand in hand.

Inventive devices in Persian gardens that are designed for distributing water or increasing the aesthetic experience of water include the *chador* (literally "shawl" in Persian, as in a "shawl of water"), a stone slab carved with geometric patterns so that the water breaks up into patterns as it falls over it. There is also the *chabutra,* a stone-seating platform that allows one who sits in a garden to be surrounded by water; this is a wonderful aid in meditation. One may see too a *chini-khana* (literally, "china cabinet"), rows of small niches carved into stone, within which a flower or a candle in a jar may be placed and over which the water falls. When such devices are combined with imaginative yet subtle lighting at dusk, it is no wonder that visitors from beyond Muslim lands are so often enchanted by the Islamic garden, such as the Russian prince who described the Shalimar Bagh in Lahore in 1842:

> The whole garden was illuminated from the edges of the fountains and water channels to the branches of the orange trees. Globes of coloured glass placed behind these candles tinged the sparkling water green or red. Add to all of this continuous fireworks, the magnificent warlike courtiers, the garden with its walks covered with Kashmiri shawls with the horses trampling upon them, the intoxicating smell of the orange blossom, and the even more intoxicating movements of the dancing girls. One felt inclined to say like Poor Tom in King Lear, "God keep us in our five senses."[24]

PEACE

It is written in the Qur'an that the only word spoken in the Gardens of Paradise is "Peace." "[In the Garden] they hear neither vain speaking nor recrimination, nothing but the saying 'Peace, Peace'" (Qur'an 56:25–26). Therefore, one of the principal functions of the earthly "Gardens of

Paradise" is to provide a place of tranquility and harmony, a retreat from the world, where the soul can let go of distracting thoughts and be at peace. The word *Islam* is related to the Arabic root S-L-M, which primarily means "peace." When taken together with its actual root, *aslama* ("to surrender, to give oneself over to another"), Islam thus means "the peace that comes when one's life is surrendered to God."[25] The traditional greeting used across the world by all Muslims, irrespective of race, nationality, color, background, or age, is *As-Salamu 'alaykum*, "Peace be upon you." The reply is, *Wa 'alaykum assalam*, "And upon you be Peace." Thus, when two Muslims greet each other, they echo the greeting that is given in the Gardens of Paradise. There is something extraordinarily beautiful about the courtesy, dignity, and sobriety of this greeting, which is both warm and reserved at the same time. It is warm because as two human beings before God, whatever our station in life, we acknowledge each other respectfully and as equals. It is reserved because the greeting requires no further communication; discretion and privacy are maintained and nothing further need be said.

Thus, when we read in the Qur'an that no words are spoken in the Gardens of Paradise except "Peace" (*Salam*), this seems perfectly natural. The human search for Paradise on Earth is essentially a search for peace, not just peace from the world, but peace from our passional soul (*nafs*), the ego and its desires—so that we may repose in our immortal soul.

The much-misused Arabic word *jihad* literally means "struggle" or "effort" and can take many forms, such as a *jihad* against intolerance and discrimination. However, according to a saying of the Prophet Muhammad, the greater *jihad* (*al-jihad al-akbar*) is the "war" within our own selves. This jihad is the struggle to transform the negative and egocentric motivations within us and to nurture positive ones. By the grace of God, this effort will eventually be rewarded by inner contentment and peace. Our longing for serenity of soul is like a vague memory of our primordial nature (*fitra* in Arabic), when the human being was at peace with the Creator in the Garden of Eden and therefore at peace with the soul. In order to regain this primordial Paradise, those who are seriously committed to the spiritual path of Islam must reach the state of constant remembrance of God (*dhikr Allah*). Few would argue that it is easier to nurture this contemplative state when surrounded by the beauties of nature or when sitting in a garden designed and planted with spiritual symbolism in mind. The traditional Islamic garden, providing as it does a sanctuary from the world and a foretaste of the Gardens of Paradise, can be a powerful aid in this remembrance.

DIVINE UNITY

The doctrine of Divine Unity (*tawhid*) is the profound message of the Qur'an that penetrates every aspect of a practicing Muslim's life. It also underpins Islamic art, architecture, and garden design. Beyond the different components of a garden—water, planting, geometry, and architecture—lies this secret force that draws them all together in a satisfying and harmonious composition. After spending some time contemplating a garden that exemplifies these principles, such as the Patio de la Acequia at the Generalife Gardens in Granada, or the smaller *chahar-bagh* in the Alacazar of Cordoba, the visitor will begin to understand that it is this secret force of *tawhid* that lies behind the sense of unity that gives an Islamic garden its special contemplative quality. This evocation of Divine Unity is evident in all traditional Islamic gardens, whether it is the magnificent Bagh-i-Fin in the Iranian city of Kashan, or one of the great mausoleum gardens of India, or the more intimate courtyard gardens of Damascus or Fez. "In Islamic art, unity is never the result of a synthesis of component elements; it exists *a priori,* and all the particular forms are deduced from it; the total form of a building or interior exists before its parts, whether they have a static function or not."[26]

After spending many hours absorbing the atmosphere of the Patio de la Acequia in the Generalife, the Court of the Myrtles and other courtyards of the Alhambra Palace, and the Azem Palace courtyards in Damascus, a realization became clear to me. For the first time, I became fully aware of the profound understanding that the Muslim designers and craftsmen of these gardens had of the harmonious relationship between architecture, geometric planning, water, and planting. All expressed the unity of the whole. I had no doubt that this understanding came about because their designers' whole way of living was permeated by *tawhid,* the central message of the Qur'an. This factor more than any other made possible their astonishing achievements in the art of garden design.

The essence of the concept of Divine Unity in Islam is the awareness that "There is no divinity but God." This statement, the first part of the *Shahada,* the Muslim testimony of faith, may also be rendered, "There is no reality but the Reality." In other words, the only reality is God. Thus, for the Muslim, existence is centered entirely on the consciousness of Divine Unity. This means that everything in the created world is transparent: behind the ephemeral beauty of the outward form, one can discern the ineffable spirit within. This eternal and transcendent quality gives the world of nature and all of manifestation their meaning: all else passes away. As Burckhardt observed:

> The most profound link between Islamic art and the Qur'an...lies not in the form of the Qur'an but in its *haqiqah,* its formless essence, and more particularly in the notion of *tawhid,* unity or union, with its contemplative implications; Islamic art—by which we mean the entirety of plastic arts in Islam—is essentially the projection into the visual order of certain aspects or dimensions of Divine Unity.[27]

TRADITION

The merging of the sacred and the secular is a crucial part of traditional Islamic culture, as it is of all traditional cultures. Tradition entails the "handing-over" of precious learning from one generation to another, which can be traced back to its ultimate source in Divine Revelation. However, Islamic gardens were not just for evoking the Unity of the Divine. They were also for pleasure and lovemaking, for political discussions and parties, and for growing vegetables and fruits. They were also for rest and refuge, and for delighting in the cooling and soothing properties of water. They were for enjoying the aesthetic and sensory delights of flowers, the scent of blossoms, the songs of the birds, and the protective shade of trees. However, all these things were enjoyed, not just for their sake alone, but also in the understanding that they were both a taste and a reflection of the joy and bliss of the Heavenly Gardens.

Thus, when one author writes, "the conclusion that the Qur'an supplied the blueprint for Islamic gardens is methodologically fallacious,"[28] she is correct in the sense that the Qur'an did not offer a "blueprint," a practical guide for measuring out one's garden as the Bible instructed Noah how to build the Ark. However, the Qur'an did offer something incommensurably deeper and more powerful than a blueprint. It offered the inward dimension, the idea behind the blueprint: the *haqiqa*, the Truth. This Truth was contained in the Divine Revelation of the Qur'an with its emphasis on *Tawhid* or Unity. When combined with a knowledge and love of the natural world, as well as the universal forms inherited from ancient civilizations, it resulted in the creation of a new art, an art that was all the more beautiful because it was true. One of the most important factors that make "Traditional" art traditional is that it is has a meaning: it performs some function, whether symbolic or practical, besides being aesthetically pleasing.[29] "Art for art's sake" has no place in the traditional world. The fact that *janna* means both garden and Paradise is indicative in itself of this lack of distinction between the sacred and the profane.

Never before in the history of humankind have there been such enormous and densely populated urban areas as there are today; and never before has there been such an intense desire to escape these areas—usually through travel to remote places "untouched" by humans—but also, on a smaller scale, through creating gardens. Increasingly, people are attempting to create their own miniature Paradise Gardens, green and secluded places that soothe the soul. These gardens are not only places of peace and quiet that are beautiful to behold, but they are also (often unconsciously) a recreation of the Heavenly Garden, itself reflected within all of us—our inner garden: "Look for the garden within yourself, in your indestructible divine Substance, which will then give you a new and imperishable garden."[30]

NOTES

(Ed.) following a note signifies that the note was added by the general editor of this set.

1. See Abu al-Fadl Jamal al-Din Muhammad ibn Manzur, *Lisan al-ʿArab* (Beirut: Dar Sadir, n.d.), vol. 10, 38–39. This early dictionary from the 13th century CE clearly indicates that for the pre-Islamic Arabs, a garden was a walled orchard that contained date palms or irrigated vineyards. (Ed.)

2. Huston Smith, *The World's Religions* (New York and San Francisco: Harper Collins, 1991), 236.

3. See especially, Qur'an 55, *Surat al-Rahman,* which will be examined in more detail below.

4. A little later (c. 1500 BCE), a garden was also the symbol of the Afterlife for the ancient Egyptians, who often placed models of gardens in their tombs.

5. The Qur'anic term *firdaws* is an Arabized version of the Middle Persian *pardis,* meaning, "garden." Thus, the plural term *jannat al-firdaws* literally means, "Gardens of the Garden," in other words, the quintessential or primordial garden. *Gana* is the Hebrew term for garden, as in *Ganat Aden,* "Garden of Eden." *Pardes* also appears in Jewish mystical texts before the coming of Islam. (Ed.)

6. The word *gul* is used as a general term for "flower" in Persian, as well as specifically for the rose. An abstracted version (the essential form) of the rose is the dominant motif in many tribal carpets from Baluchistan to Anatolia, through to the wide range of Turkomen rugs and carpets.

7. Titus Burckhardt, *Moorish Culture in Spain* (Munich: George D.W. Callwey, 1970); English translation by Alisa Jaffa (London: George Allen and Unwin, 1972), 209–210.

8. A friend made a parallel observation recently: While congregations have dwindled to an all-time low in many—if not most—churches and cathedrals in Europe, these buildings are still beautifully maintained and conserved and are lit up by floodlights from without. Paradoxically, it seems that as the "inner light" diminishes, the outer light increases. Is this another sign of the times?

9. On a recent radio program in the United Kingdom (BBC Radio 4, 14 September 2005) something that our ancient forbears understood well was acknowledged as if it were a new discovery: the environments we construct for ourselves have a powerful effect on our health and well-being.

10. Titus Burckhardt, *Art of Islam, Language and Meaning* (London, U.K.: World of Islam Publishing Company, 1976), 91.

11. In a *hadith qudsi* (non-Qur'anic divine saying) it is recorded, "Tomorrow I shall make their eyes delight in My Gardens." The key phrase in this tradition literally means, "cool their eyes," suggesting the healing effect of the color green on eyes that have become tired and sore after the heat of the desert. See *Divine Sayings: The Mishkat al-Anwar of Ibn ʿArabi, 101 Hadith Qudsi,* Arabic Text and English Translation by Stephen Hirtenstein and Martin Notcutt, (Oxford, U.K.: Anqa Publishing, 2004), 59 and Part 2, endnote.

12.   Vita Sackville-West, *Passenger to Tehran,* quoted by John Brookes in *Gardens of Paradise: History and Design of the Great Islamic Gardens* (London, U.K.: Weidenfeld and Nicholson, 1987), 13.

13.   A term from the *Fatiha,* the opening *Sura* (chapter) of the Qur'an, which Muslims recite in each of the five daily prayers.

14.   This point was captured beautifully by the poet Saadi of Shiraz (d. 1292 CE), who wrote: "To the eye of the discerning man, every leaf upon a growing tree is a book imparting knowledge of our Creator." *Poems from the Persian,* trans. J.C.E. Bowen (Oxford, U.K.: Blackwell and Company, 1958), 53.

15.   Following the teachings of the Hadith, it is traditional for Muslim men not to wear silk or gold; along with wine, these are saved for Paradise.

16.   See, for example, Martin Lings, *Symbol and Archetype: A Study of the Meaning of Existence* (Cambridge, U.K.: Quinta Essentia, 1991), 67. Al-Ghazali, the great eleventh-century Persian scholar and theologian, defined symbolism as "the science of the relation between multiple levels of reality."

17.   For further information on the Gardens of Paradise, see Emma Clark, *"Underneath which Rivers Flow": The Symbolism of the Islamic Garden* (London, U.K.: The Prince of Wales' Institute of Architecture, 1996). For a fuller explanation of *Surat al-Rahman,* see Abu Bakr Siraj al-Din, *The Book of Certainty* (Cambridge, U.K.: The Islamic Texts Society, 1992); see also, Frithjof Schuon, *Islam and the Perennial Philosophy,* trans. J. Peter Hobson (London, U.K.: World of Islam Festival Publishing Company Ltd., 1976), chap. 12.

18.   The roots of Judaism, Christianity, and Islam all start with the Prophet Abraham, father of Ishmael and Isaac. It was Abraham and Ishmael who built the Ka'ba at Mecca, the place toward which Muslims turn in their five daily prayers. The Ka'ba is symbolically the centre of the world for Muslims; its shape is almost exactly a cube. The circle that pilgrims trace in their circumambulation of the Ka'ba represents Heaven and the Ka'ba itself represents the Earth. Thus, through performing this symbolic rite, human beings reaffirm their role as the link between Heaven and Earth and as Heaven's representatives on Earth.

19.   Burckhardt, *Moorish Culture in Spain,* 209.

20.   See Russell Page, *The Education of a Gardener* (London, U.K.: Penguin Edition, 1983), chap. 2.

21.   The term, *rawda,* is applied specifically to the small area in the Prophet's Mosque at Medina between the Prophet Muhammad's tomb and the pulpit (*minbar*). It is called this because of the saying of the Prophet, "Between my house and my pulpit is a garden (*rawda*) of the Gardens of Paradise." Today, when worshippers visit the Prophet's Mosque at Medina, this area is always the most crowded, since everyone longs to be with the Prophet in his Paradise Garden.

22.   Constance Villiers Stuart, *Gardens of the Great Mughals* (London, U.K.: A. & C. Black, 1913), 42.

23.   It was only after visiting Iran and spending time in cafes at the foot of the Elborz Mountains north of Tehran that I really began to understand the importance of water and shade, and to absorb the atmosphere of what an Islamic garden means. Here, fast-running streams are straddled by cheap metal divans on which are placed rugs and cushions so that the visitor can sit cross-legged or lie on them and wait to

be served with watermelon, tea, and perhaps a *shisha* or an *argileh* (water-pipe). One sinks back into the cushions, looking up at the leaves of the *chenar* tree (*Platanus orientalis*) filtering the sunlight, and listening to the sound of water running over the pebbles below. At such times, the phrase from the Qur'an, "Gardens underneath which rivers flow," is brought alive. This experience is truly a foretaste of the Paradise Gardens that Muslims and others too no doubt, hope to be their final resting-place.

24.   Quoted by Sajjad Kausar in *Shalamar Garden, Lahore: Landscape, Form and Meaning* (Islamabad: Department of Archaeology and Museums, Ministry of Culture, Pakistan, 1990), 74.

25.   Smith, *The World's Religions*, 222.

26.   Burckhardt, *Art of Islam*, 75.

27.   Ibid., 46.

28.   See D. Fairchild Ruggles, *Gardens, Landscape and Vision in the Palaces of Islamic Spain* (University Park, Pennsylvania: Pennsylvania State University, 2000), 218–219.

29.   William Morris, the principal figure of the Arts and Crafts Movement, understood this point very well. His dictum, "Everything in the home should be both useful and beautiful" is a faint echo of the traditional perspective.

30.   Frithjof Schuon, *The Transfiguration of Man* (Bloomington, Indiana: World Wisdom Books, 1995), 103.

12

The Qur'anic Symbolism of Water

Martin Lings

In the Qur'an, the ideas of mercy and water—in particular, rain—are in a sense inseparable. With them must be included the idea of Revelation (*tanzil*), which means literally "a sending down." The Revelation and the rain are both "sent down" by God the All Merciful. Both Revelation and rain are described throughout the Qur'an as "mercy" and both are spoken of as "life-giving." So close is the connection of ideas that rain might even be said to be an integral part of the Revelation, which it prolongs, as it were, in order that by penetrating the material world the divine mercy may reach the uttermost confines of creation.[1] To perform the religious rite of ablution with water is to identify oneself, in the world of matter, with this wave of mercy, and to return with it as it ebbs back toward the principle, for purification is a return to our origins. Islam—literally "submission"—is not other than nonresistance to the pull of the current of this ebbing wave.

The origin and end of this wave lie in the Treasuries (*khaza'in*) of Water, which are "with Him [God]" (Qur'an 15:21). The Treasuries of Mercy are also spoken of in just the same terms, and it is clear that these treasuries are no less than the supreme source of mercy Himself, *al-Rahman,* God the Infinitely Good. The Qur'an also speaks of its own archetype, the "Mother of the Book" (Qur'an 13:39), which is divine omniscience, this treasury cannot be set apart from those of mercy, for it likewise belongs to *al-Rahman,* who is the source of the Book: "The Infinitely Good taught the Qur'an" (Qur'an 55:1). We have already seen the connection between mercy and comprehension, and the Treasuries of Water comprise both of these aspects of *al-Rahman,* for water is a symbol of knowledge as well as well of mercy. Abu Hamid al-Ghazali remarks in *Mishkat al-Anwar* ("The Niche of Lights") with regard to the verse, "[God] sends down water from heaven, so that valleys are in flood with it, each according to its capacity" (Qur'an 13:17), that the commentaries tell us that the "water" is Gnosis[2] and that the "valleys" are hearts.

The differentiation here is in the varying capacities of the valleys, not in the water itself, which comes directly from above and has yet to undergo the influences of soil, stone, or mineral. But water which comes up from the earth is in fact differentiated, so that it symbolizes different aspects of knowledge as in the following verse of the Qur'an: "And when Moses asked for water for his people, we said: 'Strike with thy staff the rock.' And there gushed forth from it twelve springs, and everyone knew his drinking place" (Qur'an 2:60). The differentiation here is not only in the drinkers but also in what they drink. The last five words of this verse are quoted throughout Islamic literature to refer, beyond their literal meaning, to the fact that everyone who "drinks" from the Qur'an is aware of the particular standpoint that has been providentially allotted to him whether it be that of ritual law, for example, dogmatic theology, or mysticism. It is not out of line with the literal meaning of the verse, if one remembers that in ancient Israel, each of the 12 tribes had its own particular function.

When the Qur'an tells us that at the creation, "[God's] Throne was upon the water" (Qur'an 11:7), it affirms implicitly two waters, one above the Throne and one beneath it, since the tenant of the throne is *al-Rahman* (God the Infinitely Good), with Whom are the Treasuries of Water, or rather who constitutes Himself these treasuries. This duality, the waters of the unmanifest and the waters of manifestation, is the prototype of the duality within creation of the "two seas," which are so often mentioned in the Qur'an.[3] These two seas, one sweet and fresh, the other salt and bitter (Qur'an 25:53), are, respectively, Heaven and Earth, which were originally "of one piece" (Qur'an 21:30). Parallel to this and in a sense based on it, is the Sufi symbolism of ice, for salt water and ice, both representing the nontranscendent, are "gross," albeit in different ways, when compared with fresh water. It is also true that the ocean, as the vastest of things in the entire terrestrial globe, has an altogether transcendent significance. When the Qur'an says, "If the sea were ink for the words of thy Lord, the sea would be used up before the words of the Lord were used up" (Qur'an 18:109), it is saying that the symbol is not to be compared with that which it symbolizes, namely, the "Mother of the Book," the Sea of which is in fact vast enough to contain the words of God. Nonetheless, by choosing material seas rather than any other earthly thing for this demonstration, the Qur'an affirms that they are, for the infinitude of the Divine Wisdom, the symbol of symbols; they have this symbolism in virtue of their size, apart from and, as it were, despite their saltiness, for salt water as such is always transcended by fresh water.

The significance of a symbol varies according to whether it is considered as an independent entity or in relation to some other symbol. In relation to wine, water—even fresh water—may represent the untranscendent or the less transcendent, as for example, when the Qur'an mentions that in Paradise the elect are given wine to drink whereas the generality of the faithful drink from fountains of water. This relationship between wine and water is analogous to the relationship between the sun and the moon, for wine is in a sense "liquid fire" or "liquid light"; but fire and water, inasmuch as both are elements, are on the same plane, and it is possible to consider wine and water as equal complements. Thus, in another description of Paradise, the Qur'an mentions rivers of water and rivers of wine (for example, Qur'an 47:15), without specifying any difference of level. Here it may be said that wine, being "warm," has the "subjective" significance of Gnosis in relation to the cold "objectivity" of water, which represents the Truth, the object of Gnosis. But when considered by itself, water has a total significance that transcends the distinction between subject and object, or that includes both subject and object, for inasmuch as it can be drunk, water is a symbol of Truth "subjectivized." That is, Gnosis and water can indeed claim to be "the drink of drinks." In any case, whatever the drink, water is always its basis.

The following passage of the Qur'an, the first part of which has already been quoted in connection with Gnosis, is particularly important for its illustration of the difference between the true and the false, or reality and illusion: "He sends down water from Heaven so that the valleys are in flood with it, each according to its capacity, and the flood bears the swelling foam" (Qur'an 13:17). Thus, God coins the symbols of reality and illusion. "As for the foam, it goes as scum upon the banks, and as for what profits men, it remains in the earth" (Qur'an 13:17). In light of this imagery—of the scum, which remains visible, and the water, which disappears—we may interpret the Qur'anic verse, "They know only an outward appearance of this lower life" (Qur'an 30:7). The "outward appearance" is the scum of illusion, whereas what escapes us in this world is the hidden water of Reality. We see here the significance of the fountain, which holds such an important place in Qur'anic symbolism. The bursting forth of a spring—that is, the reappearance of heaven-sent water that has become hidden—signifies the sudden unveiling of Reality, which transcends outward appearance, and the drinking of which is Gnosis. But in addition to this objective–subjective symbolism, the fountain also has the purely subjective significance of the sudden opening of an eye, which is implicit in the Arabic word 'ayn, which means both "eye" and "fountain" [or "spring"]. This subjective symbolism is in a sense more important, because the reason why men see only the scum of illusion is that their hearts are hardened; in other words, "the eye of the heart" is closed, "for verily it is not the sight that is blind but the hearts that are blind" (Qur'an 22:47). In one highly suggestive passage, the Qur'an compels us to envisage the possibility of a fountain springing from the heart: "Then even after that, your hearts grew hard so that they were like rocks, or even harder, for verily there are rocks from which rivers gush forth, and there are rocks which split asunder so that water flows from them" (Qur'an 2:74).

The presence of "a barrier beyond which they pass not" (Qur'an 55:20) between the two seas means that the waters of this world are unable to overflow into the next world and that the upper waters refrain from utterly overwhelming the lower waters. Instead, they allow them to exit as a seemingly separate domain without undue interference from above, at any rate "for a while"—to use the Qur'anic phrase, which is so often repeated to denote the impermanence of this world and everything in it. "Undue" is a necessary reservation, because the upper waters by their very nature cannot altogether be kept out of the lower waters, any more than water—to revert to the Sufi symbolism—can be kept out of ice. The upper waters, being the original substance of all creation, not only surround but also penetrate this world as its secret reality, to which it will eventually return. Thus, although the rain, symbolizing this penetration, is only sent down "in due measure," it is nonetheless the herald or portent of the hour—that is, the last day, when the barrier will be removed and the upper waters will flood this world, transforming its nature and causing the resurrection of the dead, for they are Waters of Life.[4]

Until then, any presence of life in this world means that a drop of these waters has passed the barrier, but this possibility is limited. "Verily, this lower life is but as water, which we have sent down from the sky" (Qur'an 10:24). Life is altogether transcendent in relation to this world, where it exists merely as a fleeting loan, ready to "evaporate" back whence it came as water evaporates back to the sky. Life is a passing trespass of the Beyond in the domain of the here below, a brief penetration of soul and body by the Spirit.[5] However, the Spirit is not "at home" in this world—hence the extreme precariousness of life—whereas it is indeed at home in the Beyond: "Verily, the Abode of the Hereafter, that is Life, did they but know" (Qur'an 29:64).[6]

If it were asked how this symbolism of water could be reconciled with the Earth-depopulating Flood, it must be remembered that although rainfall set the Flood in motion, the actual cataclysm is represented in the Qur'an as a stormy sea. One of Noah's sons who was drowned is said to have been swept away by a wave: agitated water is a symbol of vanity and illusion, the waves being images of accident and vicissitude, which are unreal in relation to the water itself, whose true nature they are powerless to affect.[7] It is significant that in the Verse of Darkness (Qur'an 24:40), which follows close on the better-known Verse of Light (Qur'an 24:35), the works of the infidels, having just been likened in their vanity to "a mirage in the desert which the thirsty man supposes to be water" (Qur'an 24:39), are then likened to water that has become "by accident" so remote from its true nature as to be comparable to a mirage—namely a dark, storm-tossed sea. This passage may even be taken as an inexplicit description of the Flood. In any case, there is no doubt that the waves of the flood and the waves of the Red Sea, which crashed down upon the pursuers of the Children of Israel, are a just "payment in kind" for the passionate perversity of Noah's contemporaries and of Pharaoh and his ministers. On the other hand, as regards what set the Flood in motion, the symbolism of rain is here tempered and conditioned by the number forty, which signifies death or a change of state.[8] Thus, the purifying aspect of water may be said to take precedence here over its life-giving aspect. The Earth was to be purified for a new state as the Children of Israel were to be purified by 40-years' wandering in the desert. We may also compare the purification of Lent. The waters of the Flood were an inseparable part of the Revelation made to Noah of a new religion—which is symbolized by the Ark—and as such, were waters of mercy.

Any manifestation of the Transcendent is bound to be terrible for those who refuse it, for it serves to gauge the extreme hardness of their hearts. On the other hand, for those whose hearts are not hardened, the Transcendent is always awe-inspiring; this aspect of mercy is expressed by thunder, which so often precedes the rain. "He it is who shows you the lightning, a fear and longing, and raises the heavy clouds. And the thunder extols and praises Him, as do the angels for awe of Him" (Qur'an 13:12–13).

The awe-inspiring and mysterious transcendence of the upper waters, as also their life-giving aspect, is stressed in the strange and elliptical story of Moses and al-Khidr (Qur'an 18:60–82). Moses says to Joshua: "I will not cease until I reach the meeting place of the two seas" (Qur'an 18:60). They start out as for a long journey, but they stop at a rock, which is, unknown to them, that barrier that separates the two seas. Joshua sets down for a moment the provisions he has brought, which consist of dried fish. Whether because of the extreme nearness of the Waters of Life, or because a drop of these waters actually falls on the fish, it suddenly comes to life, slips from the rock, and swims away in the sea. Moses does not notice this; and the attention of Joshua who does notice it, is immediately distracted by Satan, so that he does not mention it to Moses, and they set off once more. At length Moses, exhausted by the journey, suggests that they stop to eat. Joshua remembers that their food is gone and tells Moses about the miracle of the fish. Moses understands that the rock must have been the meeting place of the two seas, and so they retrace their steps. When they regain the rock, they find there "one of [God's] slaves unto whom We had given mercy from Our mercy and knowledge from Our knowledge" (Qur'an 18:65). This person is not named, but the commentaries tell us that it is al-Khidr, the immortal Prince of the Solitary Ones (al-afrad).[9] The symbolism of this meeting with Moses is parallel to the symbolism of the meeting of the two seas. The salt sea of this world represents, like Moses, exoteric knowledge, whereas the Waters of Life are personified by al-Khidr.[10] "Moses said unto him: 'May I follow you so that from what you have been taught you may teach me right guidance?' He said: 'Verily you cannot be patient with me, for how should you be patient in respect of that which is beyond the compass of your experience?' He said: 'God wiling, you shall find me patient, nor will I gainsay you in anything.' He said: 'Then if you go with me, question me not, until of myself I mention it to you'" (Qur'an 18:66–70).

They set out together, and al-Khidr performs three acts of mercy in disguise; but Moses, seeing only the "scandalous" outside of these acts, is too outraged not to expostulate each time. The third time, al-Khidr refuses to let Moses accompany him any further; but he explains, before they part company, the true nature of his actions. To consider this passage in any detail would be beyond the scope of our subject; but it has at least given us a glimpse of the deviousness of the exoteric path and the extreme nearness of the Waters of Life. For we are already, if only we knew it, at "the meeting place of the two seas"—witness the miracle of life that is always with us, both in us and about us, but for which the powers of illusion persuade us to take entirely for granted.

In setting before us this strange example of inadvertence and forgetfulness in respect of the marvelous incident of the fish, the Qur'an lays bare the general obtuseness of man's attitude toward life. There is only one life, that of the Living, in varying degrees of radiation, with a mere difference of intensity between the elixir that is strong enough to quicken a dried fish and the less strong elixir that suffices to enable the living to continue to "eke out for awhile" their precarious earthly existence. It is thus grossly disproportionate to marvel at the one and to remain unmoved by the other. There can be no true wisdom that does not include the enlightenment of seeing life as the miracle that it is, a supernatural interference that cannot be claimed by nature as a purely natural phenomenon. Shaikh Ahmad al-'Alawi (d. 1934) tells us that the divine mystery and miracle of life eludes us because of its extreme transcendence. It is with us, and yet at the same time it is utterly beyond us.[11] The spiritual path is in one sense not so much a journey as a gradual attunement of the soul to the presence of the Spirit, a gradual reconciliation between the natural and the supernatural, between the lower waters and the upper waters, between mind and intellect, and between Moses and al-Khidr.

In conclusion, let us consider another relevant passage, which is from the story of Solomon and the Queen of Sheba (Qur'an 27:23–44). Solomon sends for the Queen in order to convert her to the true religion, and while she and her retinue are on their way, he says to his surrounding assembly of men and jinn: "Which of you will bring me her throne before they come unto me in surrender" (Qur'an 27:38)? The throne is immediately set before him, and he gives instructions for it to be disguised:

> Disguise her throne for her; we shall see if she is on the right path, or if she is of those who are not rightly guided. And when she came it was said unto her: "Is your throne like unto this?" She said: "It is as if it were it." And Solomon reflected, "We had been given knowledge before her and had surrendered unto God; and she was barred from it by what she was wont to worship apart from God. Verily, she was from a disbelieving people." She was told: "Enter the courtyard." And when she saw it she reckoned it to be a pool of water and bared

her legs. He said: "It is a courtyard made smooth with glass." She said: "Oh my Lord, verily I have done wrong unto my soul, and I surrender with Solomon unto God, the Lord of the Worlds."

(Qur'an 27:41–44)

The gist of what this exceedingly elliptical narration tells us is that Solomon puts Bilqis—for so the Queen of Sheba is named—to two tests. She fails in both, but her failure dissolves altogether her resistance to the Truth. This in itself would require no comment. It is true that the mistakes in question are, on the surface, totally innocent. Moreover, as regards the throne, she appears to see at least partially through the disguise, since otherwise her answer would have been simply, "No." Nonetheless, it is easily imaginable that the consciousness of being mistaken might well have a profound effect upon the soul, out of all proportion to the nature of her error. However, the apparent simplicity of the facts is belied by the gravity of the Qur'an's comments on them, and the depth of the conclusions that are drawn. We are obliged to suspect that it is not merely a question of error as such, but that the particular nature of the error is all-important.

In both cases, it is a question of the failure to penetrate through a disguise. What Solomon says about his purpose in disguising the throne could be glossed: we shall see if she penetrates to the truth of things or if she is one of those who stop short at the "scum" of illusion. This gloss could also be applied to the other disguise, that of the courtyard. The "scum" in this case is the illusion that water is present when in fact it is absent. But what is the knowledge that Solomon was given "before her," and of which the condition is that he had "surrendered unto God?" It could not simply be what the words literally suggest—his knowledge that the throne was in fact that of Sheba, and that the courtyard was in fact paved with glass. Such knowledge was no more credit to him than the lack of it was a discredit to her. But we are given a key in the reason why "she was barred from it," namely, her worship of false gods. It was because she had taken illusion to be reality that she took reality to be illusion; that is, she had taken identity to be a mere deceptive likeness. Having demonstrated this last error—for although the Qur'an does not say so, we must assume that Solomon tells her that the throne is in fact hers and that what she had thought to be no more than a vague resemblance is indeed identity—he proceeds to demonstrate the opposite error that is its cause, which is her worship of false gods, her imagining divinity to be present when in fact it was absent. Here lies undoubtedly what might be called the allegorical meaning of the above-quoted verses. We must remember that when this passage was revealed, the Prophet Muhammad was undergoing great difficulties for the very reason that the chief men of Mecca were blinded to the presence of truth in his message by their erroneous belief that the truth was present elsewhere, in their own worship of false gods. There are many other passages in the Qur'an that likewise recount a historical incident that is, in one way or another, analogous to the situation of early seventh-century Arabia. Solomon here stands for the Prophet, and Bilqis sums up in herself the erring leaders of the clans of [the Prophet's tribe] Quraysh, who would not surrender to the One True God because of their involvement with a plurality of false gods. But this allegorical admonition to the chieftains of Mecca and example of repentance that it holds out to them leaves room for a deeper interpretation that throws light on some of the details that the allegory does not account for.

The Supreme Throne is below [God] its Tenant, but by inverse analogy every earthly throne may be said to transcend the king who sits on it, as is seen figured in the Seal of Solomon, if we take the apex of a triangle to be the tenant and its base the throne. Significant of the throne's transcendence is its oneness and permanence: kings come and go but their throne remains, ideally forever unchanged. The question of the throne of Sheba is not a part of the Qur'anic narrative that is directly relevant to our theme; but it cannot be set to one side, for it serves to bring out a point of general importance, namely, that a symbol that represents the Transcendent may be said to open out virtually onto the Absolute Transcendent.[12] The higher of the two seas is, strictly speaking, no more than the uppermost part of the created universe. However, the Waters of Life, as seen from below, are merged with the Treasuries of Water—that is, with the Infinite Beatitude. Since there is a certain analogy between the pairs Heaven–Earth ("the two seas") and Throne–King, the throne may be said to signify not merely the mandate of heaven, but also the source of that mandate, the Divine King, and thus ultimately the Supreme Self.

In considering Solomon's first test, it must not be forgotten that Bilqis is a queen. Her first lapse has thus to be defined, in all accuracy, as that of a queen who fails to recognize her own throne, and seen in this light it takes on a more serious aspect. Moreover, like the lapse of Moses and Joshua with regard to the miracle of the quickening of the dried fish, the incident of the throne has a general application for every man, who is by definition King of the Earth and thereby the possessor of a throne that is his mandate from Heaven. Even in these later times, men are still conscious of being kings, inasmuch as they have powers of intelligence and of will that incomparably surpass those of other creatures. However, the majority are more or less in a state of vagueness and uncertainty about their throne, and more or less forgetful that although it—that is, the mandate—is always veiled from them or "disguised," it is always one and the same. In other words, they are no longer kings except by virtuality; in actuality, they are usurpers, since veritable kingship implies an, as it were, organic connection between king and throne. For the perfect king the mandate, not his human subjectivity, is his true ego, one with the Divine Self. The failure to recognize the throne is thus a violation of the precept of Gnosis, "Know thyself," whereas fulfillment of this principle is "the knowledge" that Solomon had been given, and of which the condition is surrender (Islam) in its highest sense: that is, effacement of the human ego before the Supreme Subject.

The precise words with which Bilqis answers the question that is put to her are subtly significant in this respect, subtly because there is here a disguise, which is in a sense analogous to that of the throne. It is permissible to say, for example, that in such a sentence as "When asked the color of snow, the blind man said it was black," the word "white" is disguisedly present, because it is forced into the mind. So also, when the Queen is asked, "Is your throne like this?" and when she wrongly answers, "It is as if it were it," the right answer is forced into our minds: namely, "It is it." The Arabic words, *huwa huwa* literally mean, "He is he," for *'arsh*, "throne," is masculine. They also constitute the Arabic formula for expressing identity, and above all, liturgically, the Supreme Identity.[13]

As to Solomon's second test, which serves to demonstrate why Bilqis could not recognize her throne, the meaning remains much the same as in the allegorical interpretation. Here, however, what seems to be present but is in fact absent is the Truth as Object, whereas it is rather a question of Truth in the sense of Subjective Reality. In either case, we are reminded of the already-quoted verse that likens the works of disbelievers to "a mirage in the desert that the thirsty man supposes to be water." It will be understood from this and the other examples given of the symbolism of water why Solomon's strategy is so powerfully successful. When Bilqis lifts up her robes to avoid wetting them and steps onto the glass pavement of the court, the sudden contact of her foot with the opposite of what it had expected is directly sensed as the experience of error, which is enough in itself to produce a profound "alchemical" effect upon the soul. But this effect is aggravated beyond all measures by her consciousness that the error is, precisely, about water. Thus, her whole outlook, already shaken by her first mistake, is transformed in a moment from heresy to orthodoxy by the shock of discovering the "water" to be absent, where she had believed it to be present. In her saying, "I surrender with Solomon," these last two words are an indication that her surrender is to be understood in the same highest sense as his surrender—namely, the effacement of the self before the Self, which is the condition of his Gnosis.

NOTES

This chapter first appeared in Martin Lings, *Symbol and Archetype: A Study of the Meaning of Existence* (Louisville, Kentucky: Fons Vitae, 2005). Slight editorial changes have been made to the original for consistency of style and for purposes of clarification. The general editor of this set thanks Virginia Gray Henry-Blakemore of Fons Vitae for permission to reproduce this work.

1. Far from being a "concrete" image arbitrarily chosen by man to illustrate some "abstract" idea, a symbol is the manifestation, in some lower mode, of the higher

reality that it symbolizes and that stands in as close relationship to it as the root of a tree to a leaf. Thus, water is Mercy, and it would be true to say this even without any understanding of symbolism and even without belief in the Transcendent. Immersion in water has an inevitable effect on the soul in addition to its purification of the body. In the absence of ritual intention, this effect may be altogether momentary and superficial; it is nonetheless visible in the fact of almost any bather emerging from a lake or river or sea, however, quickly it may be effaced by the resumption of "ordinary life."

2.   *Gnosis* is the direct and immediate knowledge of God. This word, which is derived from the Greek verb "to know," is commonly used as the English equivalent of the Arabic *ma'rifa,* which literally means "knowledge." Sufis use *ma'rifa* to refer to the kind of knowledge that transcends formal, "book" learning or knowledge in general, which in Arabic is *'ilm.* (Ed.)

3.   In Genesis, too, the pure primordial substance of the created universe is water: "The Spirit of God moved upon the face of the waters." The same is true of the duality, which also appears in Genesis: "[God] divided the waters" (Gen. 1:7–8).

4.   "And you see the earth as barren and when we send down upon it water it thrills and sprouts. That is because...the Hour is coming beyond all doubt and because God raises those who are in the tombs" (Qur'an 22:5).

5.   To speak of death as "a giving up of the ghost" is thus altogether correct, and it is because life is a presence of Spirit, and therefore altogether transcendent, that it defines any scientific analysis.

6.   The great symbol of life is also very precarious over much of the earth's face, especially in those regions where the Qur'anic Revelation was first received.

7.   Ice and waves are parallel as symbols, representing, respectively, the rigidity (or brittleness) and instability of this form-bound world.

8.   The Arabic letter *mim* stands for death (*mawt*) and has the numerical value of 40. However, this letter and this number also have the sense of reconciliation and return to the principle. It is said that Seth was able to return to the Earthly Paradise and that he remained there for 40 years. See Rene Guenon, *The Lord of the World* (Ellingstring, Yorkshire, 1983), chap. 5.

9.   The *Afrad* are the few exceptional individuals who are independent of any particular religion but who represent religion in its highest aspect, being, without any effort on their part but by their very nature, as it were, throwbacks to the primordial state of man, which it is the purpose of religion to regain.

10.   The Qur'an here as it were traces from Moses only the symbolism of the lower waters, passing over his more exalted aspects, which are themes of other passages.

11.   See Martin Lings, *A Sufi Saint of the Twentieth Century: Shaikh Ahmad al-'Alawi, His Spiritual Heritage and Legacy* (Berkeley and Los Angeles: University of California Press, 1973), 134, 1n.

12.   This is an altogether universal principle of the highest practical significance. In Hinduism, for example, either Shiva or Vishnu may be invoked as Absolute, although their hierarchic station is at the level of the higher of the two seas.

13.   On this point, see Lings, *A Sufi Saint of the Twentieth Century,* 114, 2n.

13

ISLAMIC LITERATURES: WRITING IN THE SHADE OF THE QUR'AN

Shawkat M. Toorawa

The adjective "Islamic" has come both to denote practices related to the religion of Islam—such as Islamic law, Islamic dress, and the Islamic calendar—and to connote broader cultural phenomena arising from the civilization of Islam—such as Islamic architecture, Islamic medicine, and Islamic Spain. In the rubric "Islamic literatures," although the latter broader usage seems to be implied, the former narrower one is usually meant. Indeed, the term "Islamic literatures" in the wider sense is little used, although it is to be found in the title of James Kritzeck's *Anthology of Islamic Literature*[1] and in an article in the *Encyclopaedia Britannica* by Anne-Marie Schimmel, a noted scholar of Iranian and Indian Islam, who observes that the term "Islamic literatures" "virtually defies any comprehensive definition."[2] In 1986, the Pakistani English-language poet and critic Alamgir Hashmi circumvented the vexed question of the use of the adjective "Islamic" by calling his anthology of "modern and contemporary literature of the Islamic lands" *The Worlds of Muslim Imagination.*[3] His stated concern was with "the Muslim imagination, its literary engagements and manifestations, but not with Islamic pieties."[4]

"Islamic literature," then, is best understood as the *total* literary output of Muslims and those influenced by Islamic civilization. Accordingly, it comprises works in Arabic, Chinese, Hausa, Indonesian, Persian, Swahili, Turkish, Urdu, and dozens of other languages, including English. This output encompasses everything from the Qur'an,[5] an Arabic scripture that emerged with Islam in the Arabian Peninsula in the seventh century CE, to the Hebrew poetry of the Iberian Judah Halevi (d. 1145 CE),[6] to the fifteenth century Sundiata (Son-Jara) Epic of Mali,[7] to *Noor,* an English-language novel by the U.S.-based Pakistani writer Sorayya Khan.[8] Limitations of space do not permit such a comprehensive survey here. Instead, using the Qur'an as something of an axis, this chapter highlights a sampling of genres, writers, and works, with less of an emphasis on poetry as this has typically received greater attention in surveys, scholarship, and translation.[9]

In 978 CE, the Baghdad bookseller Ibn al-Nadim published *al-Fihrist* (The Catalogue), a comprehensive and annotated list of every book that he was aware of that had *ever* been written in Arabic or translated into Arabic.[10] This work has provided posterity with invaluable information about works that no longer survive (estimated at a staggering and depressing 98 percent of all works written in Islamic languages) and about the ways in which Muslims of the tenth century CE—during the so-called Golden Age of Arabo-Islamic culture—viewed their literatures. Ibn al-Nadim divides the literatures of his time into 10 categories, as follows:

1. Languages and scripts; scriptures of Muslims and other "Peoples of the Book"
2. Grammar and lexicography
3. History, belles-lettres, biography, genealogy
4. Poetry
5. Scholastic theology
6. Law and Hadith
7. Philosophy and the "ancient sciences"
8. Stories, legends, romances; magic, conjuring
9. Doctrines of the non-monotheistic creeds
10. Alchemy

Not surprisingly, script, scripture, and grammar have pride of place, appearing at the beginning of the work and altogether accounting for one-fifth of the whole catalogue. Though the *Fihrist* includes books from other languages, it only mentions these if they were translated into Arabic from their original sources. Knowledge of Arabic then, as now, was a premium for Muslims. Today, in the early twenty-first century CE, only 20 percent of the Muslim world speaks Arabic natively and an even smaller percentage is fully literate in the language. However, Arabic is just as necessary today as it was in Ibn al-Nadim's day for anyone interested in the study of Islamic civilization.[11] Knowledge of Arabic gives one access to the Qur'an in its original language, as well as to a vast output of religious and nonreligious scholarship. The *Fihrist* was itself the product of nonreligious scholarship, written by a man who was a courtier (or the son of a courtier) and a bookman. Such scholarship was possible because of the explosion of translation and writing since the ninth century CE. This birth of multiple literary forms was to a large extent due to the availability of paper,[12] a Chinese import, which in turn resulted in the various kinds of "Islamic literatures" that Ibn al-Nadim recorded.

By definition, the first example of Islamic literature is the Qur'an, a series of revelations in Arabic believed by Muslims to have emanated from God, and orally transmitted by the Archangel Gabriel to the Prophet Muhammad from the year 610 CE until Muhammad's death in 632 CE. These revelations, which were in Arabic, Muhammad's native language, were memorized and written down piecemeal by his followers, and were subsequently collected and collated into a written codex (*mushaf*). This canonizing of the "text" into what was effectively the very first Islamic book is traditionally believed to have taken place in the 650s.[13]

The Qur'an is organized into *Sura*s ("chapters"), more or less from the longest to the shortest—with the notable exception of the opening chapter, which is only seven *ayat* ("verses") long. *Sura*s are read or recited from memory in whole or in part; many pious Muslims memorize the whole Qur'an. Through its admonitory narratives of past revelations and its exemplary stories, the Qur'an also functions as a blueprint for a good and righteous life.[14] In addition to its liturgical and didactic functions, the Qur'an is also a source of law: roughly 600 of its approximately 6,200 verses are legislative. One major work on the probative nature of these legal verses was the *Risala* (Treatise) of Muhammad ibn Idris al-Shafi'i (d. 820 CE).[15]

The influence of the Qur'an on the scholarship, artistic output, and philosophy of the Islamic world, both Arab and non-Arab, is immeasurable. Its appearance accounts for the development of the Arabic script, a writing system that came to be used by almost all Muslim people. For example, Modern Persian (Farsi)—an Indo-European language—is written in Arabic script, as are the Central Asian languages Uighur and Pushtu, the South Asian language Urdu, and the African language Hausa. In the past, Arabic script was used to write Ottoman Turkish and Malay, whose Arabic script was called *Jawi* (Ar. "Javanese"). Arabic script also formed the basis for one of Islamic art and architecture's most recognizable features, Arabic calligraphy. Some modern artists today use Arabic calligraphy and other media to interpret Islamic literatures. The Algerian artist Rachid Koreïchi, for instance, has installations devoted to the Arabic works of the Andalusian Sufi Ibn 'Arabi (d. 1240 CE) and the Persian works of the Sufi Mevlana Jalaluddin Rumi (d. 1273 CE). Ibn 'Arabi's works of metaphysical Sufism are widely read, such as his *Fusus al-Hikam* (Bezels of Wisdom).[16] Rumi is the author of the influential *Divan-e Shams-e Tabriz* (The Complete Works of "Shams of Tabriz"), a 40,000 verse collection comprising quatrains (*ruba'iyyat*) and love poems (*ghazal*s), and the *Masnavi Ma'navi* (Spiritual Couplets), a poetic work of more than 25,000 couplets that is often called the most important work of Islamic literature after the Qur'an. Some mystics have even called Rumi's *Masnavi* the "Persian Qur'an," for its simplicity and profundity.[17]

Most Muslim scholars argue that by virtue of being God's word, the Qur'an is the pinnacle of literary perfection. Some concede that it is poetic in form, but they have almost unanimously rejected the idea that it is poetry. Indeed, the Qur'an itself points out that the Prophet Muhammad was not a poet (Qur'an 36:29). This is a polemical statement, however, made in the context of attacks on Muhammad by detractors for being a soothsayer inspired by supernatural forces, or a poet inspired by a supernatural muse. To Muhammad are attributed negative statements about Imru'l-Qays (d. ca. 540 CE), the great sixth-century Arab poet (who is still considered, incidentally, the greatest of all Arab poets), and whose poem "Stop, you two, and let us weep" is one of the seven Pre-Islamic classics, the *Mu'allaqat,* or so-called Suspended Odes.[18] Imru'l-Qays was a *bon vivant* whose lifestyle was certainly not in keeping with the Prophet Muhammad's moderate views. However, Muhammad himself had panegyrists of whom he approved, such as Hassan ibn Thabit (d. ca. 660 CE) and Ka'b ibn Zuhayr (fl. seventh century CE), whose "Su'ad has left" poem Muhammad so cherished that he gave Ka'b his mantle. For this reason, the poem came to be known as *Qasidat al-Burda,* "The Mantle Ode." In the thirteenth century, the Egyptian poet Busiri (d. ca. 1294 CE) wrote an expanded commentary in verse on Ka'b's poem. Though arguably of less literary value than the original, the circumstances of its writing—the paralyzed Busiri composed it after dreaming that the Prophet cured him when he placed his mantle upon him—have made it one of the most popular pieces of literature across the Islamic world. There are commentaries, super-commentaries, and imitations of this work in dozens of languages, and it is even used as a protective amulet.[19]

Debates about the nature of the Qur'an occasioned numerous works of theology and philosophy, some in the context of the infamous ninth-century "inquisition" by the Caliph al-Ma'mun (d. 833 CE), a leader remembered not only for his partiality for rationalist Greek philosophy but also for the translation of non-Arabic writings into Arabic, an activity he enthusiastically patronized.[20] Much Greek material, from Galen's medical treatises to Aristotle's philosophical ones, was rendered into Arabic by Christian translators, such as the Nestorian physician Hunayn ibn Ishaq (d. ca. 873 CE).[21] Middle Persian advice literature and wisdom literature were translated by Muslim Persian writers; many of them were state secretaries in the Caliphal administration.[22] Ibn al-Muqaffa' (d. 759 CE), for example, translated the Pahlavi work *Khwaday-Namag* (Book of Kings).[23] A verse rendering of this history, the *Shahnameh* (Epic of Kings), was made at the end of the tenth century CE by the poet Ferdowsi (d. 1020 CE) and is one of the masterpieces of Persian literature (eclipsing his other works, including his poem, "Yusuf and Zulaykha").[24] Ibn al-Muqaffa' also made famous the stories of *Kalila wa Dimna,* a collection of moral fables originally by the Indian writer Bidpai. Through such translations, Arabic literature, and later the literatures of Africa, Asia, and Europe, acquired many stories, some of which, like *Kalila wa Dimna,* emanated from the Sanskrit literary tradition.[25] Ibn al-Muqaffa' is also credited, perhaps apocryphally, with trying to imitate the Qur'an. Previously, one contemporary of the Prophet Muhammad had mocked the Prophet by saying that the stories he himself knew from the glorious Persian past were superior to the ones Muhammad was bringing in the Qur'an. This taunt is said to have occasioned the revelation of *Surat Yusuf* (Qur'an 12, "Joseph"), the only Qur'anic chapter that is a discrete and continuous narrative, and the inspiration for numerous works describing the romance between Yusuf (Joseph) and Zulaykha, Potiphar's wife.[26] The only major rival to this romance in Islamic literature is the story of the star-crossed Arab lovers Layla and Majnun, which was popularized in works such as the Persian poet Nizami's (d. 1209 CE) *Leyli va Majnun*. This story was even the inspiration for Eric Clapton's rock song, "Layla."[27] Popular South Asian romances that fall under the "Islamic" rubric include the Urdu *Dastan-e Amir Hamza* (Romance of Prince Hamza), inspired by the exploits of Hamza ibn 'Abd al-Muttalib, the Prophet Muhammad's uncle and an early martyr of Islam, and the Panjabi *Heer Ranjha* by Waris Shah (d. 1766 CE).[28] In Panjabi too is the mystical love poetry of Sultan Bahu, which is still sung today in such devotional musical forms as *qawwali* and *kaafi*.[29]

The need to understand the language of the Qur'an, accompanied by the need to understand the intent of the Prophet Muhammad's statements and actions, occasioned wider and deeper study in fields that later came to be known as "the Islamic sciences." These consisted of lexicography (*lugha*); grammar (*nahw*) and morphology (*tasrif*); metrics (*'arud*), rhyme (*qawafi*), and prosody (*sun'at al-shi'r*); rhetoric (*bayan, balagha*); literary criticism (*naqd*); legal theory and methodology (*usul al-fiqh*) and jurisprudence (*fiqh*); and philological commentary (*sharh, ma'ani, gharib*). This last genre, in a more expanded form, became the "science" of Qur'anic exegesis (*tafsir al-Qur'an*).[30] Scholars regard the monumental Arabic Qur'an commentary *Jami' al-bayan 'an ta'wil ay al-Qur'an* (The Sum of Clarity Concerning the Interpretation of the Verses of the Qur'an) by the Persian scholar Tabari (d. 923 CE) as pivotal because it combined all earlier exegetical traditions and became a major source for later commentaries.[31] Also widely consulted today are the Arabic commentaries of Zamakhshari (d. 1144 CE), Ibn Kathir (d. 1373 CE), and the handy *Tafsir al-Jalalayn* (Commentary of the two Jalals) by Jalal al-Din al-Mahalli (d. 1459 CE) and Jalal al-Din al-Suyuti (d. 1505 CE).[32] The latter work acquired considerable importance in Southeast Asia where it was translated and expanded upon by the Achenese scholar 'Abd al-Ra'uf Singkili (d. 1693 CE) in his Malay-language *Tarjuman al-mustafid* (The Influential Interpreter).[33] Also significant is *the Mafatih al-ghayb* (Keys to the Unseen) of Fakhr al-Din al-Razi (d. 1210 CE), an important theologian often viewed as equal in importance to Ibn Sina (Avicenna, d. 1037 CE) and al-Ghazali (d. 1111 CE). Ibn Sina's *Qanun fi al-tibb* (Canon of Medicine) was in wide use in the Islamic and Christian worlds for centuries, and in his *al-Shifa'* (The Cure), he systematically describes his philosophical views. Ghazali wrote a vigorous refutation of Islamic philosophy titled *Tahafut al-falasifa* (The Incoherence of the Philosophers), directed at Ibn Sina. This was itself refuted in the

Tahafut al-tahafut (The Incoherence of "The Incoherence") by another major philosopher, Ibn Rushd (Averroës) (d. 1198 CE).[34]

Ghazali held the chair in Islamic law at the premier law school of the day, the Madrasa Nizamiyya, founded by Nizam al-Mulk (d. 1092 CE), the vizier to the Seljuq Turkish rulers. Nizam al-Mulk was an author in his own right, notably of a Persian treatise on kingship, the *Siyasat Nameh* (Book of Government).[35] Like his patron, Ghazali wrote a work in the "mirror for princes" genre, the *Nasihat al-muluk* (Advice to Kings). Nizam al-Mulk, Ghazali, and the Ismaili missionary Hassan-i Sabbah (d. 1124 CE) are protagonists, together with the Persian mathematician-poet Omar Khayyam (d. 1131 CE)—whose quatrains have eclipsed his cubic equations—in the French novel *Samarcande* by Amin Maalouf, one of the few writers anywhere writing historical novels about authors of Islamic literature.[36] Ghazali's slim autobiographical treatise *al-Munqidh min al-dalal* (Deliverance from Error) is widely read, and his magisterial *Ihya' 'ulum al-din* (Revival of the Religious Sciences) has been instrumental in bridging the (apparent) rift between Islamic orthodoxy and Sufism.[37] Eight centuries later, Muhammad Iqbal (d. 1938 CE), an Indian poet and philosopher, published *The Reconstruction of Religious Thought in Islam*, based on a series of university lectures. He is also the author of the Hindustani national song, *Saare jahan se achcha* (The Finest in the World).

Important recent commentaries on the Qur'an include the Ottoman Ismail Hakkı Bursevi's (d. 1725 CE) *Ruh al-bayan* (The Soul of Eloquence), the Moroccan Sufi Ibn 'Ajiba's (d. 1809 CE) *al-Bahr al-Madid* (The Expansive Sea), Sir Sayyid Ahmad Khan's (d. 1898 CE) Urdu *Kanz-ul-iman* (The Treasure of Faith)—he is also the first Muslim to write a commentary (partial) on the Bible, Fadhlalla Haeri's English series *Keys to the Qur'an*[38] and Amin Ahsan Islahi's (d. 1997) Urdu *Tadabbur-i Qur'an* (The Organization of the Qur'an), which advances a theory of the Qur'an's structure and morphology in its canonical form based on the work of Farahi (d. 1930).[39] Although no full-length commentary on the Qur'an by a woman has yet appeared, three U.S.-based female scholars have recently given the Qur'an systematic attention: the African American convert Amina Wadud, the Pakistani-American Asma Barlas, and the Syrian Nimat Barazangi.[40] The Egyptian scholar 'Aisha 'Abd al-Rahman (d. 1974 CE) published the first partial commentary on the Qur'an by a woman, under her pen name Bint al-Shati' ("Daughter of the Seashore"). Bint al-Shati' also edited the *Risalat al-ghufran* (Epistle on Pardon) by the marvelous medieval Arab poet Ma'arri (d. 1057 CE).[41] The *Risalat al-ghufran* recounts the encounter of its protagonist (the work's addressee) with people in Paradise and Hell, into which Ma'arri casts the allegedly heretical poet Bashshar ibn Burd (d. 784 CE), among others. This is ironic, as Ma'arri was also accused of heresy and was, like Bashshar, blind. Ma'arri's *al-Fusul wa al-ghayat* (Paragraphs and Periods), because it is in rhymed prose, has been seen by some as a blasphemous imitation of the Qur'an, but the charge is no doubt an attempt to disparage this gifted author.

Commentaries on the Qur'an inspired commentaries and super-commentaries in other fields too, such as poetry and grammar. The first major Arabic book after the Qur'an was *al-Kitab* (The Book) of Sibawayhi (d. ca. 795 CE), a systematic study of Arabic grammar.[42] Countless grammar books followed, culminating in such works as the versified Arabic grammar *al-Alfiyya* (The Thousand-liner) by the Andalusian Ibn Malik (d. 1274 CE); *al-Ajurumiyya*, the Moroccan Berber Ibn Ajurum's (d. 1323 CE) eponymous condensation of all the rules of Arabic grammar; and *Bahth al-matalib* (Discussion of Grammatical Questions) by the Archbishop of Aleppo, Jermanus Farhat (d. 1732 CE). By virtue of the fact that Arabic was the language of scholarship for much of the Muslim world well into the sixteenth century CE, non-Arabic works before that time were, relatively speaking, less common—but this is not to say that they were less important. Indeed, the interplay of Arabic and Persian in particular is of great significance. Persian may have adopted rhyme patterns, for instance, from Arabic, but it gave to Arabic such forms as lyric poetry and the quatrain. Persian was also used in Muslim India, where it remained the language of culture and administration until 1835. The poet-scholar Azad Bilgrami's (d. 1786 CE) poetry—his panegyric earned him the title Hassan-i Hind (The Hassan [ibn Thabit] of India), likening him to the Prophet Muhammad's panegyrist—and his magnum opus *Subhat al-Marjan* (The Coral Rosary), a major historical–biographical–literary critical work, were in Arabic, but he wrote many more works in Persian.[43]

The Qur'an, as God's word, is held by Muslims as the standard of eloquence. It comes as no surprise therefore that it has been frequently drawn upon, thematically, textually, and structurally.[44] Textual recourse to the Qur'an involves quoting, creatively misquoting, or reworking Qur'anic passages. As might be expected, it is widely quoted by characters in novels and stories. One of the most unusual quotations is in the autobiography of 'Umar ibn Sa'id (d. 1864 CE), a West African slave and former minor Islamic scholar from North Carolina who was urged by abolitionists to write an account of his life. He begins this work, which he wrote in Arabic, with the entire text of *Surat al-Mulk* (Qur'an 67, The Dominion).[45] The modern Syro-Lebanese poet Adonis, who was born in a Shiite Muslim family, also uses Qur'anic passages, often recasting the Qur'an's words and thereby earning the disapproval of pious critics. His most recent work, like the Qur'an resonantly called *al-Kitab* (The Book), has also irked critics.[46]

Thematic recourse to the Qur'an has taken many forms. The most well known are modern uses of Qur'anic themes, such as the Algerian novelist Tahir Wattar's use of the theme of apocalyptic convulsions on Judgment Day in *al-Zilzal* (The Earthquake).[47] This novel is especially interesting for the fact that the protagonist mentions Nobel Prize–winning author Naguib

Mahfouz's *Awlad haratina* (Children of the Alley), one of the few fiction works structurally to draw upon the Qur'an.[48] *Children of the Alley* is divided into five parts, each corresponding to a character evidently based on Qur'anic and Biblical figures, but is also subdivided into 114 chapters, as is the Qur'an. The novel has been misread (and accordingly banned) as an allegorical comment on religion and the death of God. It is, rather, the converse: a reading of modern Egyptian society through the scriptural archetypes. Egyptian playwright Tawfiq al-Hakim's (d. 1987 CE) *Ahl al-kahf* (People of the Cave) is about the Seven Sleepers of Ephesus mentioned in *Surat al-Kahf* (18, The Cave) of the Qur'an.[49] Indonesian-born 'Ali Ahmad Ba-Kathir's (d. 1969) *Harut wa Marut* is about two faultfinding angels; Salman Rushdie's *The Satanic Verses*, like his subsequent *Haroun and the Sea of Stories*, is a thinly veiled critique of contemporary authoritarian Islam (in Britain in the former, in Iran in the latter) through a parody of the Prophet Muhammad and the Angel Gabriel.[50] Whether Rushdie qualifies as a writer of "Islamic Literature" will depend on the pietistic commitments of the person making the decision. Certainly, he merited inclusion in Amin Malak's recent analytical survey, *Muslim Narratives and the Discourse of English*.[51] Other authors in this work illustrate the wide sweep implicit in the notion of postcolonial Islamic literature(s). A partial list includes the Pakistani Ahmed Ali (d. 1994), who was also the translator of a widely available, if only passably good, translation of the Qur'an into English; the Somali Nuruddin Farah; the Tanzanian from Zanzibar Abdulrazak Gurnah; the Tanzanian-Canadian Ismaili writer M.G. Vassanji;[52] and the female authors, the Nigerian Zaynab Alkali and the Malaysian Che Husna Azhari.[53]

The colonial-era encounter of Islamic literatures with the West in the nineteenth century and after, principally (but by no means exclusively) through English, French, and Russian, resulted in the "importation" of the novel and the short story into the Islamic world. The novel in particular started out as a vehicle for nationalist, and sometimes secularist expression, but grew to become a major genre in Islamic literatures. Many novelists chose to write in the colonial language, as the Hashmi anthology and the Malak volume mentioned above record for English. However, prose output thrived in "Islamic" languages too. Suffice to mention here—a survey of this material is certainly a desideratum—some key figures. In Arabic, Mahfouz has been one of the most prolific and admired writers; the 1989 Nobel Prize in Literature merely confirmed his status as the dean of Arabic letters.[54] However, he has not eclipsed other great writers in Arabic, such as the Sudanese Tayeb Salih, whose 1969 *Mawsim al-hijra ila al-shamal* (Season of Migration to the North) is widely viewed as The Great Arabic Novel and is to be found on every list of postcolonial writing. A riposte to the simultaneously seductive and insidious nature of the colonial venture, it is *inter alia* a sophisticated rereading of Joseph Conrad's *Heart of Darkness* and a supple inversion of Shakespeare's *Othello*.[55] It was anticipated in 1961 by the Senegalese writer

Cheikh Hamidou Kane's French novel *L'aventure ambiguë* (The Ambiguous Adventure), which was also about the travel of a protagonist to Europe and the clash of African and Islamic cultures with European culture.[56]

The Saudi-Iraqi Abdel Rahman Munif (d. 2004) wrote poignantly in *Mudun al-milh* (Cities of Salt) about the changes wrought by modernity in an unnamed oil nation and about the excesses of politicians and business-men.[57] The Turkish novelist Orhan Pamuk has also spoken out against the status quo. His 2002 *Kar* (Snow), named one of the 10 best books of 2004 by the *New York Times,* is about the relationship between Westernism and Islamism, both typically espoused with fervor in Turkey. Pamuk came to fame with *Benim Adım Kırmızı* (My Name is Red), which is a murder mys-tery of sorts set in sixteenth-century Ottoman Istanbul.[58] Iran's most famous prose writer is Sadegh Hedayat (d. 1951). His 1937 morbid and unsettling novella *Buf-e kur* (The Blind Owl) is his masterpiece. Like *L'Etranger* (The Stranger) by Albert Camus—who was, incidentally, a *pied noir,* that is, a Frenchman born in Muslim North Africa, where most of his novels are set—the appearance of *Buf-e kur* forever changed the Iranian and international literary landscapes.[59] Modern Urdu letters boast of a number of important prose writers. Predictably, the partition of India and Pakistan features prominently, allegorically, or explicitly in their writings. Suffice to mention here the female novelist Qurratulain Hyder, whose magnum opus, *Aag Ka Darya* (River of Fire), is a historical sweep that begins before the Common Era. Like Hyder, Ismet Chugtai (d. 1991) was born in Aligarh, India, and was another major female figure in Urdu letters, but writing in India not Pakistan.[60]

As we have seen, many Muslim writers have turned to the Qur'an for inspiration. The Yemeni novelist Zayd Muti' Dammaj (d. 2001) was inspired by the Qur'anic account of Yusuf and Zulaykha (Potiphar's wife) in his novel *al-Rahina* (The Hostage). This novel is about a young man who becomes the object of affection of the sister of the governor in whose palace he is being kept prisoner.[61] The Moroccan novelist Driss Chraïbi takes on the Prophet Muhammad himself and his deeply amorous relationship with his wife Khadija in the daring but reverential *L'homme du livre* (The Man of the Book), a French novel(la) that is principally a first-person account of the thoughts of a fictionalized Muhammad on the eve of the first revelation.[62] Chraïbi includes the mysterious Qur'anic figure of al-Khidr in the novel, combining him with the Syrian monk Bahira, who was said to have seen the mark of prophecy on the young Muhammad. In the title story of his collection *The Mapmakers of Spitalfields,* the U.K.-based Bangladeshi writer Syed Manzurul Islam melds this same al-Khidr into his main character, the itinerant Brother-O Man.[63]

One antecedent for accounts about an errant or wandering character, often a rogue, who dupes those around him is the *maqamat* ("Assemblies," or "Standings"), a unique literary form in a very ornate, stylized manner, which

alternates rhyming prose with poetry. Originated in Arabic by Badi'
al-Zaman al-Hamadhani (d. 1008 CE), and expertly taken up by Hariri
(d. 1122 CE),[64] it subsequently inspired the Hebrew *Maqamat* of al-Harizi
(d. thirteenth century CE) in Andalusia and also the anonymous Spanish pica-
resque novel, *Lazarillo de Tormes* (1531).[65] *Maqamat* is usually named for a
character, a locale, or the item around which the trickery revolves. Mixing
prose and poetry (*prosimetrum*) in this genre is not uncommon. It is to be
found in scholarly, belletristic, and even popular works such as the medieval
Alf layla wa layla (The Thousand and One Nights). This is one of the most
enduring and recognizable story collections in world literature although it
has been criticized in Arabic literature because of its fabulous and salacious
content.[66] Other important story cycles in Islamic literature include the
fifteenth-century Malay *Hikayat Hang Tuah* (Tale of Hang Tuah), about
the exploits of the eponymous hero and four friends in fifteenth-century
Malacca; the sixteenth-century Turkish *Book of Dede Korkut;* a 12-story
collection of epic and heroic tales of the Turkic Oghuz people; and the medieval "Darangen Epic" of the Maranao of the southern Philippines, which is a
historical record of events from before the period of Islamization.[67]

The Algerian novelist Assïa Djebar turns to historical chronicles in *Loin de
Médine* (Far from Medina), an attempt to flesh out the lives of the women
around the Prophet Muhammad and the early Muslims. She rereads the
historical accounts preserved in such works as Tabari's monumental *Tarikh
al-rusul wa al-muluk* (History of Messengers and Kings), a world history
from creation to the mid-tenth century CE.[68] One of the many sources used
by Tabari was *Kitab Baghdad* (Book of Baghdad) by Ibn Abi Tahir Tayfur
(d. 893 CE). Only one volume of this work survives, but Jorge Luis Borges
(d. 1986), one of the many world authors drawing inspiration from Islamic
literatures, mentions it in his short story, "El Tintorero Enmascarado Hakim
de Merv" (The Masked Dyer Hakim of Merv).[69]

Djebar's and others' attempts to make sense fictionally of the Prophet
Muhammad's words and deeds mirror early Muslims' attempts to do so.
The corpus of writing that they had available was the Hadith, and they
immediately set themselves the task of verifying whether the words they had
recorded were authentically transmitted. Thus, the groundwork of the early
Hadith collectors, such as Bukhari (d. 870 CE) and Darimi (d. 869 CE), and
the Hadith transmitters, such as Nawawi (d. 1277 CE)—who produced a very
short précis of the most salient Hadith narratives in *al-Arba'in al-Nawawiya*
(The Nawawi Forty [Hadith])—was accompanied by a vigorous scrutiny of
the transmitters themselves.[70] This investigation into the personalities and
characters of the men and women involved in the transmission of Prophetic
tradition became the basis for a wider activity, namely the writing and
compiling of large biographical works, such as Ibn Sa'd's (d. 845 CE) early
compendium, *al-Tabaqat al-kubra* (The Great Generations). These biographical works were repositories of information about birth, birthplace,

education, output, reliability, and death. Some biographical works came to be devoted to a specific region; for example, Indian scholars were the subjects of 'Abd al-Hayy's (d. 1923) *Nuzhat al-khawatir* (The Promenade of Ideas). Others were devoted to a specific century, such as the Egyptian Sakhawi's (d. 1497) *al-Daw' al-lami'* (The Gleaming Lamp), which was devoted to the ninth Islamic century (fifteenth century CE). Still others were devoted to a specific profession, such as the manumitted slave Yaqut's (d. 1229 CE) *Mu'jam al-udaba'* (Encyclopaedia of Writers). Sometimes, the subjects of these books were both people and their works, as in the compilation of the top songs of Baghdad by the courtier Abu al-Faraj (d. 967 CE) in his massive *Kitab al-Aghani* (Book of Songs). Yaqut produced the alphabetically arranged *Mu'jam al-buldan* (Encyclopedia of Place-Names), which was devoted to places and locales, building on earlier geographies such as the anonymous Persian *Hudud al-'Alam* (Limits of the World).[71] Such compilations remain the principal source of information about much of medieval Islamic culture and society.[72]

Biographical compilations were complemented by book-length biographies. Ibn Hisham's (d. 833 CE) abridged edition of Ibn Ishaq's (d. 767 CE) *Sirat Rasul Allah* (The Life of the Messenger of God) is an early and widely quoted biography of the Prophet Muhammad.[73] It would become a model for later biographies, a genre out of which arose some autobiographies. Indeed, scholars frequently felt the need to write about their careers and accomplishments: to set the record straight, to serve as a model for their children and students, or, as many explicitly state, to follow the Qur'anic injunction (Qur'an 93:11) to broadcast the virtues bestowed upon them by God. The autobiography is a significant genre of Islamic literature.[74] Several authors already mentioned wrote autobiographies, such as Hunayn ibn Ishaq, al-Ghazali, Ibn Sina, Suyuti, and Azad Bilgrami. One famous autobiographer was the so-called father of sociology, 'Abd al-Rahman Ibn Khaldun (d. 1406 CE), whose six-volume world history is eclipsed by its sophisticated one-volume introduction, *al-Muqaddima* (The Prolegomenon).[75] From the fragments of the autobiography of the scholar-physician 'Abd al-Latif al-Baghdadi (d. 1231 CE), we learn a great deal about the political climate of the time and also get a glimpse of the fundamental role played by patronage in supporting literary output.[76] It is patronage that Sayyide Salme, an Omani princess who fled her home in Zanzibar, sought when she wrote under her adopted name Emilie Ruete, *Memoiren einer arabischen Prinzessin* (Memoirs of an Arabian Princess). The memoir is also a literary form with a distinguished pedigree.[77] One of the most famous of such works in all of Islamic literature is the Chaghatai *Babur-Nameh* (Book of Babur). This work contains the memoirs of Babur (d. 1530 CE), the Central Asian founder of the Mughal dynasty in India.[78] The diary is a less attested form, although the deeply personal *Kashf al-asrar* (The Unveiling of Secrets) by the Persian Sufi Ruzbihan Baqli of Shiraz (d. 1210 CE) certainly reads that way.[79]

Sufism (*tasawwuf*) accounts for a considerable literary output and, as the current interest in the poetry of Rumi suggests, is very popular. Indeed, Sufism's "popular" appeal often put it at odds with the orthodoxy espoused by the formal religious scholars (*ulama*). This explains the significance of Ghazali's espousal of Sufism, and of its incorporation into the *Han Kitab* (Chinese Writings), an early modern corpus of texts by Muslim Chinese scholars.[80] Sufi scholars wrote expositions of Sufism, such as the Persian *Kashf al-mahjub* (Unveiling the Veiled) of Hujviri (d. 1071 CE), or the *Risala* (Epistle) of Qushayri (d. 1074 CE), and biographical works (hagiographies), such as the *Tadhkirat al-awliya'* (Memorial of the Saints) by Farid al-Din 'Attar (d. 1220 CE).[81] They also wrote guides for their disciples and followers, such as the Malayo-Arabic *[al-] Sirat al-Mustaqim* (The Straight path) by the Gujarati al-Raniri (d. 1658 CE), the *Risalat al-Mu'awana* (The Book of Assistance) of the South Arabian 'Abdallah ibn 'Alawi (d. ca. 1719 CE), and Sheikh Muzaffer Ozak's (d. 1985 CE) *Ziynet-ül-kulub* (Adornment of Hearts).[82] Sufis have also written a great deal of poetry, such as the simple but searing verse attributed to the early woman mystic Rabi'a al-'Adawiyya (d. 801 CE).[83]

Poetry, the preeminent literary form of Arabic literature, may be regarded, as the literary form *par excellence* of Islamic literatures too—for the premodern period at any rate. The *qasida*, or ode, arose in the same language and region as did the Prophet Muhammad and the Qur'an (the Arabian Peninsula), but it did so before Islam. It went on, in one guise or another, to find a place in every Islamic literature. Classical Arabic scholar Stefan Sperl recognized this when he read a poem his wife was then studying, by the Pakistani poet Faiz.[84] That realization led to an anthology titled *Qasida Poetry in Islamic Asia and Africa: Eulogy's Bounty, Meaning's Abundance.* Most of the 50 poems and poets represented in this work are worth listing here, as they provide an apposite, if cursory, overview of what we might tentatively term the poetry of Islamic civilization:[85]

Arabic: Abu Tammam (d. 845 CE), in praise of an Abbasid caliph

Arabic: Mutanabbi (d. 965 CE), invective against Kafur

Hebrew: Solomon Ibn Gabirol (d. ca. 1058 CE), in praise of an unnamed person

Persian: Nasir-i Khusrau (d. ca. 1077 CE), in praise of knowledge and justice

Hebrew: Judah Halevi (d. 1141 CE), in praise of Isaac ibn al-Yatom

Persian: Khaqani (d. 1199 CE), Elegy on Mada'in

Arabic: Ibn al-Farid (d. 1235 CE), On Sufi love

Arabic: Rundi (d. 1285 CE), Elegy on the lost cities of al-Andalus

Arabic: Busiri (d. ca. 1296 CE), the *Burda* in praise of the Prophet Muhammad

Turkish: Necati (d. 1509 CE), "Rose Kaside" in praise of Sultan Bayezid II

Persian: Hayali (d. 1557 CE), "Rose Kaside" in praise of Sultan Suleyman

Persian: 'Urfi (d. 1591 CE), in praise of Abu al-Fath

Malay: Hamza Fansuri (c. 1600 CE), on Sufi teachings

Kurdish: Malaye Jaziri (d. 1640 CE), on Sufi teachings

Pashto: 'Abd al-Rahman Baba (d. c. 1710 CE), a pious *carpe diem*

Swahili: Anonymous (before 1800), in praise of a virtuous wife

Hausa: Usman dan Fodio (d. 1817 CE), in praise of the Prophet Muhammad

Urdu: Zauq (d. 1854 CE), in praise of Bahadur Shah II

Sindhi: Ghulam Haidar (d. 1861 CE), *Munajat* in praise of the Prophet Muhammad

Fulfulde: Asma'u Fodio (d. 1865 CE), in praise of Muhammad Bello

Malay: Anonymous (c. 1900), in praise of the Sufi text *Hidayatus salikin* (Guidance of the Seekers)

Urdu: Muhsin Kakoravi (d. 1905), in praise of the Prophet Muhammad

Panjabi: 'Abd al-Sattar (d. 1913), in praise of the Prophet Muhammad

Urdu: Altaf Husain Hali (d. 1914), on the Golden Jubilee of Queen Victoria

Persian: Iraj Mirza (d. 1926), criticizing the veil

Persian: Abu al-Qasim Lahuti (d. 1957), to the daughters of Iran

Arabic: Badr Shakir al-Sayyab (d. 1964), rain song

Arabic: Badawi al-Jabal (d. 1981), love and God

Arabic: Wazir Junaid al-Bukhari, elegy for Abu Bakr Bube

Turkey: Attila Ilhan, "Hell Kaside"

Persian: Khu'i, "The Imam of the Plague"

Indonesian: [sung by Arfitta Ria]: The propagation of Islam in Indonesia by the *Wali Songo* (Nine Saints)[86]

Naturally, many other important poets deserve mention in a survey of Islamic literatures. Suffice here to evoke the names of the Sufi poet 'Abd al-Rahman Jami (d. 1492 CE) and the feminist Forough Farrokhzad (d. 1967) in Persian.[87] Among the *ghazal* poets, one may cite Mir Taqi Mir (d. 1810 CE) and Ghalib (d. 1869 CE) in Urdu.[88] In Turkish poetry, mention should be made of the Ottoman Baki (d. 1600 CE), the modern Hikmet (d. 1963), and the Islamist Kisakürek (d. 1983).[89] In Swahili, one should not overlook the religious poet Seyyid Abdallah bin Nasir (d. 1820 CE) and the "secular" poet Abdillatif Abdalla.[90] Finally, writing in English were the iconoclastic Kahlil Gibran (d. 1931) and the diasporic Agha Shahid Ali (d. 2001).[91]

"Islamic literatures," whether understood broadly (the literary output of Muslims and non-Muslims influenced by Islamic civilization) or narrowly (the literary output of Muslims inspired directly by Islam), comprise a fourteen-century legacy of scripture, epic, prose, poetry, romance, and drama of a richness that is still largely untold. Together, they continue to affect and inspire the lives of well over a billion people throughout the world.

NOTES

1. See James Kritzeck, ed., *Anthology of Islamic literature: From the Rise of Islam to Modern Times* (New York: Holt, Rinehart, and Winston, 1964) and Kritzeck, ed., *Modern Islamic Literature from 1800 to the Present* (New York: New American Library, 1970).

2. Annemarie Schimmel "Arts, Islamic," *Encyclopædia Britannica* from Encyclopædia Britannica Premium Service. <http://wwwa.britannica.com/eb/article-13869> (Accessed March 1, 2006).

3. Alamgir Hashmi, ed., *The Worlds of Muslim Imagination* (Islamabad: Gulmohar, 1986), 3.

4. Ibid., 4. It should be noted that one literary movement does bear the name *al-adab al-Islami* (literally, "Islamic literature," in the singular), namely, literature produced in the context of the conservative Islamic religious revival in the Arab world. However, this "Islamic" literature, albeit prolific, has merited neither an entry in the comprehensive *Encyclopaedia of Islam,* nor in the *Oxford Encyclopedia of the Modern Islamic World,* although several paragraphs are devoted to it in the *OEMIW* entry, "Arabic Literature." Among *al-adab al-Islami*'s most famous authors are the Egyptian Najib al-Kilani (d. 1995), who defined the movement in his treatise "Islamism and Literary Movements," and Sayyid Qutb (d. 1966), whose 30-volume exegetical *Fi Zilal al-Qur'an* (*In the Shade of the Qur'an*) remains one of the most popular and widely available works in the Islamic world. See *In the Shade of the Qur'an, Vol. 30,* trans. M.A. Salahi and A.A. Shamis (London, U.K.: MWH, 1979).

5. There are approximately 60 published translations of the Qur'an into English. For a bibliography up to 1996, see A.R. Kidwai, *A Guide to English Translations of the Quran* (Port Louis: Hassam Toorawa Trust, 1997). Translations that have appeared since 1996 include: *The Quran: A New Interpretation; Textual Exegesis by Muhammad Baqir Behbudi,* translated by Colin Turner (Richmond, U.K.: Curzon Press, 1997); *The Qur'an: A Modern English Version,* translated by Majid Fakhry (Reading, U.K.: Garnet Publishing, 1997); *An Interpretation of the Qur'an: English Translation of the Meanings: A Bilingual Edition* (New York University Press, 2002); *The Quran, the First Poetic Translation,* by Fazlollah Nikayin (Skokie, Ill.: Ultimate Book, 2000); *The Qur'an, A New Translation from the Original,* by Mirza Abul Fazl [*sic*] (Hyderabad: Wakf Baitul Madina, 2002); *The Qur'an, A New Translation,* by Thomas Cleary (Chicago, Illinois: Starlatch Press, 2004); *The Qur'an, A New Translation,* by M.A.S. Abdel Haleem (Oxford; New York: Oxford University Press, 2004).

6. See Ross Brann, "Judah ha-Levi," in *The Literature of Al-Andalus,* ed. Maria Rosa Menocal, Raymond P. Scheindlin, and Michael Sells (Cambridge, U.K.: Cambridge University Press, 2000), 265–281.

7. Djibril Tamsir Niane, *Sundiata, an Epic of Old Mali,* trans. G.D. Pickett (Harlow: Longman African Writers, 1994).

8. Sorayya Khan, *Noor* (Islamabad: Alhamra, 2003).

9. For a panoramic survey, see Schimmel, *Encyclopædia Britannica*. <http://wwwa.britannica.com/eb/article-13869>; and for a short guide to further reading, see below.

10. See *The Fihrist of al-Nadim,* 2 vols., trans. Bayard Dodge (New York: Columbia University Press, 1970).

11. Kees Versteegh, *The Arabic Language* (Edinburgh, U.K.: Edinburgh University Press, 1997.

12. See Jonathan Bloom, *Paper Before Print: The History and Impact of Paper in the Islamic World* (New Haven, Connecticut: Yale University Press, 2001); see also, Shawkat M. Toorawa, *Ibn Abi Tahir Tayfur and Arabic Writerly Culture: A Ninth-Century Bookman in Baghdad* (London and New York: Routledge-Curzon, 2005).

13. On the Qur'an as a book, see Daniel A. Madigan, *The Qur'an's Self-Image: Writing and Authority in Islam's Scripture* (Princeton, New Jersey: Princeton University Press, 2001).

14. Scholarship on the Qur'an is vast. For a brief overview, see Andrew Rippin, "Koran," in *Encyclopaedia of Arabic Literature,* ed. Julie Scott Meisami and Paul Starkey (London and New York: Routledge, 1998), 2, 453–456; for in-depth information, see the *Encyclopaedia of the Qur'an,* 5 vols., ed. Jane Dammen McAuliffe (Leiden: E.J. Brill, 2001–2006).

15. See, for example, *Islamic Jurisprudence: al-Shafi'i's Risala,* trans. Majid Khadduri (Baltimore, Maryland: Johns Hopkins University Press, 1961).

16. Ibn [al-]'Arabi, *Bezels of Wisdom,* trans. R.W.J. Austin (New York: Paulist Press, 1980).

17. See *The Mathnawi of Jalalu'ddin Rumi,* ed. and trans. Reynold A. Nicholson, 8 vols. (London, U.K.: Luzac, 1925–1940). On Rumi, see Franklin Lewis, *Rumi Past and Present, East and West* (Oxford, U.K.: One World Publications, 2000). According to the 20 September 2002 issue of *Publisher's Weekly,* Rumi was the bestselling poet in the United States in 2002.

18. See *The Seven Odes,* trans. A.J. Arberry (London, U.K.: George Allen & Unwin, 1957).

19. For Ka'b's poem, see Michael Sells, *Desert Tracings: Six Classic Arabian Odes* (Middletown, Connecticut: Wesleyan University Press, 1989); for Busiri's, see *The Burda of Imam Busiri,* trans. Hamza Yusuf, 3-CD set and Casebound Book (Hayward, California: Alhambra Productions, 2004).

20. See Michael Cooperson, *Al-Ma'mun* (Oxford, U.K.: One World Publications, 2005).

21. See Dimitri Gutas, *Greek Thought, Arabic Culture* (London and New York: Routledge, 1998).

22. See Mary Boyce, "Middle Persian Literature," *Handbuch der Orientalistik, Volume 4,* ed. Ilya Gershevitch et al. (Leiden: E.J. Brill, 1968), 31–66.

23. See *History of Iranian Literature,* ed. Jan Rypka et al. (Dordrecht: D. Reidel Publishing Company), 1968.

24. Abu al-Qasim Ferdowsi, *Shahnameh: the Persian Book of Kings,* [selections] trans. Dick Davis (New York: Viking Press, 2006).

25. *Kalila and Dimna: Tales for Kings and Commoners: Selected Fables of Bidpai,* retold by Ramsay Wood (Rochester, Vermont: Inner Traditions International, 1986).

26. See, for example, the play *Yusuf va-Zulaykha* (Teheran: Sukhan, 2002) by the noted Iranian director and writer Pari Saberi (b. 1932).

27. *Layla and Majnun by Nizami,* a Prose Adaptation by Colin Turner (London, U.K.: Curzon Press, 1997). See also Maria Rosa Menocal, *Shards of Love: Exile and the Origins of the Lyric* (Durham, North Carolina: Duke University Press, 1994).

28. *The Romance Tradition in Urdu: Adventures from the Dastan of Amir Hamza,* trans. Frances W. Pritchett (New York: Columbia University Press, 1991).

29. *Death before Dying: The Sufi Poems of Sultan Bahu,* trans. Jamal Elias (Berkeley, California: University of California Press, 1998).

30. On fields of study and curricula of the Islamic sciences, see George Makdisi, *The Rise of Colleges: Institutions of Learning in Islam and the West* (Edinburgh, U.K.: Edinburgh University Press, 1981).

31. See *The Commentary on the Qur'an by Abu Ja'far Muhammad ibn Jarir al-Tabari,* partially translated by J. Cooper (Oxford, U.K.: Oxford University Press, 1987).

32. For Ibn Kathir (and Tabari), see *Interpretation of the Meanings of the Noble Quran,* trans. Muhammad Taqi-al-Din al-Hilali and Muhammad Muhsin Khan, 9 vols. (Riyadh: Darussalam, 2000). The *Tafsir al-Jalalyn* (and numerous other major Qur'an commentaries) will be available in translation at <www.altafsir.com> in coming years.

33. See Peter Riddell, *Transferring a Tradition: 'Abd Al-Ra'uf Al-Singkili's Rendering into Malay of the Jalaláyn Commentary* (Berkeley, California: Centers for South and Southeast Asia Studies, University of California at Berkeley, 1990).

34. See *The Cambridge Companion to Islamic Philosophy,* ed. Peter Adamson and Richard C. Taylor (Cambridge, U.K.: Cambridge University Press, 2005). Incidentally, Avicenna and Averroës are included by Dante in the *(Divine) Comedy.* Unlike the Prophet Muhammad, who resides in Hell, they are in Limbo, and are spared Hell.

35. Nizam al-Mulk, *The Book of Government or Rules for Kings,* trans. Hubert Darke (Richmond, U. K.: Curzon Press, 2002).

36. Amin Maalouf, *Samarkand,* trans. Russell Harris (London: Quartet, 1992). Maalouf is a Paris-based, non-Muslim Lebanese writer.

37. Ghazali, *Deliverance from Error,* trans. Richard Joseph McCarthy (Louisville, Kentucky: Fons Vitae, 1999); *The Revival of the Religious Sciences,* partial translation by Bankey Behari (Farnham: Sufi Publishing, 1972); *Ghazali's Book of Counsel for Kings,* trans. R.R.C. Bagley (London, U.K.: Oxford University Press, 1964).

38. Fadhlallah Haeri, *Keys to the Qur'an,* 5 vols., new edition (Reading, U. K.: Garnet Publishing, 1993).

39. See Rotraud Wielandt, "Exegesis of the Qur'an: Early Modern and Contemporary," in *Encyclopaedia of the Qur'an,* 2, 124–142. On Islahi, see Mustansir Mir, *Coherence in the Qur'an* (Indianapolis, Indiana: American Trust Publications, 1986).

40. Amina Wadud, *Qur'an and Woman: Rereading the Sacred Text from a Woman's Perspective* (New York: Oxford University Press, 1999); Asma Barlas, *"Believing Women" in Islam: Unreading Patriarchal Interpretations of the Qur'an* (Austin, Texas: University of Texas Press, 2002); Nimat Hafez Barazangi, *Woman's Identity and the Quran: A New Reading* (Gainesville, Florida: University Press of Florida, 2004).

41. *The Risalatu'l-Ghufran,* summarized and partially translated by Reynold A. Nicholson (London, U.K.: Royal Asiatic Society Journal, 1900).

42. For a systematic discussion of *al-Kitab*, see Michael Carter, *Sibawayhi* (London, U.K.: I.B. Tauris, 2004).

43. See Azad Bilgrami, "India as a Sacred Islamic Land," in *Religions of India in Practice*, trans. Carl Ernst, and ed. Donald S. Lopez, Jr. (Princeton, New Jersey: Princeton University Press, 1995), 556–564.

44. See A.M. Zubaidi, "The impact of the Qur'an and Hadith on medieval Arabic literature," in *Arabic Literature to the End of the Umayyad Period*, ed. A.F.L. Beeston et al. (Cambridge: Cambridge University Press, 1983), 322–343; Stefan Wild, "The Koran as subtext in modern Arabic poetry," in *Representations of the Divine in Arabic Poetry*, ed. Gert Borg and Ed de Moor (Amsterdam and Atlanta: Rodopi, 2001), 139–160; Shawkat M. Toorawa, "Modern Arabic Literature and the Qur'an: Creativity, Inimitability... Incompatibilities?" in *Religious Perspectives in Modern Muslim and Jewish Literatures,* ed. Glenda Abramson and Hilary Kilpatrick (London, U.K.: Routledge-Curzon, 2005), 239–257.

45. "The Life of Omar Ibn Said", trans. Ala A. Alryyes, in *The Multilingual Anthology of American Literature*, trans. Ala A. Alryyes and ed. Marc Shell and Werner Sollors (New York: New York University Press, 2000), 58–94.

46. Adonis' *al-Kitab* is not available in translation. For one of his works in English, see Adonis, *A Time between Ashes and Roses: Poems*, trans. Shawkat M. Toorawa (Syracuse: Syracuse University Press, 2004).

47. Tahir Wattar, *The Earthquake*, trans. William Granara (London, U.K.: Saqi Books, 2000).

48. Naguib Mahfouz, *Children of the Alley* (New York: Doubleday, 1996).

49. Tawfiq al-Hakim, *The People of the Cave [Ahl al-Kahf]*, trans. Mahmoud El Lozy (Cairo: Elias Modern Publishing House & Co., 1989).

50. Salman Rushdie, *The Satanic Verses* (London, U.K.: Viking Press, 1988); *Haroun and the Sea of Stories* (London, U.K.: Granta Books in association with Penguin Books, 1991).

51. Amin Malak, *Muslim Narratives and the Discourse of English* (Albany: State University of New York Press, 2005).

52. Ahmed Ali, *Twilight in Delhi* (Bombay: Oxford University Press, 1966). The following are the mentioned authors' most recent novels: Nuruddin Farah, *Links* (New York: Riverhead Books, 2004); Abdulrazak Gurnah, *Desertion* (New York: Pantheon Books, 2005); M.G. Vassanji, *When She Was Queen* (Toronto: Doubleday Canada, 2005).

53. Zaynab Alkali, *The Cobwebs and Other Stories* (Ikeja, Lagos State, Nigeria: Malthouse, 1997); Che Husna Azhari, *An Anthology of Kelantan Tales* (Selangor Darul Ehsan Malaysia: Furada Publishing House, 1992).

54. *Naguib Mahfouz: From Regional Fame to Global Recognition,* ed. Michael Beard and Adnan Haydar (Syracuse, New York: Syracuse University Press, 1993)

55. Tayeb Salih, *Season of Migration to the North*, trans. Denys Johnson-Davies (London, U.K.: Heinemann, 1969). See also Jamal Mahjoub, *Wings of Dust* (Oxford, U.K.: Heinemann, 1994), which is itself a response, as it were, to Saleh's book.

56. Hamidou Kane, *Ambiguous Adventure,* trans. Katherine Woods (New York: Walker, 1963).

57. Abdel Rahman Munif, *Cities of Salt*, trans. Peter Theroux (New York: Random House, 1987).

58. Orhan Pamuk, *Snow*, trans. Maureen Freely (London, U.K.: Faber and Faber, 2004); Pamuk, *My Name is Red*, trans. Erdag Göknar (New York: Alfred Knopf, 2001).

59. Sadegh Hedayat, *The Blind Owl*, trans. D.P. Costello (Repr., Edinburgh, U.K.: Rebel Inc., 1997); Albert Camus, *The Stranger*, trans. Matthew Ward (New York: Vintage Books, 1989).

60. Qurratulain Hyder, *River of Fire*, "transcreated" into English by the author (New Delhi: Kali for Women, 1998). See also *Domains of Fear and Desire: Urdu Stories*, ed. Muhammad Umar Memon (Toronto: TSAR, 1992).

61. Zayd Muti' Dammaj, *The Hostage, A Novel*, trans. May Jayyusi and Christopher Tingley (New York: Interlink, 1994).

62. Driss Chraïbi, *Muhammad, A Novel*, trans. Nadia Benabid (Boulder, Colorado: Lynne Rienner Publishers, 1998).

63. Syed Manzurul Islam, *The Mapmakers of Spitalfields* (Leeds, U.K.: Peepal Tree, 1997).

64. *The Assemblies of Al Hariri*, trans. Thomas Chenery (Repr., Farnborough: Gregg, 1969); *The Maqamat of Badi al-Zaman al-Hamadhani*, trans. W.J. Prendergast (Repr.,: London, U.K.: Curzon Press, 1973).

65. Judah al-Harizi, *The Book of Tahkemoni*, trans. David Simha Segal (Portland, Oregon: Littman Library of Jewish Civilization, 2001); *The Life of Lazarillo de Tormes: His Fortunes and Adversities*, trans. W.S. Merwin (New York: New York Review of Books, 2005).

66. *The Arabian Nights*, trans. Husain Haddawy (New York: W.W. Norton, 1990).

67. On Malay literature in general, see Sir Richard Winstedt, *A History of Classical Malay Literature* (Oxford, U.K.: Oxford University Press, 1961); *The Book of Dede Korkut*, trans. Geoffrey Lewis (Harmondsworth, Middlesex: Penguin, 1974); *Darangen: in Original Maranao Verse with English Translation*, trans. Maria Delia Coronel, 8 vols. (Marawi City, Philippines: Folklore Division, University Research Center, Mindanao State University, 1986–1995).

68. Assïa Djebar, *Far from Madina* (London, U.K.: Quartet Books, 1994); *The History of al-Tabari*, 38 vols., general editor Ehsan Yar-Shater, various translators (Albany, New York: State University of New York Press, 1985–1999).

69. Jorge Luis Borges, "Al-Hakim, the Masked Dyer of Merv," in *Borges, A Reader*, ed. Emir Rodriguez Monegal and Alistair Reid (New York: Dutton, 1981).

70. *Sahih Al-Bukhari*, trans. Muhammad Muhsin Khan, 6th ed., 9 vols. (Lahore, Pakistan: Kazi Publications, 1983); *An-Nawawi's Forty hadith*, trans. Ezzeddin Ibrahim and Denys Johnson-Davies (Beirut: Holy Koran Publishing House, 1976).

71. *The Introductory Chapters of Yaqut's Mu'jam al-Buldan*, trans. Wadie Jwaideh (Leiden: E.J. Brill, 1959); *Hudud al-'Alam, The Regions of the World*, trans. Vladimir Minorsky (London, U.K.: Luzac, 1970).

72.   On Islamic biography generally, see Michael Cooperson, *Classical Arabic Biography: the Heirs of the Prophets in the Age of al-Ma'mun* (Cambridge, U.K.: Cambridge University Press, 2000). On Abu al-Faraj's work, see Hilary Kilpatrick, *Making the Great Book of Songs* (London, U.K.: Routledge-Curzon, 2003).

73.   *The Life of Muhammad*, trans. Alfred Guillaume (London and New York: Oxford University Press, 1955).

74.   *Interpreting the Self: Autobiography in the Arabic Literary Tradition*, ed. Dwight F. Reynolds (Berkeley and Los Angeles: University of California Press, 2001).

75.   Ibn Khaldun, *The Muqaddimah: an Introduction to History*, trans. Franz Rosenthal, 2nd ed. (Princeton, New Jersey: Princeton University Press, 1967).

76.   Shawkat M. Toorawa, "Selections from the Autograph Notes of 'Abd al-Latif al-Baghdadi," in *Interpreting the Self,* ed. Reynolds, 156–164; Toorawa, "Travel in the Medieval Islamic World: The Importance of Patronage as Illustrated by 'Abd al-Latif al-Baghdadi (and other littérateurs)," in *Eastward Bound: Travel and Travelers, 1050–1550,* ed. Rosamund Allen (Manchester, U.K.: Manchester University Press, 2004), 57–70.

77.   Emilie Ruete, *Memoirs of an Arabian Princess from Zanzibar* (Princeton, New Jersey: Markus Wiener, 1989).

78.   *The Baburnama,* trans. Wheeler M. Thackston (Oxford, U.K.: Oxford University Press, 1996).

79.   Ruzbihan Baqli, *The Unveiling of Secrets: Diary of a Sufi Master,* trans. Carl W. Ernst (Chapel Hill, North Carolina: Parvardigar Press, 1997).

80.   On the *Han Kitab,* see Zvi Ben-Dor-Benite, *The Dao of Muhammad: A Cultural History of Muslims in Late Imperial China* (Cambridge, Massachusetts: Harvard University Asia Center, 2005).

81.   *The Kashf al-Mahjub of al-Hujwiri,* trans. Reynold A. Nicholson (London, U.K.: Luzac, 1936); *Principles of Sufism by al-Qushayri,* trans. B.R. von Schlegell (Berkeley: Mizan Press, 1992); *Muslim Saints and Mystics: Episodes from the Tadhkirat al-Auliya' by Farid al-Din Attar,* trans. A.J. Arberry (Chicago, Illinois: University of Chicago Press, 1966).

82.   Imam al-Haddad, *The Book of Assistance,* trans. Mostafa Badawi (Louisville, Kentucky: Fons Vitae, 1983); Muzaffer Ozek al-Jerrahi, *Adornment of Hearts,* trans. Muhtar Holland and Sixtina Friedrich (Westport, Connecticut: Pir Press, 1991).

83.   *Doorkeeper of the Heart: Versions of Rabi'a* (Putney, Vermont: Threshold Books, 1988).

84.   *Qasida Poetry in Islamic Asia and Africa,* vol. 1: *Classical Traditions and Modern Meanings,* ed. Stefan Sperl and Christopher Shackle (Leiden: J.E. Brill, 1996).

85.   *Qasida Poetry in Islamic Asia and Africa,* vol. 2: *Eulogy's Bounty, Meaning's Abundance: An Anthology,* ed. Stefan Sperl and Christopher Shackle (Leiden: E.J. Brill, 1996).

86.   *Wali Songo* (The Nine Saints) are the nine Sufis who are said to have spread Islam in Java. Their deeds are told in the sixteenth-century *Babad Tanah Jawa* (Chronicles of the Land of Java).

87.   See, for example, Abd al-Rahman al-Jami, *Yusuf and Zulaikha: An Allegorical Romance,* trans. David Pendlebury (London, U.K.: Octagon Press, 1980); and

Forugh Farrokhzad, *Another Birth: Let Us Believe in the Beginning of the Cold Season*, trans. Ismail Salami (Tehran: Zabankadeh, 2001).

88. See, for example, *Mir Taqi Mir, Selected Poetry*, trans. K.C. Kanda (New Delhi: Sterling Publishers, 1997), and *Diwan-e Ghalib*, trans. Sarwat Rahman (New Delhi: Ghalib Institute, 2003).

89. See, for example Nazim Hikmet, *Beyond the Walls*, trans. Ruth Christie et al. (London, U.K.: Anvil Press Poetry, 2002).

90. See 'Abdallah ibn 'Ali ibn Nasir, *Al-Inkishafi: The Soul's Awakening*, trans. William Hichens (London, U.K.: Sheldon Press, 1939).

91. See for example, Khalil Gibran, *The Madman: His Parables and Poems* (Mineola, New York: Dover Press, 2002), and Agha Shahid Ali, *Call me Ishmael Tonight* (New York: W.W. Norton, 2003).

SELECTED BIBLIOGRAPHY

Abramson, Glenda, and Hilary Kilpatrick, eds. *Religious Perspectives in Modern Muslim and Jewish Literatures*. London, U.K.: Routledge-Curzon, 2006.

Anthology of Islamic Literature: from the rise of Islam to modern times, Edited by James Kritzeck. New York: Holt, Rinehart, and Winston, 1964.

Arabic Literary Culture, 500–925, Edited by Michael Cooperson and Shawkat M. Toorawa. Detroit: Thomson Gale, 2005.

Arabic Literature of Africa, Edited by R.S. O'Fahey and John Hunwick, 4 vols. to date. Leiden: E.J. Brill, 1994.

Cragg, Kenneth. *The Pen and the Faith: Eight Modern Muslim Writers and the Qur'an*. London, U.K.: George Allen & Unwin, 1985.

Encyclopaedia of Islam, New Edition. Edited by H.A.R. Gibb et al., 11 vols. and supplements. Leiden: E.J. Brill, 1954–2003.

Harrow, Kenneth, ed. *Faces of Islam in African Literature*. Portsmouth, New Hampshire: Heinemann, 1991.

———. *The Marabout and the Muse*. Portsmouth, New Hampshire: Heinemann, 1996.

Hawley, John C. *The Postcolonial Crescent: Islam's Impact on Contemporary Literature*. New York: Peter Lang, 1998.

History of Persian literature: from the beginning of the Islamic period to the present day. Edited by George Morrison. Leiden: E.J. Brill, 1981.

Ibn al-Nadim, *The Fihrist of al-Nadim*. Translated by Bayard Dodge. 2 vols. New York: Columbia University Press, 1970.

Modern Islamic Literature from 1800 to the Present. Edited by James Kritzeck. New York: New American Library, 1970.

Oxford Encyclopedia of the Modern Islamic World. Edited by James L. Esposito et al. 4 vols. New York: Oxford University Press, 1995.

Qasida Poetry in Islamic Asia and Africa, vol. 1: *Classical traditions and modern meanings*, vol. 2: *Eulogy's Bounty, Meaning's Abundance: An Anthology*. Edited by Stefan Sperl and Christopher Shackle. Leiden: E.J. Brill, 1996.

Schimmel, Annemarie. *Islamic literatures of India*. Wiesbaden: O. Harrassowitz, 1973.

Winstedt, Sir Richard. *A History of Classical Malay Literature.* Oxford, U.K.: Oxford University Press, 1961.

The Worlds of Muslim Imagination. Edited by Alamgir Hashmi. Islamabad: Gulmohar, 1986.

14

MOTHS AND SCATTERED FLAMES: SOME THOUGHTS ON ISLAM AND POETRY

Daniel Abdal-Hayy Moore

Poetry is the original language of humankind. With a little imagination, it might even be said to be the original language of animals, those emotive creatures that must choose resemblances and learn to decode the meanings of things in order to survive. Or it might be the language of bees, those most poetic of insects, scanning the flowery countryside for nectar and pollen the way a good student might scan the lines of a great poem, metrically buzzing in heart and head.

I could even go so far as to say that poetry is the language of cells, who split and join, search and avoid, the way words fall into place to describe and evoke, emerging from silence. Or poetry might be the DNA language, which scans, has a recognizable meter, and a certain grammar or prosody of associations, markers, and signs. However, that might be going a bit too far, although only Allah knows how far we might go in the mysterious workings of the imagination that enters dimensions unreachable by reason alone, before we exceed or betray the truth.

Poetry is also the language of feeling, of spiritual states often and most purely beyond the reach of simple reason. In fact, in many cases symbolic or oblique language might be the best way to connect with the raw reality of things, of how things are, as well as states of intuition and realization that cannot be spoken of directly.

Allah gave Adam the wisdom of naming:

> And God taught Adam all names,
> then set them forth to the angels, and said,
> "Tell me these names, if you are truthful."

(Qur'an 2:31)[1]

Were they the names of the angels, known only to Allah before, or of everything in creation in its pre-verbalized state, animals, plants, rocks, and clouds? Adam suddenly had tongue and teeth and an articulation that brought the world into focused being, in a linguistic transparency, for the benefit of all humanity, a veritable (virtual?) dictionary of wisdom language: Poetry.

> God said, "Adam, tell them the names."
> And when he told them the names,
> God said, "Did I not say to you that I know
> the secret of the heavens and the Earth?
> And I know what you reveal,
> and what you have been hiding."

(Qur'an 2:33)

Without attempting anything like a formal commentary (*tafsir*), this verse-sign (*aya*) of the Qur'an is truly mysterious to me, and is at the heart of our being human. Were the angels unnamed before Adam named them, or, in another interpretation, did nothing have a "name" until Allah inspired Adam, may peace be upon him, with the linguistic representations of the glorious and multitudinous "things" of His creation? Did these and all other names spring from a secret that is known only to Allah? Is Allah referring only to the secrets (Ar. *sirr,* plural *asrar*) that we hold deep within our breasts? Or is it something wildly deeper, secrets of the universe so arcane that we have to struggle to name them, such that only with Allah's "dictionary of terms" can we ever hope to do so?

Rainer Maria Rilke, in the ninth of his *Duino Elegies,* echoes the Adamic mystery of this act of naming:

> Are we, perhaps, *here* just to utter: house,
> bridge, fountain, gate, jug, fruit-tree, window—
> at most: column, tower, but to utter them, remember,
> to speak in a way which the named never dreamed
> they could be? Isn't that the hidden purpose
> of this cunning earth, in urging on lovers,
> to realize, through their rapture, a rapture for all?

(William Gass Translation)[2]

Rapture: Ah, the word that really opens us up to our urge toward true and vivid utterance!

Historically speaking (whether of our physical or spiritual history is of no consequence), I have a vision of the first humans (are we speaking of the first sacred pair, when no one else existed, and their progeny, or metaphorically, the thousands for whom the sacred pair are the prophetic and Gnostic epitome?) in the great mystery of the origins of our consciousness, speaking

Adam's prophetic "poetics" of association and perception, resemblances and decodings, from the deepest source that flows both from outward to inward and from inward to outward. This is what makes poetry, where previously there was only silence or *incommunication* (a new coinage meaning, no communication at all). Observations about light spraying through the trees, the weather, the grandeur and awesomeness of the Wooly Mammoth, or whatever it might be, the death of a parent, a child, an animal. The flight of an iridescent bird. The roar of an invisible assailant. The soothing of a wound or an injustice. A falling rock. The sighting of a new star. Which sound in the night to fear, and in which to find solace? Love-stirrings. Overpowering awe at God's Terrible Beauty.

If the roots of the Arabic language are, as it is claimed, deep in the soil of the human earth, and are at their base associative and many-faceted in meaning, then this protolanguage, which is also the Arabic language that is in use today, is itself a poetics, symbolic and evocative, even if the stilted flatness of journalism and the modern media have tried to iron all of its original poetry out of it.

André Breton, the French Surrealist, said, "Astonish me!" Should not believing Muslims be in an even more constant state of astonishment than French Surrealists? Out of the void, a lush world of existence blooms with all its streamers rippling in the cosmic winds. Irrational elements arise within it—mysteries, astonishments, and buffooneries. Yes, even buffooneries! As Dante shows us in the *Divina Commedia*, our proper attitude before God is one of bewilderment, where language stutters out of control to become the tongue-tied stuttering of ecstasy, given its proper latitude in the teachings of our Prophet Muhammad, may the peace and blessings of Allah be upon him, who was no poet and did not "practice" poetry. However, his revelation has shown us the poetic scope of truth's possibilities—epic grandeur couched in a language of deep and excavatable meanings—a text, capable, through the engagement of the heart and the mind, of yielding varied interpretations from the most literal and earth-surfaced signs or *ayat,* to those that are the most deeply plumbed, esoteric, and heart-stirred. However, as the Prophet himself cautioned, this grandeur is often beyond the reach of the human understanding, the intellect, and perhaps even of the secret of the soul—the *sirr*—in which case, the only true understanding of what Allah means is by the living embodiment of His words.

Often, the isolated root words of the Qur'an go back to a resonant concrete object as an image, a life-snapshot in motion of some actuality, a glimpse of reality that goes beyond materialism to the more "abstract" numinous realities that extend past the boundaries of all the living dimensions in both this world and the unseen. A familiarity with dictionaries such as E.W. Lane's *Arabic-English Lexicon* shows an abundance of abstract concepts that arise from root words referring to concrete details (the straightforward names of things) concerning camels, swords, light, water, and so on.³ Poetic analogies or "ideas" are extrapolated from these concretions, etherealized, internalized, and made multifaceted by the grammatical extensions of the basic root letters.

From this whirling ocean of worldliness words emerge, fall into formations, and even structured formalisms to become comprehensible sentences: bursts of word combinations, exclamations, questions, longings, the whole human gamut of expression that language, even flawed language, is privy to, which can soar to the angelic, but also can descend in guttural tailspins to the demonic. However, taking into account the Spanish poet Frederico García Lorca's understanding of the *duende,* the dark under-soul of our hearts, a different and less evil understanding of "demonic" might instead mean energetic and passionate illumination. William Blake, the most "Sufi" bard of the English language, often finds the energy of Heaven and Hell interchangeable, one with the light of the other, going to the source, as it were, of visionary enlightenment. This is why I prefer Blake to T.S. Eliot, because Blake understood with visionary immediacy the depths of Gnostic understanding. The Sufi poets Rumi, Ibn al-Farid, and Hafez would probably have found in Blake a true enlightened companion, but they would have found T.S. Eliot to be perhaps too excessively Churchy, pinched, and elitist, who distrusted "inspiration" as Blake and the Sufi poets experienced it. Think of Shams of Tabriz's "transgressive" attempts to expand Mevlana Jalaluddin Rumi's heart to the true *ma'rifa* (immediate knowledge) of divine recognition.

However, words can also float on the surface of the heart-beating urge to speech, and while poetry can be very simple, at the same time it also engages one in complexities of response. Take Haiku, for example, the exquisitely wrought Japanese form of a few lines in a strict metric quantity. This has also been practiced in a way by the Iranian poet and filmmaker Abbas Kiarostami in the Persian (Farsi) language:

Autumn sunshine—
a lizard alert
on the mud-brick wall.

(*Walking with the Wind: Poems of Abbas Kiarostami*)⁴

Often, the most disarmingly unselfconscious ditty will have the most resonant meanings, as in the case of Emily Dickinson in the American tradition of poetry, or again Blake, or some of Lorca's gypsy songs. When a poem lodges in our hearts because it is strange but somehow familiar, going into a place in our consciousness like a flashlight into an attic, beaming itself in unforeseen corners, or when it seems to have such potential, then, I think, we are looking at poetry. Poetry need not be "difficult" or "esoteric" at all, and may even be all surface, when it is a matter of true vision, an entirely new perspective from an unforeseen angle as if from an otherworldly inspiration. Or it may be the torn heart in the throes of incredible yearning, a lament making up for its lack with utterance to bridge its feeling of separation.

When we look at the ecstatic poetry of Rumi (and even his more "sober" *Mathnawi* is a heart-opening, head-swirling experience), who always maintains the dimension of both loss and total unity—with jokes and asides and Gnostic teaching in-between, with giddiness, plainness, surreal but meaningful symbolism and abstract contemplation, and even a few buffooneries thrown in for good measure—we see the possibility of a true spiritual literature.

What I am getting at in a kind of irrational and impressionistic way is a very deep and passionate conviction that our most subterranean consciousness-soul is connected with the mysterious movements of the universe, and that the language of poetic utterance is what opens this connection up to us. If I say that the DNA is "reciting" poetry, or that the amoebas are poetic fiends, meandering around in a state of inspiration, I hope I can be forgiven, because it is from this conviction. Although poetic inspiration does partake of revelation, it in no way matches the Prophetic revelation, which comes unbidden and untaught through prophets and the Prophet Muhammad, may peace be upon him, whose only "poetic" skill was utter and unflagging truthfulness. In her book, *Muhammad: A Biography of the Prophet,* Karen Armstrong comes very close to saying that the divine revelation of the Qur'an was an act of creativity on the part of the Prophet. Referring to this accomplishment, she says, "To *create* (italics mine) a literary masterpiece, to found a major religion and a new world power are not ordinary achievements."[5]

I would not say this. If the state of the Qur'anic revelation may be thought of as a mode of poetic action, then Allah is the poet, not the Prophet Muhammad. Still, *wahy*—revelatory inspiration—continues to exist in Islam, and to a lesser degree by far, the poetic project can "open sesame" many treasure vaults of truthful understanding, on the molecular as well as the stellar level. We are sentient pieces of lint floating in Allah's vast universe, singing to ourselves. What are we singing? This is what touches my heart, this knowledge and the hope that what we sing elevates us to our true dimension, beyond, as Allah Most High says, that of the angels! I want to be a poet among the birds or among the high breakers of the sea. A poet of seismic convulsions and star-births. Star bursts! I can only do this by expunging myself as much as possible, by stepping aside to let the lightning speak on its own behalf, by bringing to the event a taste for language and a deepened and apprenticed skill in catching the fireflies of lightning in a mortal dimension, so that others (and myself) can view them without being burned entirely to a crisp. Prophecy and saintliness, however, do not work at "poetry." They do not carry a notebook in a little shoulder bag for noting instant inspirations. They do not type out poems or send them to magazines, hoping to be published. I cannot imagine Rumi worrying about getting published!

The Surrealists, the French mostly, but also the Latin American and Spanish Surrealists, as well as the *Mathnawi* of Rumi, were my opening to Qur'anic understanding. They went about creating expression in a new way, almost turning away their senses from the ''object'' in order to dig deeper and find a stratum unknown or unexpressed before. When Sufi poetry came along, I could recognize it for the expression of the spirit's elusiveness that it is, and hear the music of its language as if from Tahitian tom-toms, or better, from Balinese *gamelan* gongs, as if surging up from the bottom of the sea—or for the rational-minded, from the ''unconscious'' or ''subconscious''—though I dive down and find phosphorescent fish in the dark, following the glow of their headlamps.

When my wife read my first stab at the opening paragraph of this chapter, she said that she found it a bit preposterous—animals speaking ''poetry''! She felt that what made us human was the speech that no other creature has to our degree. However, I am not trying to get at the actuality of ''poetry,'' but rather at the sublingual mechanisms of a metaphorical grasp of reality. Thus, the analogy holds for me that this is what other creatures do in their own poetic way. If they do not have language, then perhaps they are even closer to nature, which is also ''non-verbal.''

Language itself is a poem that floats on top of the ''objective'' or ''concrete'' world. If we look at a blade of grass for a long time, why do we call it ''grass?'' It is this long, green, blade—but already I am using poetic word-images, ''long,'' ''green,'' and ''blade,'' to bring the thought to mind. In itself, it is simply what it is (sounds like a rap song!). I often amuse myself wondering what it might be that ''grass'' calls itself, if anything, or what ''lions'' call themselves, or ''redwood trees.'' We call other peoples by names that we have given them, and are often surprised to find that they do not call themselves by the same names at all. ''American Indians,'' for example: a name given to them by mistaken identity on the part of Columbus, who thought he had reached India. The people themselves might call themselves by a tribal name by which, somehow over time, they have become distinguished from other tribes. Very often, people in their own languages simply call themselves, ''The People,'' although it may also be a kind of naïve arrogance to say that we are the only ''real people'' and that all the rest of us are lesser creatures. Thus, a blade of grass, ''looking around,'' might think itself different from, say, a cloud, and call itself—well, you make one up. However, if you do make one up, it will be either a lovely, sibilant musical sound with no rational meaning, or a metaphorical analogy, such as ''vertical verdant eyebrow with no eye that grows upward from the ground,'' or as Walt Whitman called it, ''the handkerchief of the Lord,'' or ''the beautiful uncut hair of graves.''

All I am saying, really, is that poetry is the probing and expansive imagination living in the sounds and meanings of words. It is an act of heightened speech to make the world more transparent and its more intimate meanings to emerge, even if evanescent or emotive. It is to get down to the core, to look more deeply into the flame before flying in. Better, it is to see the Names of Allah behind every manifestation, by virtue of verbal corrective lenses, and then to go through the manifest names to He who manifests them, Allah, the unified single Name that contains all names. This gets close to what Shaykh Muhammad ibn al-Habib of Fez (may Allah protect his secret) says in his *Diwan:*

Truly created beings are meanings projected in images.[6]

For me, the purpose of poetry is illumination, a form of remembrance (*dhikr*) with transformative capabilities. In poems, illumination springs either from the humblest beginnings of simple human events or earthly objects and situations in which the poetic imagination sees the galactic dimension, as it were, or from a self-contained inspiration (*wahy*) that comes unbidden, enters the heart, lays waste to the kingdom of control, and takes over utterance into a new articulation. Illumination and ecstasy: I call my website, "The Ecstatic Exchange," hoping that the reader on the other side is the gainful bargainer. Without this yearning or urge for a new wisdom, setting out in a poem seems like a humdrum project. The model for this can even be someone like Antonin Artaud, the great, mad French poet and theatrical theoretician, whose visceral screams in words show human energy at its most fearsome, but who shows the way for a poetry that tries to go somewhere uncharted, takes risks of life and limb, and is fearless. For me, Blake does this as well. In the modern age, many of the Beat Poets showed us all to go candidly and nakedly into raw thought and its bardic yawps to awaken the hearts and heads of the world.

Sufi poetry does nothing less than this, but in a way that is, perhaps, more Apollonian, to use a Western differentiation. This is because the illumination of the Sufi saints who wrote illuminative poems was beyond the dimensions of passionate rage or frustration, although they entered the high light of intense and often delirious compression. Something cosmically impersonal happens, even though the Sufi shaykh poets were full and complete (*kamil,* "perfect" in Arabic) human beings, the likes of which we rarely see today (although I think that they have always been rare). They are the proof of divine inspiration, the inspiration I think all poets long for when they set out to express the inexpressible. We pray for divine intervention between our hearts and our pens like nothing else. "Take me over!" we cry. "Don't let any of these words originate in me alone!"

In the world, but not of it: the great masters who are also poets illuminate others by their words, which glow from a burning core, and whose passage into the world opens our hearts to the glories of Allah. In this sense, poetry is pure praise.

The Lebanese–Syrian poet Adonis says in the final essay of his book, *The Pages of Day and Night*, that with the appearance of the Qur'an, the sense of divine inspiration was co-opted. According to Adonis, the Arab poets before the Qur'an went into deeper "subconscious" states, communicated with otherworldly forces, and were inspired by the unearthly, often attributing their brilliantly metaphorical allusions to helpful spirits (*jinn*). However, with the advent of the Qur'an and Islam, this approach became suspect (the art of poetry has always been suspect in Islam), and the poets were left with expressing reflective commentaries on the Qur'an, the pinnacle of Arabic poetics having been reached and surpassed by the Qur'anic language. An analogy of this is the way poets in English have Shakespeare's shadow to contend with, either imitating it or contradicting it. (One may be either like Hart Crane, a Shakespearean poet, or like William Carlos Williams, a plain speaker breaking from Shakespearean rhetoric, with inspirational jolts from Ezra Pound.) Adonis cynically sums up his view as follows:

> Islam did not suppress poetry as a form and mode of expression. Rather, it nullified poetry's role and cognitive mission, endowing it with a new function: to celebrate and preach the truth introduced by the Qur'anic revelation. Islam thus deprived poetry of its earliest characteristic—intuition and the power of revelation—and made it into a media tool.[7]

I think that this view is overly reductive, and that the post-Qur'anic Sufi shaykh–poets like Rumi or Fakhruddin Iraqi or Yunus Emre of Turkey went into their poetic states as true messengers. They were messengers of the truth but not messengers as prophets in the Qur'anic sense. However, they helped bring forth the continuous and uninterrupted message of the Qur'an from an imaginal realm that was, nonetheless, a lesser sibling of prophecy. After all, if dreams, according to the Hadith, are a fractional part of prophecy, then the poetry that springs from the same deep soul-sources must be a fractional "part" of prophecy as well. The Prophet Muhammad, may peace be upon him, stated, "In poetry is wisdom" (*Sahih al-Bukhari*). However, he also cautioned us against poetry's low excesses and its brutish exaggerations. These faults can be found, after all, in every human endeavor.

As a coda, bringing us back to my original claim for a kind of creaturely poetry, the American poet, Robert Duncan, in his *Structure of Rime* series, writes:

"In the Hive of Continual Images the Bees, angelic swarm, build in the visible cells a language in which they dance."[8]

NOTES

This chapter first appeared online at www.deenport.com in 2005. It is reprinted here by permission of the author, who retains full rights to the chapter.

1. Thomas Cleary, *The Qur'an: A New Translation* (Chicago, Illinois: Starlatch Press, 2004), 2.

2. William H. Gass, *Reading Rilke: Reflections on the Problems of Translation* (New York: Alfred A. Knopf, 1999), 214.

3. See Edward William Lane, *Arabic English Lexicon* (1863 original repr., Cambridge, U.K.: The Islamic Texts Society, 1984), two volumes.

4. *Walking with the Wind,* Poems by Abbas Kiarostami, (Cambridge, Massachusetts/London, U.K.: A Harvard Film Archive publication, 2001), 85.

5. Karen Armstrong, *Muhammad, A Biography of the Prophet* (New York: HarperSanFrancisco, A division of Harper Collins, 1992), 52.

6. *The Diwan of Shaykh Muhammad ibn al-Habib* (Cape Town, South Africa: Madinah Press, 2001), 75.

7. Adonis, *The Pages of Day and Night,* trans. Samuel Hazo (Evanston, Illinois: The Marlboro Press/Northwestern University Press, 2000), 102.

8. Robert Duncan, *Ground Work* (New York: New Directions, 1984), 54.

15

MEDICINE AND HEALING IN TRADITIONAL ISLAM

—————————————•—————————————

Laleh Bakhtiar

Every religion emphasizes an aspect of the Truth. For Islam, the emphasis is on knowledge. With the light of grace as its source, knowledge is integrated into the principle of Unity or the Oneness of God (*tawhid*) that runs as the vertical axis through every mode of knowledge and being. The primary source of knowledge in traditional Islamic medicine is the Qur'an and the Hadith, the customs and sayings of God's Messenger Muhammad. The Sunna of the Prophet Muhammad is the Tradition of Islam. The Qur'an is the Logos or Word of God as revealed to the Prophet Muhammad over a period of 23 years. Each of the more than 6,600 verses of the Qur'an is called a Sign (*aya*), as is everything in the universe including the inner human self: "We shall show them Our Signs upon the horizons and within themselves until it is clear to them that it is the Real (the Truth)" (Qur'an 41:53).[1]

The Qur'an and the Tradition of Islam are seen as extensions of nature, in which the cosmos and the natural order overflow with divine grace (*baraka*). The cosmos is the manifested Word of God and the natural order is the macrocosmic Sunna (*Sunnat Allah,* Qur'an 48:23), the perfect model in following the Word of God. The human being's relationship with nature ideally comprises a sense of unity and oneness. Through knowledge gained by contemplating nature in all its facets, the human being learns to read God's Signs and act upon them, thus becoming a channel of divine grace. The Qur'an encourages the human being to seek knowledge in all its facets.[2] Over more than 1,400 years of Islamic history, this quest for knowledge has led to the development of what has been called the "Medicine of the Prophet" (*tibb al-nabi*) or "Prophetic Medicine" (*al-tibb al-nabawi*).

Three degrees of knowledge are expressed in the Qur'an: knowledge by inference (*'ilm al-yaqin,* "the Knowledge of Certainty," 102:5), knowledge by perception or observation (*'ayn al-yaqin,* "the Eye of Certainty,"

102:7), and knowledge by experience or intuition (*haqq al-yaqin*, "the Truth of Certainty," 69:51). The first type of knowledge depends primarily on inductive reasoning and leads to knowledge as a probability. The second type of knowledge is based on perception or empirical scientific observation. This corresponds to "the facts as I see them." The third type of knowledge depends on experience, or at times, spiritual intuition.[3]

There are many Traditions related from the Prophet Muhammad regarding knowledge. "Seek knowledge from the cradle to the grave." "To seek knowledge is the duty of every Muslim, whether man or woman." "Seek knowledge, even if it be in China." "He who leaves his home in search of knowledge walks in the path of God." "He who seeks knowledge does not die."[4] Medicine and healing in the Islamic world began with the Medicine of the Prophet and expanded over the centuries to include what is today known as "Islamic Medicine." Underlying both the Medicine of the Prophet and Islamic Medicine was a form of practical philosophy (*hikma 'amaliyya*), which today is understood as "Moral Healing."

When the Muslims encountered other cultures and civilizations that had preceded Islam, they were able to integrate the arts of medicine from these other cultures including Greece, India, and Persia. They preserved and perfected these medicinal arts at a time when, in the case of Greek knowledge; for example, the civilization that had been its basis had declined and lost its body of knowledge. Extending as it did from Spain to Southeast Asia, the Islamic world was able to incorporate much of this knowledge with just one caveat: the body of knowledge that was incorporated into Islamic medicine could not contradict the belief in One God. This was true of many sciences, including the science of medicine and healing.

One of the greatest Muslim theologians, Abu Hamid al-Ghazali (d. 1111 CE), taught that the study and practice of medicine is *fard kifaya:* it is necessary for a sufficient number of Muslims to learn medicine in order to meet the community's needs. Many practitioners of Prophetic Medicine expressed the view that "after faith, the practice of medicine is the most meritorious service in God's sight."[5]

THE MEDICINE OF THE PROPHET

The goal of the Medicine of the Prophet is to restore the nature created by God (*fitrat Allah*) from imbalance back to balance. This nature is referred to in the Qur'an: "Set thy face, [oh Muhammad], as a primordial monotheist (*hanifan*), toward the nature of God (*fitrat Allah*), upon which He has created the human being. There is no changing the creation of God. That is the upright religion, but most people know it not" (Qur'an 30:30). In the view of Islam, the human being is not born in a state of original sin, but in a state originated by God. This natural disposition is a nature that has the potential to sense the order, balance, harmony, and equilibrium in the universe as well as within the self. The acceptance of this nature originated by God comes from the covenant that the human being accepted when God formed the human soul (*nafs*) by blowing the Divine Spirit into it (Qur'an 7:172). This is what gives meaning to the human being. Having accepted the covenant at creation as part of the nature originated by God, the human being was then given the trust of nature as God's representative on Earth (Qur'an 33:72).

As the trustee of the natural world, human beings have certain duties and obligations that were acknowledged as part of their original nature. Prophets are sent by God to remind human beings of their duties and obligations and the rewards or punishments for performing or not performing these obligations. In this sense, every revealed book sent by Allah through a Prophetic Messenger is a reminder (*dhikra*). Revelation is of two kinds: First, the created order is itself a revelation, and second, the Revealed Books of Allah's Messengers are an additional kind of revelation that serve as a reminder and a source of guidance from God.

Many verses of the Qur'an refer to God as the ultimate Healer and to the Qur'an as a means of healing. "When I am ill, it is [God] who cures me" (Qur'an 26:80). "We reveal from the Qur'an that which is a healing and a mercy for the believers" (Qur'an 17:82). "If God touches you with affliction, none can remove it but He" (Qur'an 6:17). "Oh humankind! There has come to you counsel from your Lord and a healing for what is in your hearts; this is a guidance and a mercy for the believers" (Qur'an 10:57).

The Qur'an also gives guidance that promotes good health: "Oh people, eat what is lawful and wholesome from [the foods of] the Earth" (Qur'an 2:168). The Qur'an also counsels people to select the best foods (Qur'an 18:19) and enjoy them: "Eat of the good things that we have provided for you" (Qur'an 7:160). Moderation is stressed: "Eat and drink, but do not be profligate" (Qur'an 7:31), as well as the avoidance of excess (Qur'an 20:81). Muslims are also enjoined to fast from food and drink during the daytime hours of the month of Ramadan, to learn self-restraint (Qur'an 2:183).

Prohibited actions in the Qur'an that lead to an imbalance in health include the eating of pork and alcohol consumption.[6] The Qur'an also forbids excessive eating, which leads to obesity and other medical problems: "Eat and drink, but do not be excessive" (Qur'an 7:31). Good health is considered a great blessing in Islam. On the Day of Judgment, the human being will be questioned about how she respected and maintained the blessings of God that she received: "Then you will be questioned about [God's] blessings on that day" (Qur'an 102:8). The Qur'an establishes three general rules for the maintenance of health and well-being: the preservation of bodily health, the expulsion of harmful substances, and protection from harm that might occur to the body from unlawful or injudicious actions. In his book, *Medicine of the Prophet,* the noted Hanbali scholar Ibn Qayyim al-Jawziyya (d. 1350 CE) comments on how the Qur'an applies each of these rules:

> In the Qur'anic verses on fasting, the preservation of health is emphasized as a greater requirement than the religious obligation to fast. "If any of you are ill or on a journey, [then fasting should be made up from] a set number of other days" (Qur'an 2:184). Ibn Qayyim comments, "[God] permitted a sick person to break the fast because of illness, and [He permitted] the traveler [to break the fast] in order to preserve his health and strength. [This is because] fasting while traveling might cause injury to health through the combination of vigorous movements and the consumption of vital bodily energy, which often is not properly replaced due to lack of food. Thus, He permitted the traveler to break his fast."[7]

With regard to the expulsion of harmful substances, the Qur'an states: "If any of you are sick or has an ailment in his head, then [he can make] compensation [for not being able to complete the Hajj pilgrimage] by fasting, almsgiving, or sacrifice" (Qur'an 2:196). Ibn Qayyim explains: "[God] gave permission to the sick and to anyone with an ailment in his head...to shave his head while in the state of pilgrim sanctity (*ihram*). This was to evacuate the harmful vapors that brought about the ailment to his head through being congested beneath the hair. When the head is shaved, the pores are opened and these vapors make their way out. This kind of evacuation is used to draw an analogy for all other kinds of evacuation where the congestion of matter would cause harm."[8]

Ten actions of the body considered to cause imbalance when they are blocked or restrained are the following: the blood when agitated, the semen when moving, urine, feces, gastric gases, vomiting, sneezing, sleep, hunger, and thirst. Ibn Qayyim continues: "The Most High drew attention to the least significant [aspect of impurity]—the vapor congested in the head—to indicate the importance of evacuating what is more serious. Such is the method of the Qur'an: to give instruction about the greater through mentioning the lesser. In the verse of ablution the Most High refers to protection from harm: 'If you are sick or on a journey, or one of you comes from the privy, or you have been in contact with women, and you can find no water, then take for yourselves clean sand or earth' (Qur'an 4:34). He permitted the sick person to desist from using water and to use earth instead, in order to protect the body against harm. Here again, attention is drawn to take the necessary precautionary measures against anything which could harm the body internally or externally."[9]

Treatment of illness by the Prophet Muhammad as recorded in the Hadith was of three kinds: treatment with natural medicines, treatment with "divine medicines" (recitation of the Qur'an and prayers), and treatment with a combination of these two. However, a traditional doctor or a physician (*hakim*) never treated a physical illness without paying attention to the moral aspect of healing as well. As one of the better-known exponents of the Medicine of the Prophet, Ibn Qayyim commented that the moral dimension of healing was part of God's Law (*Shari'a*): "As for the guidance of the Prophet on physical medicine, it came as a completion of his religious law (*al-Shari'a*) and was equally to be used when needed."[10] At another place in the text, he noted, "Restoration of the body without restoration of the heart is of no benefit. However, damage to the body when the spirit is restored brings only limited harm, for it is a temporary damage that will be followed by a permanent and complete cure."[11]

A tradition from Usama ibn Sharik reported the following discussion: "I was with the Prophet when a Bedouin came and asked him, 'Oh Messenger of God, do we have to take medicine for treatment of illnesses?' The Prophet said, 'Yes. Oh servants of God, take medicine, for God Almighty has not created a disease without having created a remedy for it except one disease.' When they asked what this disease was, he said, 'Old age.'" Ibn Qayyim comments on this tradition:

> It is possible that [the Prophet's] words, "For every disease there is a remedy," are to be taken in a general sense, so as to encompass fatal illnesses and those which no physician can cure. In that case, God the Most Glorious has appointed remedies to cure them but has concealed the knowledge of such remedies from humankind, and has not given the human being the means to discover them. For created beings have no knowledge, except what God teaches.
>
> Therefore, the Prophet indicated that healing is dependent on the concurrence of the medicine with the illness. For every created entity has an opposite and every disease has an opposite as a remedy by which it can be treated. The Prophet also indicated that the cure is dependent on the suitability of the remedy to the disease, in addition to its mere existence. For when a medicine is too potent for the illness or is administered in excess, it transforms the original illness into another. When [the cure] is insufficient for the illness, it does not fully combat it and the treatment is defective; when the healer is unable to identify the right medicine, healing does not result. When the body is not receptive [to the medicine] or the faculties are incapable of bearing it, or there is some other factor preventing its influence, a cure will not be obtained, because of the lack of compatibility. But when there is complete compatibility, a cure must inevitably occur. This is the best of the two assumptions in the traditions.
>
> The second assumption is that within the general meaning it is the particular which is intended, especially seeing that what is contained within an expression is much greater than what comes out from it and this is common usage in every language. Thus, the meaning would be: God has not made any disease that can be treated without making a remedy for it. This does not include those diseases which are not receptive to medicine.[12]

As for those who are reluctant to seek any treatment at all for their illnesses, Ibn Qayyim reassures them that seeking treatment does not negate trust in

God's will (*tawakkul*) any more than does eating or drinking to repel hunger or thirst. He states: "The reality of the divine unity is only made complete by direct use of the means that God has appointed as being essential to bring about certain effects, according to God's command and the Shari'a."[13]

From the time of the revelation of the Qur'an, the Prophet and many of his followers would recite verses of the Qur'an to a sick person as a method of healing. This practice was known as *ruqya*. The Medicine of the Prophet sees the healing effects of the recitation of the Qur'an to be achieved in two ways: through the meaning of the Qur'an for those who understand it and through the sound of the Arabic words of the Qur'an, even for those who do not understand.

The Traditions also refer to the healing power of scents: "A sweet scent is the nourishment of the spirit; the spirit is the instrument of the faculties, and the faculties increase with scent. For it is beneficial for the brain and the heart and the other internal organs; it makes the heart rejoice, pleases the soul, and revitalizes the spirit."[14]

Listening to singing was also recommended as a means of healing by some physicians. According to the Egyptian scholar Jalal al-Din al-Suyuti (d. 1505 CE): "Listening to singing is the scent of souls, the calmer of hearts, and the food of the spirit. It is among the most important kinds of psychological medicine. It is a cause of pleasure, even for some animals. Pleasure in moderation purifies the innate heat [of the body], strengthens the function of the faculties, slows down senile decay by driving out diseases, renders the complexion clearer, and refreshes the whole body. By contrast, an excess of pleasure makes the illnesses of the body increase."[15] There was a difference of opinion on the legality of listening to music. Some scholars saw a benefit in music, but others could not differentiate between music that inflamed the passions and music that fostered spirituality and healing. Ibn Qutayba (d. 889 CE), who was perhaps the most famous cultural historian of the Abbasid period (750–1258 CE), fully approved of the psychological and medicinal effects of music and especially singing. He wrote, "Songs and harmonious chants clarify the brain, sweeten the character, animate the soul, clear the blood, improve and help persons with thick diseases, and develop all the natural qualities of a human being. Listening to singing is recommended in the treatment of some diseases, especially those due to spleen."[16]

However, the main method of treatment associated with the Medicine of the Prophet was with drugs made from plants and herbs, which were known as "simples" in Islamic pharmaceutical vocabulary. Muslim physicians divided drugs into two categories: "simples" (*mufradat*) and "compounds" (*murakkabat*). Simples are drugs in their natural state, and which have not been combined with other drugs to make compounds. Each "simple" drug was thought to possess its own nature and interacted with the four elements of earth, water, fire, and air, to bring the bodily humors back into balance. The use of simple drugs was thus related both to the temperament of the patient and to the temperament of the drug itself, which derived from the nature of its source in a particular plant or herb. The Medicine of the Prophet relied mostly on simples. Knowledge of the nature of simple drugs and their herbal sources played a major role in the traditional pharmacology of medieval Islam. Some modern scholars use the term "pharmacognosy" to characterize this knowledge, because it combined empirical knowledge of the properties of plants with a subtler and more esoteric knowledge of their natures.[17]

Another method used in the Medicine of the Prophet was incantation. A tradition that is reproduced in the *Sunan* of Abu Dawud, the *Musnad* of Ahmad ibn Hanbal, and the *Sunan* of Tirmidhi states that a person asked the Prophet Muhammad: "Oh Messenger of God, do you consider incantations a suitable means of treatment, and are they useful for protection? Do they turn back anything from God's decree?" He replied, "They are part of God's decree."[18] Even today, many Muslims in traditional communities continue to rely on prayer, fasting, incantations, and the recitation of certain verses of the Qur'an as approaches to healing. In the past, treatments based on the medicinal properties of minerals and plants were supplemented by charms that were based on the science of letters and numbers. Talismans or amulets were often used as alternative forms of treatment in the Medicine of the Prophet.

The underlying philosophy in the treatment of illness as expressed in the Medicine of the Prophet and later in Islamic Medicine was that the body has the power to preserve and restore balance through its God-given power of self-preservation. Therefore, the role of medicine and the physician was to help this power function by removing any obstacles that may be present in the body that obstruct the natural balance of humors and the flow of bodily fluids. In this view, regaining health is achieved by the body itself and any form of treatment simply helps this process by assisting the natural life force.

THE *HAKIM:* THE ISLAMIC PHYSICIAN

In the early centuries of Islamic history, physicians were usually of Jewish, Christian, or Zoroastrian background. The use of Christians and Jews as physicians continued well into the medieval period. However, Muslims began to enter the profession in the second century of Islam (mid-eighth century CE). Eventually, the position of physician evolved into that of the *hakim* (wise person or sage), who was both a physician and a philosopher and often a master of other Islamic sciences as well. Many famous Muslim philosophers were also physicians. These included three of the most famous philosophers in Islam, Muhammad ibn Abu Zakariyya al-Razi (Rhazes, d. 925 CE), Abu 'Ali Ibn Sina (Avicenna, d. 1037 CE), and Muhammad Ibn Rushd (Averroes, d. 1198 CE). Theoretical studies of the Medicine of the

Prophet and Islamic Medicine were often taught in a traditional school of higher education, the *madrasa*. Clinical medicine, however, was taught in hospitals, which were often attached to a *madrasa* that specialized in medical subjects.[19] Private instruction was also available, especially in the area of pharmacology.

Wherever the physician was taught, he was required to develop certain personal characteristics in order to practice his craft. The following is a description of the attributes of a physician from the famous work, *Chahar Maqala* (Four Treatises):

> The physician should be of a tender disposition and a wise nature, and excelling in acumen, this being a nimbleness of mind in forming correct views; that is to say, a rapid transition to the unknown from the known. No physician can be of a tender disposition if he fails to recognize the nobility of the human soul; nor can he be of a wise nature unless he is acquainted with logic, nor can he excel in acumen unless he is strengthened by God's aid. He who is not acute in conjecture will not arrive at a correct understanding of any ailment, for he must derive his indications from the pulse, which has a systole, a diastole, and a pause intervening between these two movements.[20]

The well-known *Ethics of the Physician* (*Adab al-Tabib*), by Ishaq ibn 'Ali al-Ruhawi, gives directives on medical ethics and what today would be called "bedside manners." Ruhawi discusses what the doctor should ask of the patient and the nurse, what the patient may conceal from the physician, and what the physician should inform the patient under his or her treatment. The contemporary Islamic scholar Seyyed Hossein Nasr sums up the attributes of the traditional Islamic physician in the following way: "The physician was expected to be a man of virtuous character, who combined scientific acumen with moral qualities, and whose intellectual power was never divorced from deep religious faith and reliance upon God."[21]

The Egyptian writer Suyuti refers to many traditions that showed that in the time of the Prophet Muhammad, women were permitted to give medical treatment to men, even though they were not close relations. Some of these traditions are recorded in the reliable collection called *Sahih Muslim*, such as when one woman reported: "We journeyed with the Prophet Muhammad in seven raids. I traveled in the rear with the baggage. I prepared their food and I treated the sick and wounded." Another tradition recounts: "The Prophet once made a raid and took with him Umm Saylam, and with her came the womenfolk of the Helpers. They used to carry round the drinking water and treat the wounded."[22] Imam Ahmad ibn Hanbal (d. 855 CE) said that it was lawful for a male physician to examine a woman, even though she was not a relative, and even in forbidden places.[23] Suyuti similarly said that it was lawful for a woman to look at the forbidden parts of a man in case of necessity. He then concludes his section by saying, "If a man dies among women or a woman dies among men, the women are allowed to wash the corpse of the man and the men that of the woman."[24]

The job of the Islamic physician is to learn to read the signs of imbalance in both its empirical and its qualitative aspects. Whereas the empirical aspects of systemic imbalance appear in the sensible world and allow direct observation and experimentation, the qualitative aspects can only be known indirectly by the effects that they produce. Whereas empirical knowledge speaks through the signs of outer forms and observed reality "on the horizons," the qualitative dimension of knowledge speaks through signs of meaning that appear more subtly, within the nature of the patient himself or herself. In the words of the Holy Qur'an: "We shall show them our signs on the horizons and within themselves until it becomes manifest to them that it is the Truth" (Qur'an 41:53).

ISLAMIC MEDICINE: THEORY

Islamic Medicine deals with the inborn nature of the patient in an attempt to maintain health and restore the person to health whenever the inner equilibrium of the patient is lost. The work of the physician is to achieve a dynamic balance between all aspects of the human person. This approach is holistic in theory, practice, diagnosis, and treatment.[25] Ibn Sina (Avicenna), the famous Islamic philosopher and physician and the author of the influential textbook *al-Qanun fi al-Tibb* (The Canon of Medicine), defines medicine as the branch of knowledge that deals with the states of health and disease in the human body for the purpose of employing suitable means for preserving or restoring health. According to Ibn Sina and other traditional physicians, the theory of Islamic Medicine is divided into four parts: the constitution of the patient, the state of the body of the patient, the etiology of disease, and symptoms or signs of disease in the patient.

The Constitution of the Patient

The constitution of the patient has seven components: (1) the four elements and their qualities, (2) temperament, (3) the four humors, (4) the fundamental organs, (5) the souls, (6) the faculties, (7) the functions of attraction and repulsion.

The Four Elements and Their Qualities

The concept of the four elements was inherited by Islamic Medicine from the Greek medical tradition, through the translated works of Hippocrates, Dioscorides, and Galen.[26] The four elements are earth, air, fire, and water. Earth and water are heavy, and air and fire are light. The heavy elements are considered strong, negative, passive, earthly, and female. The light elements are weak, positive, active, heavenly, and male.

The element of earth is located at the center of our existence. It is made of gross matter (*madda*). Because of the inherent weight that this element possesses, it remains at rest while the other elements are pulled toward it by means of attraction. Ibn Sina explained the force of gravity as the "attraction" or "inclination" (*mayl*) of lighter objects toward the heavy earth.[27] The element of earth within our bodies fixes and holds our bodies in place. Its gross materiality forms the building block of the skeleton.

The element of water allows things to be shaped, molded, and spread. It has a tendency to sag or droop and forms the building block of the muscles. The element of air refines things and makes them lighter so that they can ascend easily. It is the building block of the circulatory system. It is also the building block of the breath (*nafas*, related to *nafs*, "soul"), as it moves in and out of the physical form of the body, making involuntary movement possible. The element of fire rarifies, refines, and mixes things. It penetrates air and overcomes the coldness of earth and water. It forms the basic building block of the liver.

Each of the four elements has two primary qualities. Earth is cold and dry, water is cold and wet, air is hot and wet, and fire is hot and dry. Many descriptions of the four elements can be found in medieval medical and scientific texts from the Islamic world. It is clear from all of these texts that the four elements of Islamic Medicine are not what we call earth, air, water, and fire. They are more than the earth we walk on, the air we breathe, the water we drink, and the fire we use to cook our food. Rather, they are manifestations of primary matter, subtle qualities that our bodies contain. The quality of moisture within the elements of water and air dispels dryness and protects things from crumbling; the quality of dryness in earth and air prevents moisture from dispersing. The four elements are continuously in motion, making changes within the body. These changes can be either cyclical or progressive. The changes involved in eating food, digesting food, and eliminating waste are cyclical because they are repeated in the same manner. The growth of a cancerous tumor, however, is an example of progressive change because it creates a condition in the body that has not existed before.

Substances (sing. *jawhar*) are either simple or compound. The four elements are simple substances that provide the primary matter for the components of the human body. It is through these four elements and their qualities that bodies gain shape and mass. However, mass needs energy to move. This energy comes from the properties of heat and cold, which act upon the elements in the body. Heat and cold are active properties of energy, while moisture and dryness are passive qualities of matter. Although a person can speak of these qualities separately, in action they are inseparable. For instance, heat provides kinetic energy to the atoms of the body because it possesses both rapid and random motion.

Temperament

Temperament is unique to each individual. In Islamic Medicine, no two persons can be treated alike medically because they have different temperaments. Temperament refers to the metabolic constitution of a person and one's pattern of behavior. Temperament was thought to be partially dependent on one's astrological sign or constellation at birth and on one's place of conception. If the temperament is balanced, there is no need for medical treatment. An illness creates an imbalance in the temperament. There are eight different kinds of imbalance in temperament. Four are simple: an imbalance in heat, cold, dryness, or moisture. Four are compound: an imbalance in the combination of heat and dryness, an imbalance in the combination of heat and moisture, an imbalance in the combination of cold and dryness, and an imbalance in the combination of cold and moisture.

The temperament of a person comes about primarily from the interaction of the qualities of the four elements acting on the components of the body. For example, blood is hot and moist. If a person were to sleep excessively or to become exposed to cold, the natural heat of the blood would dissipate and the result would be too much moisture. The diagnosis of this condition would be an "imbalance of the hot temperament of the blood," and treatment would be given accordingly. The breath, blood, and liver are considered the hottest components of the body. When they are out of balance by being too hot, herbs with the quality of cold are given to restore balance. Hair, bones, and cartilage are considered the coldest components of the body. Oil, fat, and the brain are considered wet components, while ligaments, tendons, and the serous membranes are dry components. A "hot imbalance" is hotter than it should be but not moister or drier. A "cold imbalance" is colder than it should be but not moister or drier. A "dry imbalance" is drier than it should be but not hotter or colder. A "moist imbalance" is wetter than it should be but not hotter or colder.

An imbalance in temperament can be either qualitative or material. If the imbalance is qualitative, it does not affect an organ directly. For example, a fever is a qualitative imbalance of temperament because it does not affect a particular organ of the body. A material imbalance directly invades an organ of the body and causes change. A cancerous tumor causes a material imbalance in temperament because it directly affects a particular part of the body.

The Egyptian scholar Suyuti considered the temperament of the Prophet Muhammad to have been the most balanced of human temperaments. This was because his moral character and the temperament of his body were in perfect equilibrium. A tradition related from 'A'isha, the wife of the Prophet, states, "His character is the Qur'an." Since the Qur'an, as God's revelation to humanity, is the embodiment of divine justice and truth, the Prophet's temperament was also justly balanced because his character corresponded to God's justice and truth. Conversely, if the Prophet's temperament were the most balanced of temperaments, then his character must have been the best of characters as well.[28]

The Humors

Each of the four elements relates to a corresponding humor, substances that are made up of quasi-material or semi-gaseous vapors. The humor of blood (Sanguineous Humor) relates to air, so that it is hot and moist when balanced. The humor of phlegm (Serous Humor) relates to water, so that it is cold and moist when balanced. The humor of yellow bile (Bilious Humor) relates to fire, and is hot and dry when balanced. The humor of black bile (Atrabilious Humor) relates to earth, so that it is cold and dry when balanced.

The four humors were first observed by the Greek physician Hippocrates, who noticed four mixtures in the blood. The red portion of the blood he related to the humor of blood, the white material mixed with the blood he designated as the humor of phlegm, the yellow froth on top of the blood he called the yellow bile humor, and the black bile humor was related to the heavy part of the blood that settles to the bottom when the blood is precipitated. The four humors were later refined by Galen, who observed that all illness and disease were the result of an imbalance in the humors. The Muslim philosopher and physician Ibn Sina added two fluids to the humors as secondary humors: intracellular fluids and extracellular fluids. He further observed that the four primary humors arise out of the digestive process. He believed that the primary humors and the fluids were used as nutrients for the maintenance, growth, and repair of the organs, as well as for supplying the energy necessary to do work.

Existing as they do in a kinetic state, the humors are continuously adjusting and mixing with the body's organs, fluids, and tissues. The preservation of the vital force or immune system of the body depends on the balance of the humors. Any treatment given for an imbalance in the humors is to help the body regain this ability. According to the theory of humors, the four humors arise in the liver, depending on the nature of the food that one eats and the degree of digestion that follows. The liver first forms the blood humor (hot and moist) from the best of the nutrients in the food that has been eaten. Then the phlegm humor (cold and moist) arises as part of the next stage of the digestive process. In normal digestion, the phlegm humor changes into mucus, saliva, and gastric and intestinal mucus. If there is a problem at this stage because of the quality of the food ingested, excess mucus is formed, which is then classified as sweet, sour, thick, or thin.

The coarser and less refined products of the digestive process form the yellow bile humor (hot and dry). This humor is stored in the gall bladder, renders the blood subtle, and helps it pass through the narrow channels of the veins and arteries. Part of the yellow bile humor is carried to the bowels and produces the color of the feces. The sediment that is left over comes from the least digestible and least usable parts of the nutrients ingested; these materials form the black bile humor (cold and dry). When balanced, the black bile humor feeds the spleen and forms the bones. Part of the black bile humor passes to the opening of the stomach, where it creates stomach acidity and the hunger for food. This humor was considered the most toxic of the four humors and was thought to be responsible for cancerous growths in the body. When it is out of balance, the black bile humor passes out of the liver in the form of ash or it mixes with the other three humors and causes various morbid conditions.

The Fundamental Organs

The organs of primary importance are the brain, the heart, the liver, and the generative organs, the testicles or ovaries. The nerves serve the brain, the arteries serve the heart, the veins serve the liver, the spermatic vessels serve the testicles, and the fallopian tubes serve the ovaries. The vital power or innate heat of the body comes from the heart. Mental faculties and the powers of perception and movement are located in the brain, whereas the source of the nutritive and vegetative faculties is the liver. The generative organs, the testicles and ovaries, produce masculine and feminine genders and form the elements of reproduction.

The Souls

The psychological aspect of Islamic Medicine is based on the concept of two souls, or more accurately, one soul that is divided into secondary souls or functions. The first of these souls is the rational soul (*al-nafs al-ʿaqliyya*), which governs the cognitive system and the ability to reason. The second is the animal soul (*al-nafs al-hayawaniyya*), which governs the instincts and passions, especially the attraction to pleasure and the instinct to repel harm or danger. This soul is called the animal soul because the instincts and passions are shared by both human beings and animals. The goal of traditional psychology, or the "science of souls" (*ʿilm al-nufus*) in Islam, is to maintain a balance between these two souls.[29] As in physical Islamic Medicine, the medicine of souls sees health as a state of equilibrium, in which the instincts, desires, and impulses that act on the human being are controlled and are in balance.

When the rational soul and the animal soul are in equilibrium, the emotions are balanced by reason. Simple imbalances occur because of a "quantitative" imbalance, in which certain aspects of the soul become too active or too passive, or they may occur because of a qualitative imbalance, in which one of the aspects of the soul is missing or not utilized. Compound imbalances result from the rational soul and the animal soul acting together in such a way that the passional aspects overcome the rational aspects.

The desire for pleasure, a major aspect of the animal soul, is known as the "affective system." It is the most basic aspect of the animal soul and is the first to develop in the human personality. Its purpose is to preserve the human species. This aspect of the animal soul comes into play when one yields to the influence of inner passions or outer stimuli. The virtue that restores a sense of balance to the passions and the desire for pleasure is temperance. Too much desire shows itself as greed; too little desire connotes a lack of self-esteem; a lack of emotional responsiveness or affect may indicate envy.

The avoidance of pain is another important aspect of the animal soul. This instinct (*ghariza*) forms the psychological basis of the "behavioral system." Shared by both humans and animals, the instinct of pain avoidance exists in order to preserve the life of the individual. Because it is an instinct, it is pre-conscious, and thus capable of being disciplined, whereas the affective system that governs passion and desire is unconscious. The virtue that brings the "fight or flight" tendencies of this aspect of the soul into balance is courage. Too much courage shows itself as anger or recklessness and may lead to the love of power and ambition. Too little courage results in cowardice and imaginary fears or phobias.

When they are given too much free rein in the human personality, the affective and behavioral systems of the animal soul may corrupt the rational soul. This results in the loss of reason and the inability to rationally exercise free will; by themselves, these aspects of the animal soul do not utilize reason. As preconscious instincts or unconscious processes, they instead utilize inner impulses and the imagination to move the self toward seeking pleasure or avoiding harm. The psychic "motion" that they cause within the self is what we call emotion. The affective system seeks love and pleasure whereas the behavioral system avoids hate and pain. Both systems were thought to be located in the heart. However, the affective system receives its energy from the liver. This energy flows through the veins, causing the attraction to pleasure. The desire for pleasure is the most basic drive of human nature. Unlike the affective system, the behavioral system receives its energies from the heart through the arteries.

Reason (*'aql*), the property of the rational soul, belongs to the human being alone. While the purpose of the affective system is to preserve the species and the purpose of the behavioral system is to preserve the individual, the purpose of the cognitive system is to preserve consciousness. Consciousness is defined as the exercise of free will and the development of a conscience with which to balance free will. Whereas the animal soul is instinctive and is fully formed at birth, the rational soul develops as one grows and matures. The nature of its quantitative and qualitative development depends upon the processes of nurturing and education. The highest virtue achieved by the rational soul is wisdom (*hikma*). Too little wisdom shows itself as ignorance (*jahl*); the development of knowledge without wisdom leads to hypocrisy (*nifaq*). A lack of the qualitative function of the rational soul results in disbelief in God (*shirk* or *kufr*). The goal of Islamic psychology is the same as the goal of Islamic Medicine as a whole: to maintain balance, harmony, and equilibrium between the rational soul and the animal soul. The outward sign of inner balance is when a person manifests a sense of fairness and justice. Such a person is then referred to as being "centered."[30]

The Faculties and Energies

The faculties of the human body are the natural faculties, the vital faculties, and the nervous faculties. In Islamic Medicine, the human being is considered as a complete system that makes use of the energy transformed from food and air to satisfy its various natural dispositions. Energy moves from perception to motivation and motivation to perception. Motivation is the seat of impulses toward inclinations, which are imprinted on the external and internal senses. Then, through filtering into the practical intellect, a response is given. Three sources of energy are active in this perspective: natural or physical (venial) energy, vital (arterial) energy, and nervous energy. These transformed energies are distributed throughout the body.

Natural or Physical Energies: The natural or physical energies are twofold. One, located in the liver, where the humors are also formed, is responsible for the preservation of the individual and therefore supplies energy for nutrition and growth. The other is located in the testicles and ovaries and is responsible for the sexual functions to preserve the human race. The nutritive function works through subordinate systems: retention, digestion, assimilation, and expulsion. The humors move by natural energy through the veins carrying sustenance to the body. A natural appetite, guided by nature in its mode of operation, instructs these various energies.

Vital Energy of the Heart: Some natural energies and humors enter the cavity of the heart through transformation. There, they become vital energy, a substance that is less gross than the humors in the liver. The heart is the seat of life, of heat, of pulse, of the vital energies, and of nature in its mode of operation. It is the organ that lives first and dies last. Vital energies are carried to the organs of the body by arteries. They make life possible. They are transformed in the brain, where they become nervous energy. This makes perception and motivation possible.

Nervous Energy: Nervous energy arises in the brain from the vital energy that reaches it from the heart. The brain, where the cognitive functions are located, is the center of motivation and perception. Motivation stimulates movement, and perception consists of the external and internal senses. In the cognitive system, vital energy from the heart is distributed to the nervous system, whereas the affective system receives natural energy through the veins and the behavioral system receives vital energy through the arteries.

During the early stages of human development, before the cognitive system is fully formed, the systems of affect and behavior use the natural and vital energies for nutrition, growth, and development. They invest energy in objects that appear to fulfill the needs of attracting pleasure and avoiding harm. However, because the systems of affect and behavior do not function cognitively, when their needs are not met, they automatically seek to displace their energies toward another object. Through observation and imitation, most often under the guidance of parents, the individual gradually develops cognition. Cognition allows the person to become selective and to choose what best satisfies the basic needs. The cognitive system is endowed by nature with the ability to identify and match the mental image arising out of a need with a real perception that will satisfy a natural disposition. Whereas the affective and behavioral systems cannot differentiate between the impression of a desired object and the object itself, the cognitive system may come to know through learning that the impression and the real object are different and that the impression must conform to something real. The moral and religious training imparted by prophets, spiritual masters, and other teachers builds on this basic training or education (*tarbiyya*).

The Functions

The primary functions or responses associated with the body and the human personality are attraction and repulsion. Both relate to the functions of the animal soul and its interaction with the humors and faculties. They are closely related to the behavioral and affective systems, especially with the desire to seek pleasure and the instinct to avoid harm.

The State of the Body

The human body may subsist in three possible states: health, disease, and a condition that is neither health nor disease, namely, convalescence or old age. The Prophet Muhammad said, "He who wakes up in the morning healthy in body and sound in soul and whose daily bread is assured, is as one that possesses the world."[31]

The Etiology of Disease

Islamic Medicine identifies six causes of disease: (1) air, (2) foods and drinks, (3) bodily movement, (4) emotional movement, (5) wakefulness and sleep, and (6) excretion and retention. Air is the essential element that keeps the body in equilibrium. Bad or polluted air disturbs the balance and equilibrium of the body. Hot food and drinks increase the heat of the bodily system; cold foods and drinks cool the bodily system. Movement increases the warmth or heat of the body. The "movement" of the emotions sets the soul in motion and may cause an internal disequilibrium that is visible symptomatically, such as with outward signs of disease. Strong emotional states such as anger, fear, grief, or extreme joy may be dangerous to the equilibrium of the body. Sleep was thought to cause the soul to "bubble" within the body, while cooling the body from the outside. Wakefulness heats the body. Finally, a balance between excretion and retention processes is thought to protect the body. Excessive excretions such as diarrhea dehydrate the body and upset natural balances, whereas infrequent excretions may keep damaging or poisonous substances within the body rather than expelling them to the outside.

Symptoms of Disease

The practitioners of Islamic Medicine saw the symptoms of disease as external signs (*'alamat*) that provided evidence of internal states of imbalance or disequilibrium. Such signs could be "read" inductively, much as the world of signs (*ayat*) could be "read" to deduce the existence of God's presence behind it. An example of how such signs of disease were understood can be found in the Egyptian scholar Suyuti's book on the Medicine of the Prophet: "An excess of flesh is a sign of heat combined with moisture. Excess of fat is a sign of cold combined with moisture. In the same way, excessive desire for sleep is a sign of moisture, whereas a diminished desire for sleep is a sign of dryness. Similarly, the appearance of the organs [bulging through the skin] is a sign. Capacious organs are signs of heat, and the opposite is a sign of coldness. In the same way, dreams show temperaments. Seeing the colors yellow or red, or seeing flashes of light are all signs of heat. Their opposites are signs of coldness. Again, an excess of body odor is a sign of heat; the lack of it is a sign of cold."[32]

ISLAMIC MEDICINE: PRACTICE

Diagnosis

The diagnostic process in Islamic Medicine is dependent on observation and physical examination. The most common sign of illness is fever. According to the theory of Islamic Medicine, fever is a heat the body develops in order to compensate for a long-standing lack of heat within the body. A fever quickly hastens to refine the accumulated superfluous matters in the body by "ripening" them so that they can be eliminated. There are many types and kinds of fever, each requiring a different type of treatment.

To determine the relative harmony of the life force within the body, the *hakim* or physician evaluates the pulse. The pulse is a sign of the movement of the blood in the heart and the arteries, which expand and contract. Every beat of the pulse consists of two movements and two pauses: expansion-pause and contraction-pause. The quality of expansion and contraction is measured according to the length, width, and depth of the artery carrying the blood. The physician examines the quality of the pulse, the duration of its cycle, the duration of its pauses, and variations in the quality of the expansion of the arteries. The physician also checks the compressibility of the artery, the moisture and temperature of the body when he takes the pulse, and its regularity: in other words, whether its rhythm is normal or disordered.

Pain is a sign of an imbalance in the body. Fifteen types of pain are identified in Islamic Medicine, each calling for a different treatment. In *The Canon of Medicine* (*al-Qanun fi al-Tibb*), Ibn Sina described the effects of pain on the body from the perspective of Islamic Medicine. The effects of pain include (1) dissipation of the faculties, (2) interference with the functions of the organs, and (3) the alternation of heat and cold in the affected organ. The coldness of the organ that comes about with the persistence of pain is due to the dispersion of vital forces and the decrease of innate heat.[33] Pain may be removed by a variety of substances: (1) *Resolvents* act in a way that is contrary to the cause of pain, thus removing the cause. Such resolvents may include anethum or linseed, which is made into a poultice and applied over the painful place. (2) *Narcotics* are agents that counteract the acrimony of the humors by soothing the body, inducing sleep, or dulling the sensitive faculties and lessening their activity. Narcotics used in Islamic Medicine include inebriants, milk, oil, and aqua dulcis. (3) *Analgesics* produce cold and thus increase the insensitivity of the affected organs. In addition, the body takes in nutrients, metabolizes them, and expels the wastes. Islamic Medicine stresses the importance of eliminants of the body and also uses them as a key in determining a diagnosis.[34]

Treatment

Diet and herbal remedies are emphasized in the treatment of illness in Islamic Medicine. Through diet, incorrect foods causing imbalances in bodily systems are eliminated; herbal remedies help restore balance of the body. The first step in treatment is to detoxify the body of any superfluous matters that have gathered in the body, causing obstruction to the natural flow of the humors. The physician does this by cleansing the stomach and bowels in order to restore the digestive process. Elimination processes are important for the restoration of health. The body takes in nutrients and metabolizes them, and the by-products must be carried away. Often, the urine was examined as a form of diagnosis. The quality of the urine was determined by color, transparency, and clearness, and also by the thickness, form, sediments, and residues that appear in the urine.

Ibn Sina developed a Formulary that was one of the most important handbooks of medicinal treatments in the Middle Ages. It contained special prescriptions and antidotes. It also discussed the forms they should take, such as pills, powders, syrups, decoctions, confections, or elixirs, and their method of preparation. It also contained thorough discourses about laxatives, purgative and nonpurgative powders, medicinal powders, dosages, potions and thickened juices, jams and preserves, pills, herbs and cereals, lotions, ointments, and dressings and prescriptions for the treatment of different diseases.[35]

ISLAMIC MEDICINE: MORAL HEALING

In Islamic Medicine, issues of morality are treated much like physical illnesses. Classical Islam did not have a simplistic notion of sin. Islamic morality and ethics made a distinction between occasional lapses of judgment or morality, which are designated by the Arabic term *dhanb*, and the willful breaking of moral rules, which is termed *ithm*. The moral consequences of an *ithm* are much greater than those of a *dhanb*. Furthermore, the Qur'an and Islamic traditions are quite clear that the person must take full responsibility for one's failings. It was very difficult in Classical Islam to avoid personal responsibility by saying, "The Devil made me do it." Chronic moral failings were treated as medical conditions, much like physical diseases. Just as physical diseases were caused by imbalances in the humors or in the working of the bodily systems, chronic moral problems were seen as psychic diseases that were caused by imbalances as well. According to the Shiite philosopher, scientist, and ethicist Nasir al-Din Tusi (d. 1274 CE) the theory of the treatment of a moral malady is the same as the theory of the treatment of a physical malady: "It must be understood that the professional rule in treating imbalances is as follows: first, to know the classes of imbalances, then to recognize their causes and symptoms, and finally to proceed to restoration thereof. Moreover, imbalances are constitutional declinations from (a state of) equilibrium, while their treatment is the restoration of such constitutions to equilibrium by technical skill."[36]

Because moral diseases were seen as analogous to physical diseases, moral imbalances were treated by the same four categories of treatments as used in Islamic Medicine to heal physical ailments. One of Tusi's most famous works was a handbook on the ethics and treatment of moral maladies known as *The Nasirian Ethics*. According to this work, "General remedies in medicine are effected by the use of four categories of treatment: diet, medication, antidote, and cauterization or surgery. In psychical [*sic*] disorders, too, one must make use of the same system."[37] The first stage of treatment in Tusi's approach to Islamic Moral Medicine begins with the awareness of a moral imbalance and the honest attempt by the afflicted person to own up to one's negative traits and behaviors:

> One should first clearly recognize the harm of the negative trait one seeks to change [i.e., gain cognitive consciousness of it]. There should be no doubt about it in order to have the necessary motivation to effect change. One should become aware though imagery of the harmful effects the negative trait has on the self, whether in one's faith or in one's worldly affairs. Then, at the next stage one should shun the learned negative trait by the use of will-power. If one's purpose is attained, well and good. If not, one must constantly concern oneself with the application of the positive trait corresponding to that negative one, going to great lengths to repeat, in the most excellent way and the fairest manner, the acts pertaining to that function. Such remedies, generally speaking, correspond to treatment by diet as practiced by physicians.[38]

Once one has become conscious of a moral malady, it is necessary to seek its cause. According to the teachings of Islamic Medicine, moral imbalances may be caused by improper diet, just as the imbalances that cause physical diseases may be caused by diet. On the other hand, moral imbalances might also be caused by factors that we today would call "psychological." In such cases, the "medication" for the disease consists of techniques that are analogous in many ways to modern psychotherapy. Key to this process is to use certain positive tendencies and motivations within the bodily system to overcome other more destructive tendencies. This acts as a sort of antidote to the cause of the moral malady. Tusi explains:

> If, however, by this sort of imbalance [i.e., diet] the imbalance is not balanced, one must proceed to consciously chide and revile, to humiliate and reproach the self for the act in question, either in thought or by word or deed. If this does not produce the desired result and one's purpose is to adjust one of either the two functions—behavioral or affective/emotive, then one must effect this change by the use of the other function, for whenever one is dominant, the other is dominated. Moreover, just as the natural, created purpose of the affective/ emotive function is to preserve alive the individual and the species, so the purpose of the behavioral function is to defeat the onslaught of "attraction to pleasure." Thus, when they neutralize and compensate each other, the cognitive function has scope for distinction. This category of restoration to balance is analogous to the giving of medication by medical physicians.[39]

The use of an "antidote" in the treatment of a moral malady consists of restoring the balance of the moral system by applying remedies that act in opposition to the imbalance that created the moral malady in the first place. Thus, negative traits are countered by positive traits, hoping thereby that the interaction of these two traits will restore the psychological balance or mean. However, in moral treatment, as in all medical treatment, care must be taken so that the patient does not "overdose" on the remedy. An excessive zeal to apply virtue may be just as dangerous in its own way as an excessive weakness for vice:

> If, again, the imbalance is not eliminated by [the previous] method, then, in order to eliminate it, one must seek help from the entrenched negative trait by consciously developing the opposite negative trait. However, one must always closely observe the condition of the self and notice any adjustment made in the condition. That is to say, when the [deeply entrenched] negative trait begins to decline [in terms of intensity] and approaches the mean, which is the place of the positive trait, the moral-seeker must abandon the course on which he has embarked in order not to incline from equilibrium to the other end of the continuum and thereby fall into another imbalance. This category of restoration to moral balance corresponds to the poisonous remedy to which the medical physician does not put his hand unless he is compelled to do so; and when he does, he recognizes the obligation to careful observation and monitoring the disorder so that there be no declination of the one disorder towards its opposite. "As for him who fears to stand in the presence of his Lord and keeps the self from passion, then surely paradise—that is his abode." Prophetic traditions too command resisting the passions. The teaching of the Divine Law [does so] also. The Divine Law also enjoined the removal of negative traits from the self by good acts of the body. This constitutes the source of the specific form of opposition found in the ethics of [the Sunni theologian Abu Hamid] Ghazali, etc., that is, the removal of a negative trait by removing its causes and the removal of causes by means of their opposites.[40]

The fourth stage in the restoration of moral balance is similar to surgery, in that it involves the elimination or "cauterization" of the portion of the self that is diseased. This amounts to emergency treatment because it addresses a mortal threat to the moral life of the person: "If this type of restoration to moral balance [i.e., antidote], too, proves insufficient, the self constantly returning to the repetition of the [same] negative trait, then it must be consciously chastised and deadened. Difficult and arduous tasks must be imposed upon it to effect change. Furthermore, one should set about making vows and covenants that are difficult to implement after becoming aware of the negative effects upon the self. This category of restoration to moral balance is like the cutting-off of limbs in medicine or the cauterization of the extremities. The final remedy is surgery."[41]

The ultimate goal is the unity of the self: "The goal of self in practical philosophy is unity, which is achieved by the self when it completes the perfection of nature in its mode of operation in the self. As the self seeks balance, it learns to read the Signs of guidance through creation and guidance through revelation, on the way to completing the perfection of nature in its mode of operation. The stages are: becoming conscious of self; becoming centered in positive traits; benefiting another person; and practicing guiding the development of positive traits and preventing the development of negative ones in other and in the self."[42]

The Medicine of the Prophet and Islamic Medicine are branches of the tree of knowledge that grew in the Islamic world over a period of more than 1,400 years. Although its origins were in Greek approaches to medicine such as those of Hippocrates and Galen, Islamic Medicine eventually synthesized the theory and practice of Greek medicine and those of other civilizations such as India and China. Eventually, just as in other branches of science, Muslims came to excel in medicine and added their own important contributions to medical knowledge. This can be seen in the widespread influence of Ibn Sina's (Avicenna's) *The Canon of Medicine* throughout medieval Europe. Western theories of scientific medicine have now taken over most of the Islamic world, so much so, in fact, that doctors may even become the leaders of countries, such as former Prime Minister Mahathir Muhammad of Malaysia. However, Islamic Medicine is still a living tradition in many areas of the Islamic world. One can find numerous practitioners and even clinics of Islamic Medicine in countries such as Iran, Pakistan, Bangladesh, and India.

NOTES

1. "Scientific knowledge comes from the study of natural phenomena. These natural phenomena are the signs of God." See M.M. Sharif, *A History of Muslim Philosophy* (Wiesbaden: Otto Harrassowitz, 1963), vol. 1, 147.

2. See, for example, the following Qur'anic verses: 2:164,219; 3:190; 6:95–99; 10:3–6; 13:2–4; 17:12; 30:20–27; 45:3–6.

3. See Sharif, *A History of Muslim Philosophy*, 146–147.

4. These are common traditions, and are known to virtually every Muslim. See, for example, the hadith in *Sunan al-Tirmidhi*, "He who leaves his home in search of knowledge walks in the path of God." Abu 'Isa Muhammad al-Tirmidhi, *Jami' Sunan al-Tirmidhi* (Beirut: Dar al-Ma'arif, 2000), 39:2.

5. Fazlur Rahman, *Health and Medicine in the Islamic Tradition* (Chicago, Illinois: ABC International Group, 1998), 38.

6. The consumption of alcohol is known to increase the incidence of several cancers and inflammatory conditions of the alimentary tract, cirrhosis of the liver, pancreatitis, heart muscle damage, and various disorders of the central and peripheral nervous systems. See Shahid Athar, *Islamic Perspectives in Medicine* (Indianapolis, Indiana: American Trust Publication, 1993), 118.

7. Ibn Qayyim al-Jawziyya, *Medicine of the Prophet*, trans. Penelope Johnstone (Cambridge, U.K.: The Islamic Texts Society, 1998), 4.

8. Ibid., 5.

9. Ibid., 17.

10. Ibid.

11. Ibid., 10.

12. Ibid., 10–11.

13. Ibid., 11.

14. Ibid., 199.

15. Jalal al-Din 'Abd al-Rahman ibn Abu Bakr al-Suyuti, *Traditional Medicine of the Prophet,* trans. Cyril Elgood (Istanbul, Dar al-Fikr, 1999), 145.

16. Ibid., 146; see also, Abu Hamid Muhammad al-Ghazzali, *On Listening to Music* (Chicago, Illinois: Great Books of the Islamic World, 2002).

17. For a discussion of "pharmacognosy" and a description of works on the subject, see Seyyid Hossein Nasr, *Islamic Science: an Illustrated Study* (London: World of Islam Festival, 1976), 187–189.

18. See al-Tirmidhi, *Jami' Sunan al-Tirmidhi,* "Kitab al-Tibb," hadith no. 21.

19. For the history and development of hospitals in the Muslim world, see Nasr, *Islamic Science,* 154–156.

20. Nizami 'Arudi of Samarkand, *Chahar Maqala,* trans. E.G. Browne (London, U.K.: Luzac, 1921), 76.

21. Seyyed Hossein Nasr, *Science and Civilization in Islam* (Chicago, Illinois: ABC International Group, 2001) 185.

22. Imam Muslim ibn al-Hajjaj, *Sahih Muslim,* trans. Abdul Hamid Siddiqi (Lahore, Pakistan: Sh. Muhammad Ashraf, 2001), vol. 3, 1004 (no. 4462) and 1001 (no. 4454).

23. Quoted in Suyuti, *Traditional Medicine of the Prophet,* 103.

24. Ibid.

25. Islamic Medicine also formed the basis of medicine in the medieval Western world through the influence of Ibn Sina's (Avicenna's) *The Canon of Medicine* (al-Qanun fi al-Tibb), which was translated into Latin soon after its publication in Arabic. For 700 years, Ibn Sina's *Canon* was the most important textbook on medicine in Europe. It also formed the basis of the work of Samuel Hahnemann (d. 1897 CE), the founder of homeopathy.

26. See, for example, Sami K. Hamarneh, "The Life Sciences," in *The Genius of Arab Civlization: Source of Renaissance,* ed. John R. Hayes, 2nd ed. (Cambridge, Massachusetts: MIT Press, 1983), 173–200.

27. See Vincent J. Cornell, "Religion and Philosophy, " in *World Eras Volume 2: The Rise and Spread of Islam 622–1500,* ed. Susan L. Douglass (Farmington Hills, Michigan: The Gale Group/Manly Inc., 2002), 324–399.

28. Suyuti, *Traditional Medicine of the Prophet,* 19.

29. On the medicine of souls and traditional "psychotherapy" in Islam, see Laleh Bakhtiar, *God's Will Be Done: Traditional Pyschoethics and the Personality Paradigm* (Chicago, Illinois: Institute of Traditional Psychology, 1994), volume 1 of the series *God's Will Be Done.*

30. "To find the real center, which entails absolute moderation, is difficult to attain. To remain at this center and to preserve the balance is even more difficult." See Muhammad Mahdi ibn Abi Dharr Naraqi, *Jami' al-sa'adat,* trans. Shahyar Sa'adat (Tehran: Foundation of Islamic Thought, 1989), 70. The Prophet Muhammad also said, "*Sura Hud* has made an old man of me" (*shaykh,* "old man" or "wise person") because of the verse, "Tread the Straight Path as you have been commanded, as well

as those who are repentant with you, and do not transgress. Verily, [God] is the Seer of whatever you do" (11:112).

31. *Sunan al-Tirmidhi,* "Kitab al-Zuhd" (Book of Asceticism), 34.

32. Suyuti, *Traditional Medicine of the Prophet,* 22–23.

33. Avicenna, *The Canon of Medicine,* trans. O. Cameron Gruner and adapted by Laleh Bakhtiar (Chicago, Illinois: Great Books of the Islamic World, 1999), 251.

34. Ibid.

35. Ibid., 5.

36. Nasir al-Din Tusi, *Nassirian Ethics,* trans. G. Wickens (London, U.K.: George Allen & Unwin, 1966), 182. On the intellectual environment in which Tusi lived and worked, see "Conservation and Courtliness in the Intellectual Traditions, c. 1258–1503," in Marshall G.S. Hodgson, *The Venture of Islam: Conscience and History in a World Civilization, Volume 2: the Expansion of Islam in the Middle Periods* (Chicago and London: University of Chicago Press, 1977), 437–500.

37. Tusi, *Nassirian Ethics,* 175.

38. Ibid.

39. Ibid.

40. Ibid.

41. Ibid., 182.

42. Ibid.

INDEX

About the Editor and Contributors

———————————— • ————————————

VINCENT J. CORNELL is Asa Griggs Candler Professor of Middle East and Islamic Studies at Emory University. From 2000 to 2006, he was Professor of History and Director of the King Fahd Center for Middle East and Islamic Studies at the University of Arkansas. From 1991 to 2000, he taught at Duke University. Dr. Cornell has published two major books, *The Way of Abu Madyan* (Cambridge, U.K.: The Islamic Texts Society, 1996) and *Realm of the Saint: Power and Authority in Moroccan Sufism* (Austin, Texas: University of Texas Press, 1998), and over 30 articles. His interests cover the entire spectrum of Islamic thought from Sufism to theology and Islamic law. He has lived and worked in Morocco for nearly six years and has spent considerable time both teaching and doing research in Egypt, Tunisia, Malaysia, and Indonesia. He is currently working on projects on Islamic ethics and moral theology in conjunction with the Shalom Hartmann Institute and the Elijah Interfaith Institute in Jerusalem. For the past five years (2002–2006), he has been a key participant in the Building Bridges Seminars hosted by the Archbishop of Canterbury.

LALEH BAKHTIAR has a PhD in Educational Psychology and is a nationally certified counselor and licensed psychotherapist in the state of Illinois. She is the coauthor of *A Sense of Unity: The Sufi Tradition in Persian Architecture* (1973) with Nader Ardalan and is the author of *Sufi: Expressions of the Mystic Quest* (1976, reprinted in 2004). She has also published three volumes of the set *God's Will Be Done:* Volume 1, *Traditional Psychoethics and Personality Paradigm;* Volume 2, *Moral Healer's Handbook: The Psychology of Spiritual Chivalry;* and Volume 3, *Moral Healing Through the Most Beautiful Names* (1994). Dr. Bakhtiar's other published works include *Muhammad's Companions: Essays on Some Who Bore Witness to His Message* (1993), *Encyclopedia of Islamic Law* (1996), and *Sufi Women of America: Angels in the Making* (1996).

TITUS BURCKHARDT (1908–1984) was a leading member of the Traditionalist or Perennialist school of thought. In his early twenties he lived in Fez, Morocco, where he entered Islam as Sidi Ibrahim 'Izz ad-Din, attended courses on the traditional sciences at al-Qarawiyyin University, and was received into Sufism by the spiritual master Mulay 'Ali ibn al-Tayyib al-Darqawi. With his extensive knowledge of Arabic, Burckhardt prepared authoritative French translations of Sufi classics such as Ibn 'Arabi's *Fusus al-Hikam* (Bezels of Wisdom), 'Abd al-Karim al-Jili's *al-Insan al-Kamil* (The Universal Man), and Mulay al-'Arabi al-Darqawi's *Rasa'il* (Letters). From 1972 to 1977, Burckhardt served as UNESCO Special Advisor to the Moroccan government, with particular reference to the preservation of the unique architectural heritage in Fez, a city whose political, cultural, and spiritual history he recounted in his book *Fez: City of Islam* (First German Edition 1960, English Translation, The Islamic Texts Society, 1992). Burckhardt was a tireless defender of the traditional arts and crafts in the face of ever-encroaching mass production technology and presented several lectures at international conferences to defend this position. His major work in this field is the widely acclaimed *Art of Islam: Language and Meaning* (1976). Portions of this work are reproduced in the present volume. An international colloquium was held in Marrakech in 1999 to commemorate the exceptional achievements of his life's work.

EMMA C. CLARK specializes in designing Islamic gardens both in the United Kingdom and in other countries. She has written many articles on Islamic art and architecture, in particular on the Islamic garden and garden carpet, and two children's books on Muslim heroes. Her latest book, *The Art of the Islamic Garden,* was published in the winter of 2004. An earlier monograph, *Underneath Which Rivers Flow: Symbolism of the Islamic Garden,* was published in 1996 by the Prince of Wales' Institute of Architecture. She is also a lecturer and tutor in the Visual Islamic and Traditional Arts Programme (VITA) at the Prince's School of Traditional Arts in London, where she focuses on teaching the universal principles of sacred and traditional arts.

VIRGINIA GRAY HENRY-BLAKEMORE is the director of the inter-faith publishing houses Fons Vitae and Quinta Essentia. She is a writer and video producer under contract with the Book Foundation, U.S. director of photography and children's book publisher Dar Nun, and cofounder and trustee of the Islamic Texts Society of Cambridge, England. She is an accomplished lecturer in art history, world religions, and filmmaking. She has taught at Fordham University, Cairo American College, and Cambridge University. She is also a founding member of the Thomas Merton Center Foundation. Virginia Gray Henry-Blakemore received her BA from Sarah Lawrence College, studied at the American University in Cairo and Al-Azhar University, earned her MA in Education from the University of Michigan, served as Research Fellow at Cambridge University from 1983 to 1990, and is scheduled to receive her PhD from Canterbury, Kent, in 2008.

MARTIN LINGS (1909–2005), also known as Abu Bakr Siraj al-Din, was one of the twentieth century's most influential writers on Islamic thought and spirituality. He was educated at Oxford University and his interest in Islam and the Arabic language took him to Egypt in 1939. In the following year he was given a lectureship at Cairo University. In 1952, he returned to England and completed a doctorate in Arabic at the University of London. From 1970 to 1974, he served as Keeper of Oriental Manuscripts and Printed Books at the British Library in London. He had previously been in charge of manuscripts of the Qur'an at the British Museum since 1955. Dr. Lings was the author of many important books, including the widely read biography of the Prophet, *Muhammad: His Life Based on the Earliest Sources* (1983). His first book, *A Sufi Saint of the Twentieth Century: Shaikh Ahmad al-'Alawi* (1961; latest edition Islamic Texts Society, 1993), is widely regarded as a classic monograph on Sufism and Sufi doctrine. His final work, *A Return to the Spirit*, was completed just before his death in May 2005 and will be published by Fons Vitae of Louisville, Kentucky.

JEAN-LOUIS MICHON is a French scholar who specializes in Islam in North Africa, Islamic art, and Sufism. Dr. Michon has spent years living and working in various Muslim cities and countries, including Damascus, Cairo, and throughout Morocco. He has translated, edited, and written many works on Sufism and art, including *Le Soufi marocain Ahmad ibn 'Ajiba et son mi'raj* (English translation: *The Autobiography* (Fahrasa) *of a Moroccan Sufi: Ahmad ibn 'Ajiba, 1747-1809*, Fons Vitae, 1999), *Lights of Islam: Institutions, Cultures, Arts, and Spirituality in the Islamic City*, and *Sufism: Love and Wisdom*. Dr. Michon has translated the Qur'an into French for the World Wide Web and is preparing a print version as well. He has acted as a consultant on several UNESCO projects on Islamic art, particularly in Morocco, and has been an important contributor to the maintenance and restoration of traditional Islamic arts and crafts. Dr. Michon was associated with Frithjof Schuon, whose perspective Michon has incorporated into his own writings and works.

DANIEL ABDAL-HAYY MOORE is a widely regarded American Muslim poet. His first book of poems, *Dawn Visions*, was published by Lawrence Ferlinghetti of City Lights Books in San Francisco (1964). He became a Sufi Muslim in 1970, performed the Hajj in 1972, and lived and traveled in Morocco, Spain, Algeria, and Nigeria. Upon his return to California, he published *The Desert is the Only Way Out* in 1985 and *Chronicles of Akhira* in 1986. A resident of Philadelphia since 1990, he has published *The Ramadan Sonnets* (1996) and *The Blind Beekeeper* (2002). He has also been the major editor for a number of works, including *The Burda of Shaykh Busiri* (2003), translated by Hamza Yusuf, and *State of Siege* (2004), the poetry of the Palestinian poet, Mahmoud Darwish, translated by Munir Akash.

FRITHJOF SCHUON (1907–1998) was known in the Muslim world as Shaykh 'Isa Nur al-Din Ahmad al-'Alawi al-Maryami. For most of his life, he was the leading exponent of the Traditionalist or Perennialist school of comparative religious thought. In his youth, he traveled to Algeria, where he embraced Islam and was initiated into Sufism by the celebrated Shaykh Ahmad al-'Alawi (d. 1934). Schuon visited North Africa many times in subsequent years and later became the spiritual master of a branch of the Shadhiliyya–Darqawiyya–'Alawiyya Sufi order. Schuon's branch of the 'Alawiyya, which was called the Maryamiyya, was known for its emphasis on the Islamic image of the Virgin Mary as a symbol of spirituality, its strong emphasis upon universality and essentiality, and its wide dissemination in the West. Schuon was the author of over 25 books on metaphysics, philosophy, comparative religion, art, and spirituality. His acknowledged masterpiece in the field of Islamic studies is *Understanding Islam,* which has been translated into 13 languages. This book has been referred to by Seyyed Hossein Nasr of George Washington University as "the best work in English on the meaning of Islam."

SHAWKAT M. TOORAWA is Associate Professor of Arabic Literature and Islamic Studies at Cornell University. His publications include a translation of Adonis' *A Time Between Ashes and Roses* (2004) and the historical study, *Ibn Abi Tahir Tayfur and Arabic Writerly Culture: A Ninth-Century Bookman in Baghdad* (2005). In 2006, Dr. Toorawa received a Mellon New Directions Fellowship to pursue his study of the Arabic literature of eighteenth- and nineteenth-century India.